Perception and Prejudice

Perception and Prejudice

Race and Politics in the United States

Edited by Jon Hurwitz and Mark Peffley

Yale University Press

New Haven and London

Set in Adobe Garamond type by The Composing Room of Michigan, Inc., Grand Rapids, Michigan
Printed in the United States of America

Library of Congress Cataloging-in-Publication Data
Perception and prejudice : race and politics in the United States
    edited by Jon Hurwitz and Mark Peffley.
        p.   cm.
    Includes bibliographical references and index.
    ISBN 0-300-07143-4 (cloth : alk.paper)
        1. United States—Race relations.   2. Racism—Political aspects—United States.   3. United States—Politics and government—1993–Attitudes.
    I. Hurwitz, Jon.   II. Peffley, Mark.   4. United States—
    1993 5. Whites—United States—
    E185.615.P415   1998
    305.8'00973—dc21   97-44948
                                                                              CIP

A catalogue record for this book is available from the British Library.

The paper in this book meets the guidelines for permanence and durability of the Committee on Production Guidelines for Book Longevity of the Council on Library Resources.

10 9 8 7 6 5 4 3 2 1

Contents

Preface

In one way or another, all the contributors to this volume examine how whites see and evaluate African-Americans, and what difference such judgments make. But the chapters are united by more than a substantive focus—they are, additionally, all the product of the Race and Politics Study (RPS), and consequently share an intellectual framework that developed in the course of planning and executing this project.

In many respects, the success of the RPS is attributable to the vision and tireless energy of Paul Sniderman and Thomas Piazza. In 1985, they applied to the National Science Foundation (NSF) for funds to study public attitudes in what is, inarguably, the most contentious and salient issue domain in America—race. But although everyone agrees on the importance of racial attitudes, they also agree about the difficulty of studying them. Not only are such opinions complex, but they are also often disguised and notoriously unyielding to conventional survey approaches. To effectively gauge attitudes in this domain, Sniderman and Piazza argued, requires a survey design considerably more advanced than those which surrender only correlational data.

Instead, the design must incorporate numerous experiments, unobtrusive measures, and multiple measurement strategies which, collectively, provide exceptional leverage for those attempting to unpack the complex opinions in this area.

The NSF responded with funds for Sniderman and Piazza to apply these methods in a pilot study, the 1986 Bay Area Study, most of the results of which were reported in *The Scar of Race* (1993). Having validated the measurement and methodological strategies in the Bay Area project, they reapplied to the NSF, which awarded Grant SES-8508937 to Sniderman, Piazza, and Philip Tetlock for the purpose of greatly expanding this project nationally.

To their credit, the recipients shared the wealth by inviting a group of scholars to help in planning and executing this massive study. They deliberately selected an interdisciplinary group, representing psychology, sociology, and (most numerously) political science, and, anticipating the multistrategic approach that the survey instrument would display, they also selected individuals with varying methodological traditions and skills.

It is important to note that most of the contributors to this volume were not simply handed the data and instructed to analyze it. To the contrary, many were involved in the development of the project from its genesis. The planning group met first at the Survey Research Center at the University of California at Berkeley in October 1989. During this "brainstorming" session participants determined the scope and parameters of the study. A second meeting, held in Pope Valley, California, in January 1992, was used to discuss results of a national pretest and to make additional changes to the instrument. Quite clearly, the generosity of Sniderman and Piazza allowed the chapter authors of this volume to become full participants in all stages of the Race and Politics Study, from design to execution.

We are deeply indebted to Paul and Tom, and it is no exaggeration to state that this book could not have been written without them. Paul Sniderman's generous sharing of resources resulted in a study that has been uncommonly constructed from the input of some of the most innovative minds working in the area. As the manager of statistical services at the Survey Research Center at the University of California at Berkeley, Tom Piazza was at the center of the planning and design process, and should be credited with a good number of the methodological and measurement innovations embedded in the RPS.

Many others, of course, also deserve our thanks. Philip Tetlock (formerly of the Department of Psychology at Berkeley, now at the Ohio State University) was one of the principal investigators of the RPS project and, consequently, responsible for many of its virtues. Frank Scioli of the NSF provided invaluable assistance and advice regarding the grant proposal. Two other individuals at the Survey Research Center lent their considerable efforts and expertise to the survey as it was being developed and executed: Karen Garrett (the manager of survey services) and J. Merrill Shanks (the director of the Program in Computer Assisted Survey Methods).

As the editors of this volume, we are particularly indebted to John Covell, senior editor at Yale University Press and a man of remarkable patience. He and his editorial assistant, Patricia Anders, along with Manuscript Editor Harry Haskell, offered invaluable editorial and technical assistance that contributed immeasurably to this book. We also thank Brad Canon, Paul Goren, Pia Knigge, Stephanie Muraca, Ray Owen, B. Guy Peters, Ellen Riggle, Bert Rockman, and Todd Shields for their assorted acts of generosity. Funding from various sources (the University of Kentucky College of Arts and Sciences, Office of Research and Graduate Studies, and Office of Graduate Affairs, and the University of Pittsburgh Center for American Politics and Society) helped bring this project to fruition. Of course, none of the above-mentioned individuals or agencies is responsible for any remaining shortcomings. We share that responsibility, as we have shared the work of putting together this volume, equally.

Finally, we are grateful to our families—Rebecca Dick-Hurwitz, Kathy Kalias, Joanna Hurwitz, Rebecca Peffley, Rhoda and Sid Hurwitz, and Louise Peffley—who, years ago, stopped taking us and our work seriously, and we are the better for it.

Chapter 1 Introduction

Jon Hurwitz and Mark Peffley

In 1957, while most teenage girls were listening to Buddy Holly's "Peggy Sue," watching Elvis gyrate, and collecting crinoline slips, I was escaping the hanging rope of a lynch mob, dodging lighted sticks of dynamite, and washing away burning acid sprayed into my eyes.

During my junior year in high school, I lived at the center of a violent civil rights conflict. In 1954, the Supreme Court had decreed an end to segregated schools. Arkansas Governor Orval Faubus and states' rights segregationists defied that ruling. . . .

On our first day at Central High, Governor Faubus dispatched gun-toting Arkansas National Guard soldiers to prevent us from entering. Mother and I got separated from the others. The two of us narrowly escaped a rope-carrying lynch mob of men and women shouting that they'd kill us rather than see me go to school with their children.

As one of the nine black children selected initially to integrate Little Rock's Central High School, Melba Pattillo Beals (1994) has a compelling story to tell in *Warriors Don't Cry*—a story that is remarkable in its capacity to remind us of errors that have been made and sins that have been committed. When Beals recounts the events of May 17, 1954, the day the U.S. Supreme Court issued its *Brown v. Board of Education of*

Topeka decision, she does not remember feeling triumph or celebration; rather, she recalls her seventh-grade teacher dismissing class early so that the children could run home before the lynch mobs had an opportunity to congregate outside the school. Her account is both stunning and sobering to those unaware of the era.

In large measure, we are shocked by such stories precisely because they appear so unreal, given the extraordinary changes witnessed in the United States over the intervening years. A partial litany of government outputs would include legislative mandates such as the Civil Rights Acts of 1957, 1960, 1964, and 1968; the Voting Rights Act of 1965; and such judicial decisions as *Bolling v. Sharpe* (1954), *Heart of Atlanta Motel v. United States* (1964), *Swann v. Charlotte-Mecklenburg Board of Education* (1971), and, of course, *Brown*. Collectively, these decisions dismantled de jure segregation of public schools and accommodations and enfranchised millions of African-Americans who had previously not enjoyed the rights of electoral participation.

To these legal changes we must add well-documented changes in public attitudes: dwindling minorities who endorse such blatantly bigoted beliefs as black genetic inferiority, increasing acceptance of neighborhood integration and social intercourse, and growing percentages who claim that they would be willing to support African-American candidates for public office (see, for example, Schuman et al. 1988).

It seems impossible that the overt forms of hostility and prejudice that Beals describes could have existed in America in the relatively recent past. Thus her account is a useful reminder of the nearly revolutionary legislative, judicial, and social changes that have occurred since the 1950s. More important, it recalls the utter simplicity of the lines of contention that were drawn in the early days of the civil rights movement. Looking back, it is an easy matter to identify good guys and bad guys. The good guys, quite simply, wanted to end racial segregation and discrimination and the bad guys did not.

The bad guys were recognizable not only because of what they did but because of the blatancy of their language and actions. Mainstream political leaders such as Dixiecrat presidential candidate Strom Thurmond, Alabama governor George Wallace, and Arkansas governor Orval Faubus not only did everything possible to preserve a segregated America but justified their behavior with words and arguments that even they (at least publicly) later disavowed. Their motivations, moreover, were strikingly ugly; with few exceptions, they were driven by unconcealed bigotry and prejudice.

Today, the battles of racial politics are fought on a field marked by fuzzier lines. Soon after passage of the landmark civil rights legislation of the 1960s, conflict over racial issues shifted from guaranteeing the equal rights of African-Americans to a variety of *remedial* programs designed to right the wrongs of the past. Support for these policies—from social welfare programs designed to assist minorities, to affirmative action, to an enhanced federal role in enforcing equal treatment policies—reflected not only one's commitment to the goal of racial equality but also the priority one assigned to other, often conflicting values, such as self-reliance, fairness, attitudes toward the federal government, and so on. Consequently, in attempting to understand the mainstream "liberals" and "conservatives" of the politics of race (leaving aside the minority of whites who continue to oppose the principle of racial equality), we have discovered only that their motives are far more obscure.

To be sure, the agendas of the racial conservatives—those more likely to oppose affirmative action, traditional welfare programs, and leniency on crime—can be, and have been, interpreted as a more subtle continuation of the overt prejudice displayed in earlier decades. According to this "new" (or "symbolic") racism thesis, (see, for example, McConahay and Hough 1976, Kinder and Sears 1981), now that blatant bigotry is unfashionable, racists couch their sentiments in more socially acceptable guises. Kinder and Sears argue that symbolic racists may oppose redistributive programs such as welfare or, for that matter, resist any "change in the racial status quo" because of their "moral feelings that blacks violate such traditional American values as individualism and self-reliance, the work ethic, obedience, and discipline" (p. 416).

The attraction of this perspective is that it offers a simple litmus test for identifying racism and prejudice in contemporary public opinion. Whites who agree with statements like "It is wrong to set up quotas to admit black students to college who don't meet the usual standards" or "The streets are not safe these days without a patrolman around" are well on their way, according to the criteria established by the symbolic racism thesis, to becoming modern racists. In other words, conservatism on contemporary issues such as affirmative action, welfare, and crime is largely *assumed* to be motivated by prejudice on its face. A study of the connections between prejudice and policy attitudes appears redundant, since the latter—if they lean in the conservative direction—are taken as an indication of the former.

Although the new racism thesis has gained acceptance in some quarters, it is by no means uncontroversial. Without entering into the debate over the strength of the thesis—a controversy more adequately addressed elsewhere (Bobo 1983, 1988; Fazio 1996; Kinder 1986; Sniderman and Piazza 1993; Sniderman and Tetlock 1986; Sears 1988, 1994; Tetlock 1994), we note only that, taken to an extreme, the new racism thesis obscures some important individual differences between racial conservatives. Even if the prejudicial underpinning of some racial conservatives is acknowledged, there are no doubt countless others whose concerns about more liberal policies stem more from their philosophical beliefs about the proper role of government than from antipathy toward African-Americans.

The point is not that racial conservatism is *never* motivated by indefensible bigotry or more subtle forms of prejudice. Rather, it is that the foundations of conservatism are numerous and varied, ranging from the sophisticated ideological arguments of the libertarian right to the angry denunciations of welfare of the white supremacist groups. Granted, our views of the players in the current racial debates may change with time. But one thing seems certain: forty years from now we will not brand all opponents of affirmative action or welfare in the same pejorative way that we brand the segregationists of the 1950s. Today, we continue to have nothing but sympathy for the fictional Atticus Finch as he fights the losing battle to defend an obviously innocent black man accused of rape. We continue to speak admiringly of Hubert Humphrey for admonishing the Democrats for indifference to civil rights at their 1948 convention, and of Chief Justice Earl Warren for the courage he demonstrated in crafting the *Brown* decision in 1954. Most of all, we continue to see their adversaries as being not only wrong but simply mean-spirited and ugly. In forty years, however, will we regard current racial conservatives—at least as a cohesive group—with the same degree of contempt?

Clearly, racial conservatives are *not* a cohesive group. As the subsequent chapters in this book make plain, some of their policy positions stem undeniably from racial animosity and horrendous stereotypes. But given the diversity of racial conservatism, and the complexity of racial attitudes in general, it makes far more sense to investigate connections between racial prejudice and political attitudes empirically rather than simply to *assume* that such connections either do not exist or, as the modern racism thesis holds, that they invariably do.

RACIAL PERCEPTION AND PUBLIC POLICY

Although we contend that it is a mistake to assume that all opposition to racial programs is motivated by prejudice, it is also a mistake to assume that racial prejudice is not an important undergirding of contemporary political attitudes toward race-related issues. The new racism thesis drastically oversimplifies an extremely complicated phenomenon, but it is quite useful in another sense: it reminds us of the importance of perception and stereotyping in shaping the political views of whites on racial issues. The premise of this book is that prejudice against blacks is alive and well today, some forty years after the passage of civil rights legislation designed to solve the "race problem" in this country. Exactly where the prejudice exists, however, and how it affects the political thinking of whites on racial issues are not at all obvious. Quite clearly, to understand public opinion on racial issues, we need to know much more about the manner in which white Americans perceive, and evaluate, blacks.

This book is, fundamentally, about the link between racial perception and policy choices—about the images of African-Americans that whites hold and the political consequences of these images. We do not maintain that this focus is original; on the contrary, it has been explored for centuries. Alexis de Tocqueville (1956), Gunnar Myrdal (1944), Gordon Allport (1954), Winthrop Jordan (1968), George Fredrickson (1971), George Takaki (1979), and numerous others have come to quite similar conclusions—that the politics, economy, social structure and, indeed, even the culture of American society has, to a remarkable extent, been shaped by whites' pejorative images of blacks. Without such judgments, slavery and segregation surely could not have been justified.

According to Schuman et al. (1988), the relationship between racial stereotyping and public policy became more explicit during the late nineteenth and early twentieth centuries. The Jim Crow laws that multiplied near the end of the 1800s were commonly justified by "highly intellectualized theories of 'biological racism'" (p. 8). At the heart of the social Darwinism movement was the stereotype of African-Americans as genetically and socially inferior, an assumption which encouraged many whites to believe that blacks could not, and should not, become integrated into the white world. Quite simply, racial segregation became the preferred policy because the assumed biological inferiority of blacks necessitated their own separate set of rules.

If surveys are to be believed, the great majority of whites today, in stark contrast to forty years ago, reject the notion that African-Americans are genetically, intellectually, or otherwise biologically deficient (Schuman et al. 1988). The National Opinion Research Center (NORC), for example, found that although in 1942 only 47 percent of white Americans believed blacks to be as intelligent as whites, twenty-two years later the proportion had increased to more than eight out of ten.

Racial stereotyping, however, has not disappeared. To the contrary, as Chapter 4 of this volume makes plain, stereotypes have simply evolved. Biological stereotypes have given way to behavioral stereotypes, as large minorities (in some cases even majorities) of whites today perceive blacks to be "undisciplined" or "violent." These perceptions matter in the important sense that they frequently translate into a series of political and policy attitudes.

Thus, just as the politics of slavery, of reconstruction, and of twentieth-century segregation were shaped by whites' stereotypes of blacks, so too are many of the political debates of more recent times. Quite clearly, there is no one-to-one correspondence between racial images and policy preferences. Whites who perceive blacks negatively will not inevitably oppose welfare and affirmative action, and whites who perceive them more favorably will not inevitably support such policies. Policy preferences are far more complicated than that. As noted above, racial policy conservatism (and liberalism) have many antecedents other than whites' simple stereotypes. Our task in this book, then, is to explore not just *whether* racial perceptions matter but, of equal importance, *when, why,* and *how* they matter.

THE RACE AND POLITICS STUDY

Fortunately, new methodologies have been developed in the social sciences in recent years that make such an inquiry possible. Each chapter in this volume makes use of one of the newest and most innovative instruments ever developed for the purpose of examining racial attitudes—the Race and Politics Study (RPS) administered by the Survey Research Center at the University of California at Berkeley. In 1989, Paul Sniderman, funded by the National Science Foundation, assembled an interdisciplinary team of political scientists, psychologists, and sociologists to develop an attitudinal survey that fully exploited recent technological advances. Over the next two years, the group crafted the RPS, taking full advantage of computer-assisted telephone interviewing (CATI) technologies—technologies that enable survey researchers to utilize experimental, unobtrusive, and interactive procedures to a far greater extent than previously possible.

As will become clear in the remaining chapters, CATI technology combines the advantages of the traditional cross-sectional survey (such as generalizability) with the advantages of experimental design (control and internal validity), both of which are essential for unraveling public opinion on racial issues. Although the use of survey experiments in the study of racial attitudes did not originate with the development of CATI (see, for example, Schuman and Bobo 1988), computer-assisted designs have permitted much greater flexibility and complexity in design construction than the conventional split-ballot questionnaire. In contrast to the classic public opinion survey, which usually emphasizes standardization—asking all respondents the same questions, in the same way, and in the same order—one advantage of the CATI system is that it makes it easy to construct a variety of survey experiments, where respondents are randomly assigned to different "treatment" or question-wording groups, making it possible to attribute differences in responses exclusively to the manipulated differences in question wording.

Because neither the respondent nor the interviewer is aware of alternative question wordings, the manipulations are fairly unobtrusive. Thus, by systematically varying the racial referent and other characteristics of various stimuli in the questions (for instance, asking about black versus white welfare mothers, or about welfare programs designed to benefit blacks and minorities versus immigrants from Europe), CATI experiments combine the benefits of control and internal validity gained from experiments with the generalizability gained from cross-sectional surveys (within the limits of sampling error for each experimental condition). Moreover, because probes or follow-up questions can be tailored to initial responses with computer-assisted interviewing, the CATI system allows the analyst to transform the interview from a passive collection of preconceived ideas and opinions to an interactive process that permits greater insights into the dynamics of political reasoning (Piazza, Sniderman, and Tetlock 1991).

A common feature of the work presented in this volume is the authors' use of innovative measures and methodologies to solve chronic problems confronting students of race and politics. One such problem results from the sheer complexity of contemporary public opinion on racial issues. In contrast to the politics of segregation a generation ago, where public divisions seemed clear, public opinion on contemporary racial issues—from the explicitly racial issue of affirmative action to the racially "coded" issues of crime and welfare—seems infinitely more complex and elusive. Not only do individuals often seem ambivalent and conflicted in their opinions, being pulled by opposing considerations and values, but their responses to questions of race may also be distorted by social desirability pressures that militate against honest answers to interviewers' questions.

A further complexity stems from the fact that stereotypes and prejudice rarely translate into political behavior in any simple way. Whether people's judgments about specific issues (such as welfare) and individuals (welfare recipients) are driven by stereotyping and prejudice is likely to depend on a variety of limiting conditions, such as the way the issue is framed and the way the target individual is described.

THE PLAN OF THE BOOK

These problems—and, more important, the use of the RPS to gain leverage over them—are addressed in Chapter 2 by Paul M. Sniderman, Thomas Piazza, and Hosea Harvey. They begin by describing in detail the intellectual and academic roots of the systematic study of race, prejudice, and politics, dating back to the influential *Scientific American* studies published over a two-decade span beginning in the mid-1950s. Although these reports provided considerable room for optimism, subsequent studies attacked their findings on a number of fronts, which the authors of Chapter 2 discuss.

Historically, definitions of prejudice have been plentiful; conceptual clarity on what exactly constitutes prejudice, on the other hand, has been in short supply. Sniderman, Piazza, and Harvey seek to clarify our understanding of the phenomenon by first identifying points of agreement in different definitions of prejudice and then addressing points at which they diverge.

This "recovery of the concept of racial prejudice," which is the first theme of their argument, is followed by a careful discussion of the "contingency of political judgments"—by which they mean the reality that political attitudes are highly dependent upon the specific characteristics of the people, places, and things that serve as the stimuli of questions posed to respondents. The analytic and measurement features of the RPS, they contend, have been carefully designed to unpack the circumstances under which racial judgments do and do not affect public policy attitudes.

The discussion of prejudice in Chapter 2 is useful for highlighting the fact that the different authors of this volume all, in one way or another, deal with different aspects of prejudice (stereotypes, affect, social distance, and so on), even if they do not always use the same labels and measures. Thus, rather than adopting a "one size fits all" approach to prejudice and politics, different authors emphasize different aspects of prejudice that help to explain public opinion on racial issues.

Sniderman, Piazza, and Harvey's discussion is also useful for underscoring the considerable overlap between racial prejudice and racial stereotyping. Although the two concepts are not identical, negative stereotyping is certainly a better measure of prejudice than many of the current alternatives—notably, the modern or symbolic racism scale. Used not only by political scientists (Kinder and Sears 1981) but by some social psychologists as well (Devine et al. 1991), the modern racism scale confounds political attitudes with racial attitudes and then, quite tautologically, uses this prejudice measure to predict policy attitudes. By contrast, stereotypes are far enough removed from policy attitudes to avoid this tautology. Moreover, negative stereotypes adhere to the common properties of prejudice identified by Sniderman, Piazza, and Harvey: they are clearly evaluative (as in describing blacks as "lazy" or "violent"), over-generalized (as in attributing such traits to "most blacks" or "blacks in general"), and highly resistant to change (as are stereotypes in general).

Of course, no single measure is capable of capturing all of what scholars mean by a multifaceted concept like prejudice. In Chapter 3, James Kuklinski and Michael Cobb explore a different dimension of prejudice with one of the few unobtrusive measures of prejudice devised for a mass telephone survey. One of the most important innovations of the RPS is its use of unobtrusive measurement, or the ability to assess opinions without the knowledge of the respondent—an important consideration in measuring racial attitudes in today's climate. The randomized experiment is one unobtrusive way to detect racial bias in whites' opinions about blacks; the "list experiment," devised by Kuklinski, is another. With this procedure, fully exploited in Chapter 3, a random half of the sample is read a list of three situations unrelated to race (for example, athletes being paid multimillion-dollar salaries) and asked to indicate the number of situations that "anger" them. Another random half of the sample is read a list that contains a fourth situation which is race-relevant (such as "a black family moving next door"). Differences in the mean number of anger-provoking conditions between the baseline group and the test group, then, can only be attributed to the racial animosities of the respondents. Using this unobtrusive measure of prejudice, Kuklinski and Cobb are able to calculate the prevalence of bigotry both in the country as a whole and in strategic subsets of it. The authors find, for instance, that, despite the presumed convergence between north and south in recent decades, sharp regional differences in prejudice continue to exist, with white southern males expressing extremely high levels of anger at the thought of a single black family moving next door.

In Chapter 4, Mark Peffley and Jon Hurwitz turn to an exploration of the content, antecedents, and political consequences of shared racial perceptions—otherwise known as stereotypes. Judging from the results of the RPS, many whites continue to hold negative stereotypes of African-Americans nearly forty years after the civil rights movement. Negative stereotypes are more prevalent in the South and among the less educated, but the most powerful predictors of racial stereotyping, the authors find, are different components of ethnocentrism—social intolerance, conformity, and anti-Semitism.

Much of the extant research on racial stereotyping focuses on how whites feel about generic blacks and the policies—such as welfare, affirmative action, and crime—that affect minorities. Peffley and Hurwitz shift the focus of this work by investigating how whites with different expectations of African-Americans respond to counterstereotypical information in the explosive contexts of welfare and crime. Using CATI, the authors manipulate both the race and other attributes of welfare mothers, welfare recipients, and drug suspects to determine how two groups of whites—those who embrace and those who reject negative racial stereotypes—respond to counterstereotypical individuating information. Specifically, what happens when whites who embrace negative stereotypes of blacks are confronted with scenarios in which blacks do not fit the pejorative impression? Does positive individuating information have any impact on their political judgments of blacks? Conversely, how do whites who reject such stereotypes respond in the presence of blacks who are stigmatized and who correspond to quite negative images? Are their more positive views of blacks in the abstract mere window dressing, which they quickly abandon when confronted with stigmatized blacks?

Among which sector of the polity are such images most consequential? It has been widely assumed that racism is more rampant among Republicans and conservatives than among Democrats and liberals; after all, most of the notorious racial hard-liners have come from the right wing of the political spectrum. In Chapter 5, however, Carmines and Layman put a new and largely counterintuitive spin on this question: they show that negative stereotypes are almost as prevalent on the left as they are on the right. More important, they find these negative images of blacks to be much more consequential for Democrats than for Republicans. Although prejudice—or the endorsement of negative racial stereotypes—makes little difference in whether Republicans support policies such as affirmative action and welfare assistance for blacks, they make a remarkable difference for Democrats and their support for these same programs. Paradoxically, then, the authors conclude that even if prejudice is somewhat more common on the political right, it is more powerful on the political left. After documenting the nature, depth, and location of divisions over racial issues in the Democratic party, the authors are in a strong position to speculate on the power of race to shape the future political landscape in this country.

While Chapters 3–5 focus on the content and distribution of racial perceptions, Chapters 6 and 7 explicitly spotlight policy attitudes. Laura Stoker examines the contentious "wedge" issue of affirmative action in Chapter 6, demonstrating convincingly the ambivalent and highly conditional nature of opinion on this matter. When surveys indicate that X percent of Americans favor (or oppose) affirmative action programs, the findings are not necessarily wrong; they are, however, capable of revealing only a small portion of the picture. In her analyses of experiments pertaining to affirmative action in the workplace and in university admissions, Stoker reveals that support among whites is strongly influenced by both the rationale given for the program and racial prejudice. Notably, programs consistent with Supreme Court rulings upholding affirmative action programs as "a remedy for past discrimination" receive a much larger measure of support from whites than do the great bulk of surveys that either provide no rationale or describe such programs pejoratively as "quotas" or "special treatment" programs. Also in contrast to prior studies, Stoker finds that prejudice plays an important role in conditioning support for affirmative action, though in ways that diverge from prior studies.

Martin Gilens turns, in Chapter 7, to the important question of whether whites' opposition to ostensibly race-neutral issues like welfare stem, in part, from their dislike of blacks. This is an important question, Gilens argues, because although numerous studies have investigated links between racial attitudes and explicitly racial issues, such as busing and affirmative action, few have examined the racial components of racially "coded" issues like welfare and crime that play upon whites' negative views of blacks without ever explicitly raising the "race card" (Edsall and Edsall 1991). Gilens exploits the power of CATI to disentangle the racial versus class dimensions of whites' antagonism to welfare policies. Using identical questions about whites' perceptions of black and white welfare recipients, for example, he shows that negative views of black (but not white) welfare mothers are strongly related to opposition to welfare. The analysis is both elegant and convincing, made possible, in part, by the design of the RPS survey.

It is one matter to establish the existence of prejudice (and its link with social policy), but quite another to understand its character. In Chapter 8, Kathleen Knight begins to address this issue by asking how whites, in their own words, describe African-Americans and talk about racial issues. Typically, responses to closed-ended questions offer respondents little opportunity to display the complexity and ambivalence that have become the hallmarks of contemporary feelings about race. In the RPS, however, respondents are asked to discuss, at length, their own explanations of a central issue fueling racial discord: why are blacks typically less well off than whites? As will be shown, explanations of black conditions differ dramatically among our respondents. Particularly relevant is the division between whites who attribute black misfortune to environmental and sociological factors (such as discrimination or a lack of opportunity) and those who see the condition as self-inflicted. In the course of her analysis, Knight explores both the antecedents of attributions of the black dilemma and some of the consequences of such attributions. We choose to conclude this volume with Knight's analysis because the richness of insights gained from such open-ended responses leaves readers with a remembrance of the "human element" that fixed-choice surveys often obscure. This human element, it is hoped, will remind readers both that race is something with which well-meaning individuals struggle on a regular basis and, more important, that prejudice is more than merely a statistic.

Readers will notice that, overall, the methodological and substantive foci of the book go hand in hand. Computer-assisted interviewing allows the analyst to probe and manipulate responses to gain a more conditional view of public opinion. In fact, a more nuanced view of the impact of prejudice on political opinions is exactly what emerges from the chapters in this book. In contrast to earlier views of prejudice as an all-pervasive force in American politics directed indiscriminately by all whites toward all blacks under all circumstances, the common substantive theme of this book is that the impact of prejudice on political attitudes is dependent on numerous extenuating circumstances. Thus, the linkage between prejudice and politics is stronger for some policies than others (see Stoker and Gilens), for some policy frames than others (see Stoker), among Democrats than among Republicans (see Carmines and Layman), for some descriptions of blacks than for others (see Peffley and Hurwitz), and so on. This more conditional view of the power of prejudice in public opinion is a natural outgrowth of a more sensitive methodology that is capable of probing responses. Importantly, however, this more conditional view in no way diminishes the importance of prejudice in American politics. To the contrary, a more complex and sometimes more insidious view of the effects of prejudice emerges from our study.

As Sniderman, Piazza, and Harvey explain in Chapter 2, and as readers of subsequent chapters will rapidly realize, the analyses in this volume are wide-ranging substantively and eclectic methodologically. Not only are the contributors from different disciplines, but the RPS makes possible an extremely rich and varied assortment of methods, ranging from analyses of experimental data to open-ended responses to unobtrusive measurements.

Readers will also note the impressive breadth and diversity of the RPS. The telephone interviews with a national probability sample of more than two thousand individuals have been supplemented by an additional battery of items mailed to respondents and returned to the Berkeley Survey Research Center for analysis. The total number of variables provides a range of items unavailable in any existing national study of race. One of our goals in this book, consequently, is to encourage the scholarly community to familiarize itself with, and take advantage of, one of the most innovative and comprehensive instruments ever developed in the social sciences, let alone in the field of race.

Despite the considerable contributions of the RPS, it does, like any other, have its limitations. In the first place, the focus is clearly on the perceptions of white Americans, ignoring the obviously important racial judgments of African-Americans. This restriction to whites' perceptions is based on two considerations, the first being that the RPS survey includes only a small subsample of black respondents (N = 201), making statistical comparisons somewhat suspect. More important, however, is our firm belief that Gunnar Myrdal's (1944) conviction that the problem of race and prejudice in the United States is a white person's problem is still largely true today. At the same time, however, we acknowledge the enormous contribution that a range of studies on black political attitudes and behavior makes to a more complete understanding of the problem of race in this country (see, for example, Bobo and Kluegel 1993; Dawson 1994; Sigelman and Welch 1991; Smith and Seltzer 1992; Tate 1993).

Second, we acknowledge that the insights into public opinion included in this volume are time-bound in the sense that they represent only a snapshot analysis reflecting public reactions to politics at a particular moment. Race in America is notable, ironically, both because of its remarkable continuity of importance and because of its constantly changing and fluid nature. Historically, it has been impossible to understand American politics without appreciating the central role race has played in shaping public thinking on issues that have polarized the country. Recent political developments serve as grim reminders that the politics of race on the contemporary scene has, in many ways, intensified rather than abated.

One is struck by the sudden willingness of politicians across the political spectrum to jump on the political bandwagon to dismantle a range of affirmative action programs originally enacted by bipartisan majorities as a remedy to discrimination against blacks. We have also recently witnessed dramatic reversals in the Supreme Court's willingness to uphold the constitutionality of a variety of policies designed to benefit blacks, including not only affirmative action programs (as in *Adarand Constructors v. Pena* [1995]) but black-majority congressional districts (*Shaw v. Reno* [1993]) and school desegregation plans (*Missouri v. Jenkins* [1995]). Such political backsliding is particularly troubling in light of the continuing need to confront persistent problems of racial segregation (Massey and Denton 1993), racial inequalities in income and wealth (Sigelman and Welch 1991), and urban decay in the inner city (Wilson 1987).

In the contemporary context one is also struck by the strong racial undercurrents that characterize debates on such prominent and emotional issues as crime and welfare. Although neither issue is explicitly racial in the same fashion as affirmative action or busing, both become linked to race because white Americans (inaccurately) tend to see the typical welfare recipient and criminal as being black. Such perceptions are, of course, promoted by news coverage that portrays the typical welfare recipient or criminal suspect as African-American and by the political rhetoric of politicians who incite whites' fear and loathing of blacks by talking about welfare and crime in racially coded terms. Prominent examples include the Willie Horton ads shown during the 1988 presidential election, which linked an African-American to fears of violent crime, and the ads of David Duke (among others), which linked blacks to resentment of welfare.

Developments in the scientific community must also be termed regressive, in a sense. To cite just one example, the publication of *The Bell Curve* (Herrnstein and Murray 1994), despite the book's several scientific shortcomings, has helped to promote the idea that programs designed to help blacks are doomed to failure, in part because racial differences in achievement, according to the authors, may be rooted in the lower average intelligence of African-Americans compared to whites.

In short, race relations, public policies, political debates, and virtually everything else in the environment continue to evolve, rendering the attitudes that we chart today an important part of a time series that must continue to be gauged into the future. Thus, just as the analyses included in this volume represent a starting point rather than a culmination of the Race and Politics Study, the RPS itself is not, and must not be, an end-point to the scholarly analysis of race in America.

REFERENCES

Allport, Gordon W. 1954. *The Nature of Prejudice*. Garden City, N.Y.: Doubleday Anchor.
Beals, Melba Pattillo. 1994. *Warriors Don't Cry: A Searing Memoir of the Battle to Integrate Little Rock's Central High*. New York: Pocket Books.

Bobo, Lawrence. 1983. "Whites' Opposition to Busing: Symbolic Racism or Realistic Group Conflict?" *Journal of Personality and Social Psychology* 45:1196-1210.

―――. 1988. "Group Conflict, Prejudice, and the Paradox of Contemporary Racial Attitudes." In *Eliminating Racism: Profiles in Controversy,* ed. Phyllis A. Katz and Dalmas A. Taylor. New York: Plenum.

Dawson, Robert. 1994. *Behind the Mule: Race and Class in African-American Politics.* Princeton, N.J.: Princeton University Press.

Devine, Patricia G., Margo J. Monteith, Julia R. Zuwerink, and Andrew J. Elliot. 1991. "Prejudice without Compunction." *Journal of Personality and Social Psychology* 60:817–30.

Edsall, Thomas B., and Mary D. Edsall. 1992. *Chain Reaction: The Impact of Race, Rights, and Taxes on American Politics.* New York: W. W. Norton.

Fazio, Russell H., Joni R. Jackson, Bridget C. Dunton, and Carol J. Williams. 1995. "Variability in Automatic Activation as an Unobtrusive Measure of Racial Attitudes: A Bona Fide Pipeline?" *Journal of Personality and Social Psychology* 69:1013–27.

Fredrickson, George M. 1971. *The Black Image in the White Mind: The Debate on African-Americans' Character and Destiny, 1817–1914.* New York: Harper and Row.

Herrnstein, Richard J., and Charles Murray. 1994. *The Bell Curve: Intelligence and Class Structure in American Life.* New York: Free Press.

Jordan, Winthrop D. 1968. *White Over Black: American Attitudes Toward the Negro, 1550–1812.* Baltimore: Penguin.

Kinder, Donald R. 1986. "The Continuing American Dilemma: White Resistance to Racial Change 40 Years After Myrdal." *Journal of Social Issues* 42:151–71.

Kinder, Donald R., and David O. Sears. 1981. "Prejudice and Politics: Symbolic Racism Versus Racial Threats to the Good Life." *Journal of Personality and Social Psychology* 40:414–31.

Massey, Douglas S., and Nancy A. Denton. 1993. *American Apartheid: Segregation and the Making of an Underclass.* Cambridge, Mass.: Harvard University Press.

McConahay, James B., and James C. Hough. 1976. "Symbolic Racism." *Journal of Social Issues* 32:23–45.

Myrdal, Gunnar. 1944. *An American Dilemma: The Negro Problem and Modern Democracy.* 2 vols. New York: Random House.

Piazza, Thomas, Paul M. Sniderman, and Philip E. Tetlock. 1991. "Analysis of the Dynamics of Political Reasoning: A General-Purpose Computer-Assisted Methodology." *Political Analysis II.* Ann Arbor: University of Michigan Press.

Schuman, Howard, and Lawrence Bobo. 1988. "Survey-Based Experiments on White Racial Attitudes Toward Residential Integration." *American Journal of Sociology* 2:161–207.

Schuman, Howard, Charlotte Steeh, and Lawrence Bobo. 1988. *Racial Attitudes in America: Trends and Interpretations.* Cambridge, Mass.: Harvard University Press.

Sears, David O. 1988. "Symbolic Racism." In *Eliminating Racism: Profiles in Controversy,* ed. Phyllis A. Katz and Dalmas A. Taylor. New York: Plenum Press.

―――. 1994. "Ideological Bias in Political Psychology: The View from Scientific Hell." *Political Psychology* 15:509–29.

Sigelman, Lee, and Susan Welch. 1991. *A Dream Deferred: Black Attitudes Toward Race and Inequality.* Cambridge: Cambridge University Press.

Smith, Robert C., and Richard Seltzer. 1992. *Race, Class, and Culture: A Study in Afro-American Public Opinion*. Albany, N.Y.: SUNY Press.

Sniderman, Paul M., and Thomas Piazza. 1993. *The Scar of Race*. Cambridge, Mass.: Harvard University Press.

Sniderman, Paul M., and Philip E. Tetlock. 1986. "Symbolic Racism: Problems of Motive Attribution in Political Science.". *Journal of Social Issues* 42:129–50.

Takaki, Ronald T. 1979. *Iron Cages: Race and Culture in Nineteenth-Century America*. Seattle: University of Washington Press.

Tate, Katherine. 1993. *From Protest to Politics: The New Black Voters in the American Electorate*. Cambridge, Mass.: Harvard University Press.

Tetlock, Philip. 1994. "Political Psychology or Politicized Psychology: Is the Road to Scientific Hell Paved with Good Moral Intentions?" *Political Psychology* 15:509–29.

Tocqueville, Alexis de. 1945 [1835]. *Democracy in America*, vol. 1. Trans. Henry Reeve. New York: Vintage.

Wilson, William Julius. 1987. *The Truly Disadvantaged: The Inner City, the Underclass and Public Policy.* Chicago: University of Chicago Press.

Chapter 2 Prejudice and Politics: An Intellectual Biography of a Research Project

Paul M. Sniderman, Thomas Piazza, and Hosea Harvey

The specific studies presented in this book, each conceived on its own terms, are part of a larger framework on the analysis of prejudice and politics. We want, in this chapter, to call attention to this framework by sketching the intellectual background of the Race and Politics Project and commenting on its deeper-lying analytical themes. We hope, by engaging the classic studies of prejudice and politics, to illuminate three themes at the center of this book as a whole: the recovery of racial prejudice as a problem worthy of study, the inescapably contingent character of political judgments about issues of race, and the necessity (in a field of study that has made a virtue of repetition of measures) of innovations in measurement.

AN INTELLECTUAL CHRONOLOGY

Beginning slowly and suffering many reversals, the civil rights movement became a national force in the 1950s. Even so, the official apparatus and public practice of racial segregation, with its heraldry of apartheid, appeared fixed in place. The Supreme Court had announced, in the *Brown* decision, the end of the era of "separate but equal" in schools (*Brown v. Board of Education of Topeka,* 1954). But between the self-interested timidity of public officials and the self-righteous hostility of White Citizen Councils, Southern schools remained segregated. Yet, only a short time later, the landmark Civil Rights Act was passed in 1964, the Voting Rights Act in 1965.

Social science a generation ago provided both a record of the social and political change and an interpretation of its meaning. For generations, Americans who have never heard of Gunnar Myrdal have thought of race as an American dilemma. The issue of race, they recognized, has political and economic aspects, but it goes deeper than either. At its core, it represents a fundamental moral contradiction—between the highest principles that Americans, as Americans, held and the institutionalized practice of racial segregation. And, immediate obstacles notwithstanding, the outcome of this contradiction seemed certain: Americans, if forced to choose, would favor liberty, equality, and fair play.

Americans, according to the first generation of systematic research on racial attitudes, increasingly did choose in favor of tolerance and equality. In an extended series of reports published in *Scientific American,* beginning in the mid-1950s and running through the 1970s, Herbert Hyman, Paul Sheatsley, and their colleagues tracked changes in the racial attitudes of white Americans, concentrating on public support for explicit racial segregation—for separate school systems, public accommodations, seating sections in public transportation, and residential areas. The first *Scientific American* study documented a historic transformation. An example will suffice: in 1942, only one-third of whites believed that white students and black students should go to the same schools, and less than half opposed the idea that there should be separate sections for Negroes in streetcars and buses; by 1956, one-half of whites favored desegregation of schools, and nearly two-thirds supported desegregation of public transportation (Hyman and Sheatsley 1956).

Continuing studies, by Hyman, Sheatsley, and their colleagues (Hyman and Sheatsley 1964; Greeley and Sheatsley 1971; and Taylor, Sheatsley, and Greeley 1978) and then by Howard Schuman and his (see Schuman, Steeh, and Bobo 1985), made two further fundamental points. First, the progressive trend, so far from being a mere decade spurt, continued through the sixties, seventies, and eighties. Second, the trend, rather than being narrowly confined to the institutions of Jim Crow, represented a broad movement in favor of tolerance. There was, conspicuously, a collapse of popular support, initially in the North and later in the South, too, for racial segregation. But the change in social norms also extended to private interactions, with the barriers to blacks being invited as guests to a white's home, or being allowed to live in the same neighborhood, or marrying a white, being breached, albeit more slowly and in the face of more resistance than for more public and impersonal forms of interaction. Indeed, so far from being restricted to issues of race, the movement in favor of tolerance was being swept along by a broad current of open-mindedness, which unmistakably showed itself in increasing public support for the political rights of unpopular or controversial political or social groups, including communists, atheists, and homosexuals.[1]

The sweep and seemingly irresistible momentum of the trend in favor of tolerance suggested that fundamental social processes were at work. In his classic study of political tolerance, *Communism, Conformity, and Civil Liberties,* Samuel Stouffer captured the spirit of this transformation of the society as a whole. "Great social, economic and technological forces," he declared, "are operating slowly and imperceptibly on the side of spreading tolerance. The rising level of education and the accompanying decline in authoritarian child-rearing practices increase independence of thought and respect for others whose ideas are different. The increasing geographic movement has a similar consequence, as well as the vicarious experiences supplied by the magic of our ever more powerful media of communications" (1992, p. 236). Here was the basis for a generation's optimism. The last of the *Scientific American* reports, in particular, focused on a trio of factors promoting racial tolerance—the entrance of new age-cohorts, increased educational opportunities, and the liberalization of the general climate of opinion in American society (Taylor, Sheatsley, and Greeley 1978, pp. 42–49). Fundamental and very nearly automatic social processes were driving forward the liberalization of American society.

It would be quite wrong to give the impression that the *Scientific American* reports were insensitive to complexity or lacking in qualification. The series repeatedly showed that white opinion was far from uniform. The willingness to accept blacks in public places did not carry with it a comparable readiness to accept them in private ones, and if Americans were markedly more tolerant than they had been, it did not mean that they had become tolerant in any absolute sense. Moreover, even if the account of change was predominantly social and mechanistic, it was not entirely so. Contrasting school districts within the South that had achieved significant desegregation with those that had resisted it, the *Scientific American* investigators observed that the more the public schools had in fact desegregated, the more public support there was for racial desegregation, suggesting that public action in favor of school desegregation can lead to increases in public support for it, as well as the other way around. As they remarked, "Apparently, the pattern is that as official action works to bury what is already regarded as a lost cause, public acceptance of integration increases because opinions are readjusted to the inevitable reality" (Hyman and Sheatsley 1956, p. 21). Their argument, if right, throws a direct light on the role of local leadership in the dynamics of societal change. Instead of capitalizing on a sense of inevitability in the wake of the *Brown* decision, a large percentage of local officials made evident their reluctance to press ahead with school desegregation, in the process not only forgoing the momentum in favor of desegregation but legitimizing opposition to it.

There is a broader point, obscured in subsequent studies. The authors of the *Scientific American* reports were well aware of the resistance, in the North as well as the South, to racial change. Through the 1960s and 1970s, they took pains to detail, among other things, local conflicts over school integration; the national drama in Little Rock in 1957; George Wallace's ominous success in northern as well as southern presidential primaries. Their argument was not that the American dilemma had been resolved but rather that one measure of the strength of the progressive trend in favor of racial tolerance was precisely its continuation in the face of all the controversies over race.

THE REVISIONIST WORK

The *Scientific American* studies, with their demonstration of a gathering momentum of the movement to racial tolerance, represented the high-water mark of faith in the power of American idealism. Before the last of the studies even had appeared, however, the studies came under fire. From the 1970s on, critics rejected or radically qualified the reports' optimism. And the next generation of research changed the climate of opinion. A belief that the strongest force in favor of racial progress was the commitment of white Americans to decency and fair play gave way to a skepticism, even a cynicism, about their professions of support for the principles of racial equality and tolerance.

The revisionism of the second generation was woven out of distinct strands of argument, and we want, therefore, to lay out three of the most influential lines of criticism. The first was formulated by Sears and his colleagues (Kinder and Sears 1981; McConahay and Hough 1976; Sears and Kinder 1971). Curiously, the starting point of their criticism of the argument of the *Scientific American* reports was acceptance of the findings contained in them. Citing the studies, Sears and his colleagues declared that "white America has become, in principle at least, racially egalitarian" (Kinder and Sears 1981, p. 416). Yet resistance to racial change persisted. There were the flashpoint issues of busing, crime, and poverty, and, increasingly, of affirmative action, not to mention the evident handicap under which black candidates for public office had to labor (Sears, Hensler, and Speer 1979). Large numbers of white Americans, though approving the idea of racial equality, were resisting nearly every active effort to achieve it. Racism in its overt form was no longer a major political force, the *Scientific American* studies had showed: but if racism of the traditional stripe did not lie behind white resistance to racial equality for blacks, what did?

The answer, according to Sears and his colleagues, was a new racism. Like the old racism, it centered on dislike of blacks. Also like the old, it appeared early in the developmental cycle, during pre-adult years, and once acquired persisted through adulthood. But unlike the old racism, which expressed itself in overtly derogatory evaluations of blacks, the new racism was subtle. It took the form of beliefs that on their face were not necessarily racist. Before, racists would say blatantly that blacks were lazy. Now, they would say instead that if blacks were only willing to work hard, they could be as well off as whites. If challenged, new racists would protest that, so far from being racists, the whole point was that they believed blacks could achieve as much as whites if they were willing to apply themselves.

The new racism also is new in a second and still more significant respect. Rather than having to rely solely on its own strength, it has now been fused with a whole array of traditional American values, above all individualism. So understood, modern or symbolic racism "represents a form of resistance to change in the racial status quo based on moral feelings that blacks violate such traditional American values as individualism and self-reliance, the work ethic, obedience, and discipline" (Kinder and Sears 1981, p. 416). It would be a shame to overlook the fine irony of this formulation. By positing the existence of a new racism in addition to, and independent of, the old, it is possible to accept the validity of the *Scientific American* findings of increased racial tolerance, and yet turn Myrdal's confidence in the American Creed on its head. The eclipse of overt racism, captured in initial public opinion studies, would have seemed to confirm the buoyancy of the first generation of public opinion research on racial attitudes. But these findings, the argument now runs, do not offer reason for optimism—indeed, if anything, the opposite. The eclipse of overt racism has been counterbalanced by the advent of a new, more modern racism. And modern racism, though no less noxious than the old, is more subtle and now has the backing of "the proudest and finest of American values" (Sears 1988, p. 54).

Myrdal's thesis can also be challenged by challenging the *Scientific American* findings outright, and toward the end of the 1970s Mary Jackman and her colleague took this route (Jackman 1978; Jackman 1981; and Jackman and Muha 1984). Racial tolerance, they contended, manifests itself at two distinct levels: support for the principle of tolerance, and support for the principle in practice, by backing public policies to achieve it. The *Scientific American* studies concluded that education promoted tolerance. But if better-educated people are more likely to have a genuine and well-grounded commitment to tolerance *because* they are better educated, then the better educated people are, the more consistent they should be in translating their general support for the principle of tolerance into specific policies to achieve it. But, Jackman contended, although the more educated are more likely to favor general tolerance, they are not more likely to support applied tolerance, and what is more, the connection between general and applied tolerance is no tighter for the more educated than for the less.

The *Scientific American* studies, if Jackman's argument is correct, are tracking not a stronger commitment to racial integration but "a greater familiarity with the appropriate democratic position on racial integration" (Jackman 1978, p. 322). Education may teach a lesson of tolerance but, if Jackman is right, the lesson is learned only superficially. Well-educated whites are more likely to know the "right" thing to say; perhaps more likely even to believe it the right thing to do. But their commitment to racial tolerance and equality is superficial. And when they must choose between racial tolerance and competing values, as inevitably they will in the swirl of democratic politics, they choose to give up racial equality. Thus the appearance of racial progress the *Scientific American* reports recorded, though not quite a sham, is largely an illusion.

If the first two lines of criticism did not suffice to rebut the optimism of the first generation of public opinion research on race, there was a third, led by Schuman, Steeh, and Bobo (1985). The hinge of their analysis was a contrast of white racial attitudes at the levels of principle and of policy. In a uniquely panoramic analysis, Schuman and his colleagues first documented the continuing momentum in favor of racial desegregation among whites at the level of principle.[2] But then, as a second step, they tracked white racial attitudes toward a large array of specific policies intended to achieve racial equality (for example, whether the federal government has a responsibility to assure fair treatment in employment for blacks or to see that white and black children should go to the same schools). The patterns for the two, they show, differ. At any one point in time, there always is markedly less public support for policies intended to make the principle of racial equality a reality than for the principle in the abstract. Still more tellingly, over time, although support for the principle of racial equality has shot up, support for policies to realize equality has either remained flat or, in some instances, even fallen off (Schuman, Steeh, and Bobo 1985, table 3.2 [pp. 88–89]).

Why the difference between principle and policy? Unlike Sears and his colleagues, Schuman and his do not see it as a sign of a new form of racism. Unlike Jackman and hers, they do not read it as evidence of the superficiality of white Americans' commitment to the principle of racial equality. Instead, they reason that if whites resist government programs to assist blacks in becoming equal even in the face of a genuine belief of racial equality, there must be a sticking point. The exact nature of this sticking point is not entirely clear, Schuman and his colleagues observe. It is unlikely that ordinary citizens resist government activism in the area of race either because they have strongly held views about government activism across the board, since whether they favor or oppose government intervention seems to have much to do both with the particular domain of policy and their own political point of view. Nor is it likely that they resist government activism on race because of a loss of confidence in government efficacy and honesty, since public resistance to government efforts to achieve racial equality in particular does not appear to be rooted in a general cynicism about government. Nor, finally, is it likely that they resist it because of a specific aversion to federal intervention, since resistance to local initiatives to assure racial equality (for example, in the form of fair housing laws) is just as marked. Instead, as an explanation of the principle-policy puzzle, Schuman and his colleagues offer their "own tentative interpretation . . . that it is constraint of any kind that is disliked, and that the extent to which respondents accept constraints is heavily influenced by the degree to which they support a particular policy goal" (Schuman, Steeh, and Bobo 1985, p. 189).

On at least three different grounds, then, the second generation of public opinion research on American racial attitudes questioned the optimism of the first. The values of the American Creed would not bring about racial fairness because they were themselves implicated in a new racism (the position of Sears and his colleagues); or because they had only a superficial hold on Americans (the argument of Jackman and her colleagues); or because they were frustrated by an aversion to constraint (the hypothesis of Schuman and his colleagues). It may have been difficult to agree with all three. It was not, however, hard to accept any two. And even if one concurred with only one, the conclusion to draw was the same: pessimism about the prospects for racial progress.

THE CONCEPT OF PREJUDICE

It may be premature to judge whether this verdict of pessimism was justified or not, but it is timely to consider whether it has limits. There is, most obviously, the question of whether the second generation of research was well done. Early on we looked at much of it.[3] In preparing for this study, however, instead of only critically evaluating what had been done, it seemed to us crucial to bring into focus what had yet to be done.

The first thing to do stood out at once: to pay attention to racial prejudice. Over the last two decades nearly every aspect of American racial attitudes has been measured except the most important: racial prejudice. As Schuman and his colleagues have pointed out, in all the major studies through the 1970s and 1980s, of the three principal sources of trend data, only one, the NORC, has information at all on white attitudes toward blacks, and the information it has is limited to a single question, which was in any event discontinued after 1968.

Why racial prejudice, of all things, was omitted from the study of racial attitudes is far from clear. One reason, it has been suggested, was a belief that merely to ask the questions necessarily had "racist overtones."[4] Another followed from the symbolic-racism research program of Sears and his colleagues. Traditional prejudice, they believed, had all but disappeared (Kinder and Sears 1981, p. 416). It therefore made little sense, it seemed to follow, to see if a substantial number of whites would agree with frankly derogatory assertions about blacks.[5] Whatever the reason, the consequence was the same. Whether racial prejudice was common or scarce in the 1970s and 1980s; whether racial prejudice is more pervasive in some parts of American society than in others; even so essential a question as whether there now is less racial prejudice than there was twenty years ago—all are unanswerable questions now because the right questions were not asked then.

Which made it necessary for us to determine—since racial prejudice manifestly needed to be recovered in the study of racial politics—what racial prejudice means. Below, we list a number of conceptual definitions of prejudice.[6]

- Prejudiced attitudes . . . are irrational, unjust, or intolerant dispositions toward others. They are often accompanied by stereotyping. This is the attribution of supposed characteristics of the whole group to all its individual members (Milner 1975, p. 9).

- It seems most useful to us to define prejudice as a failure of rationality or a failure of justice or a failure of human-heartedness in an individual's attitude toward members of another ethnic group (Harding, Prochansky, Kutner, and Chein 1969, p. 6).
- An emotional, rigid attitude, a predisposition to respond to a certain stimulus in a certain way toward a group of people (Simpson and Yinger 1985, p. 21).
- Thinking ill of others without sufficient warrant (Allport 1954, p. 7).
- Ethnic prejudice is an antipathy based upon a faulty and inflexible generalization. It may be felt or expressed. It may be directed toward a group as a whole, or toward an individual because he is a member of that group (Allport 1954, p. 9).
- An unsubstantiated prejudgment of an individual or group, favorable or unfavorable in character, tending to action in a consonant direction (Klineberg 1968, p. 439).
- A pattern of hostility in interpersonal relations which is directed against an entire group, or against its individual members; it fulfills a specific irrational function for its bearer (Ackerman and Jahoda 1950, pp. 2–3).
- Hostility or aggression toward individuals on the basis of their group membership (Buss 1961, p. 245).
- Group prejudice is now commonly viewed as having two components: hostility and misinformation (Kelman and Pettigrew 1959, p. 436).
- An unfavorable attitude toward an object which tends to be highly stereotyped, emotionally charged, and not easily changed by contrary information (Krech, Crutchfield, and Ballachey 1962, p. 321).

Four points of agreement stand out. First, prejudice refers to a response to members of a group by virtue of their membership in the group. Milner, for example, speaks of "the attribution of . . . characteristics of the whole group to all its individual members" (see Duckitt 1992, table 2.1 [p. 10]); Allport (1954, p. 9) of a response "based on . . . generalization . . . directed toward a group as whole, or toward an individual because he is a member of that group"; and Jones (1986) of a "generalization from a group characterization (stereotype) to an individual member of the group" (cited by Dovidio and Gaertner 1986, p. 3). It makes sense, in ordinary language, to speak of one person being prejudiced against another without an attribution of membership in a group necessarily being invoked. For our purposes, however, the concept of prejudice presumes a response directed toward individuals by virtue of their membership in a group.

Second, prejudice involves an evaluative orientation. In principle, an evaluative orientation can be positive as well as negative, and there are indeed studies of "in-group bias"—the disposition to reward members of the same group as oneself—as well as of "out-group bias"—the disposition to sanction members of a group different from oneself (Tajfel 1970). Nonetheless, as the definitions of prejudice enumerated above make plain, archetypically the evaluative orientation characteristic of prejudice is negative. Notice the references to dispositions that are "unjust or intolerant" (Milner 1975, p. 9), "a failure of human-heartedness" (Harding, Prochansky, Kutner, and Chein 1969, p. 6), a "pattern of hostility" (Ackerman and Jahoda 1950, pp. 2–3), or "hostility or aggression toward individuals on the basis of their group membership" (Buss 1961, p. 245). In sum, feelings of contempt, disdain, antipathy, dislike, distaste, and aversion toward members of a group, by virtue of their membership in the group, are at the center of the concept of prejudice.

Third, prejudice involves a negative evaluative orientation toward a group or member of a group that is incorrect. The presumption of an attribution that is not only negative but also erroneous is critical, and is conveyed in a variety of ways—in references, for example, to "the attribution of supposed characteristics" (Milner 1975, p. 9); "thinking ill of others without sufficient warrant" (Allport 1954, p. 7); to "a faulty generalization" (Allport 1954, p. 9); to "misinformation" (Kelman and Pettigrew 1959, p. 436). In saying that prejudice involves a faulty attribution, we are not suggesting that the exact sense in which an error is being made is clear, only that it is unequivocally clear that prejudice involves an erroneous attribution of a negative characteristic to a group as a whole (or to a member of a group by virtue of his or her membership).

Fourth, there is a requirement of consistency. By way of analogy, consider judging whether a particular person is politically a liberal. To learn that he took a liberal position on one issue on one occasion offers little help; the question is, rather, whether he reliably and predictably takes liberal positions on issues of the day. In saying this, we are not suggesting that a liberal is perfectly consistent, only that the more consistently liberal a person's political choices, the more liberal he or she is considered to be. Exactly the same principle holds for prejudice. It is one thing to categorize a person as a bigot because he offers, on a particular occasion, a negative judgment of a particular social group; it is another if he does so regularly and predictably. Evaluative consistency—above all, consistency in the application of negative attributions to social groups—is the mark of prejudice.

In sum, it is widely agreed that prejudice consists in attributions (1) about groups or members of groups, by virtue of their membership in the group, that are (2) disparaging and hostile, (3) false, or at least without warrant, and (4) consistently made. Accordingly, by prejudice we mean a readiness consistently to attribute negative characteristics (or to decline to attribute positive ones) to a group or to members of a group by virtue of their membership in the group. The more consistently a person attributes negative characteristics (or declines to attribute positive ones) to a group, the more prejudiced he or she is.

Prejudice, so understood, is the focal point of this study, integral to the pioneering analyses of negative judgments of blacks by Peffley and Hurwitz (Chapter 4), the unobtrusive measurement of racial anger by Kuklinski and Cobb (Chapter 3), the interaction of prejudice and ideology by Carmines and Layman, and the linkage between prejudice and welfare by Gilens (Chapter 7).

THE CONTINGENCY OF JUDGMENTS

If one irony of the second generation of research on the politics of race is a neglect of racial prejudice, a second is the neglect of politics itself. The analyses of Jackman, for example, omit expressly political considerations, most conspicuously political ideology, and when it is taken into account (Jackman 1978), the principle-policy gap turns out to be rooted not in racial hypocrisy but in ideological consistency. A principal contribution of this study, however, is to drive home the centrality of politics by highlighting the contingency of political judgments.

Political judgments can be contingent in one of two senses. In the first, to say that people's political judgments are contingent is to say that in making political choices, instead of depending on their general political orientations, they rely on the specific framing of the choice. In the second and stronger sense, to say political judgments are contingent is to say that, in making their political choices, people take account of the framing of issues in light of their general political orientations.

Contingency, in the first sense, is the centerpiece of the chapter by Stoker. Public opinion surveys, she argues, characteristically canvass citizens' evaluations of public policies in the abstract, but judgments about public policy are inherently contextual. The courts, conspicuously, do not reach a judgment about the propriety of public policies in the abstract. Instead they weigh the merits of claimants in the context of justifications advanced in specific cases. By extension, Stoker suggests, citizens' judgments about a policy may be responsive to the specific justifications given in its behalf.

In a surprising move, Stoker applies this conception of the inherent contingency of political judgments to white attitudes toward racial quotas; surprising because, if whites have staked out a position on any issue, they surely have on this issue. Yet, as she shows, even when affirmative action involves explicit quotas, support can be significantly bolstered depending on its specific justification.

Contingency in the strong sense is the centerpiece of the chapter by Carmines and Layman. Their starting point is a fundamental puzzle in the politics of race. Judged by the size of the (zero-order) correlations between whites' feelings toward blacks and their positions on public policies dealing with blacks, the impact of racial prejudice is modest (Sniderman and Carmines 1997). But surely the conclusion that prejudice is only a minor factor does not quite ring true. By exploring the contingency of political judgments, Carmines and Layman show just where it goes wrong.

The politics of race, they observe, is defined by the party system. The Democratic and Republican parties, at their core, are committed to competing points of view. On issue after issue the Democratic party favors, and the Republican party opposes, centrally directed ameliorative programs. Just for this reason, it has become common to suggest that the Republican party and the conservatism it espouses are driven by racism. In an ingenious analysis, Carmines and Layman turn this suggestion on its head. Republicans, if they share their party's creed, have a reason to oppose activist welfare programs, and this reason is as relevant if they feel positively toward blacks as if they feel negatively toward them. By contrast, Democrats, if they feel negatively toward blacks, will resist programs to benefit blacks that they know, as Democrats, they should support. The paradoxical consequence: although prejudice is more common on the right, it is more powerful in shaping the political thinking of the left.

METHODOLOGICAL INNOVATIONS
IN THE STUDY OF RACE

The second generation of research, for all its criticism of the interpretations of the first, stayed within the same measurement framework—and thereby was bound to the same conceptual framework. The third characteristic of this research program, by contrast, is innovation—and, in consequence, discovery.

This commitment to innovation takes many different forms. Its fundamental underpinning, however, is the use of computer-assisted interviewing to refashion the role of experimentation in public opinion surveys. Until the development of computer-assisted interviewing, public opinion polls had to rely on paper-and-pencil questionnaires. Because these questionnaires had to be printed in advance, experiments were highly constrained in design, typically involving only a single variation of a single factor. In turn, design constraints translated into constraints in objectives, with the so-called split-ballot experiments overwhelmingly restricted to questions of measurement rather than substance.

By contrast, through the facilities of the Computer-Assisted Survey Methods Program (CSM) and the Survey Research Center (SRC) of the University of California, a new approach to experimentation was developed. In a computer-assisted regime, the questionnaire is a dynamic instrument controlled by a computer program. Test items are "composed" at the moment of application. At the moment of application, the computer program selects at random from among the values assignable to each experimental facet. In consequence, each experiment can have multiple facets; each facet can take on multiple values; each study can carry out multiple experiments each independent of each other. It is worth remarking that, notwithstanding the complexity of the experiments now possible, their administration is effortless for the interviewer and invisible to the respondent.[7]

What distinguishes this study is the innovative use of this new methodological platform for the substantive analysis of both its principal concerns—the role of prejudice and the contingency of political judgments. Consider three examples. In Chapter 4, Peffley and Hurwitz explore the impact of attitudes toward blacks in general on evaluation of blacks as individuals. In thinking about the impact of racial prejudice, the question conventionally posed is: To what extent are responses to matters of race predictable, given knowledge of how negatively whites feel toward blacks? But in real life, it is rarely a matter of responding to a person who is black—and only black. They have, in addition to being black, other characteristics, some inviting a positive response, others a negative one. Taking advantage of computer-assisted interviewing, Peffley and Hurwitz present a set of innovative experiments exploring, for the first time in general population surveys, the conditional influence of racial prejudice. Their findings are, we think, strikingly original. If whites' attitudes toward blacks in general are positive, it makes remarkably little difference if the particular black to whom they are responding has a negative characteristic; but if their attitudes toward blacks in general are negative, it makes a big difference if he or she has a positive characteristic. This asymmetry, if confirmed by subsequent studies, has manifestly important implications.

As a second example of innovation, consider the chapter by Kuklinski and Cobb. The problem they tackle is one of the most vexing in the study of racial attitudes. Surely some white Americans, when asked how they feel about black Americans, will say not what they really think, but what they think is appropriate to say. But if we cannot take them at their word—and in a public opinion interview all we have are their words—how can we tell if they mean what they say? Again taking advantage of computer-assisted interviewing, Kuklinski and Cobb set out an imaginative experimental procedure capable of persuading respondents that they can express anger about matters of race without anyone, very much including the person interviewing them, being able to tell that that is what they are doing. This procedure was devised by Kuklinski, and he and his colleagues have cross-validated it in a long series of studies: so here we want to say a word not about method but about substance.

The first generation of research took it for granted that the problem of race, though surely not confined to the American South, was especially acute there. Over the last generation, the distinctiveness of the South is presumed to have disappeared. The politics of race is treated as essentially the same, in both character and extent, throughout the country. Indeed, on the public platform, the claim is made that the new South can be a model to the country as a whole in establishing cordial and candid relations between blacks and whites. Using their new procedure to measure racial sentiments unobtrusively, however, Kuklinski and Cobb throw an arresting light on the persisting distinctiveness of the South on matters of race.

Kathleen Knight's chapter, "In Their Own Words," offers counterpoint methodologically and substantively. Distinctively, she focuses on the understanding of Americans, black as well as white, of why blacks remain worse off than whites when both are free to define the problem in the terms they think appropriate. It is worth underlining how pioneering a venture this is. A generation ago, the thematic analysis of open-ended responses was woven into the theoretical pattern of the seminal study of voting, *The American Voter*, by Angus Campbell and his colleagues (1960). It is difficult to think of a major work in survey research since then that has treated the original analysis of open-ended data as trump to take intellectual tricks.[8] By demonstrating the power of computer-assisted interviewing to facilitate recording, retrieving, and coding verbatim responses, Knight's chapter contributes to the larger study's effort at innovation in measurement.

Substantive discovery is the test of methodological innovation, and Knight's analysis meets the burden of proof twice over. The standard public opinion survey relies entirely on respondents choosing between a small number of fixed alternatives formulated in advance. The alternatives, since they must be administered to everyone in the same way, must be not only comprehensible but also acceptable to everyone. There is thus a double loss, one well recognized, the other not. The well-recognized loss is that there is no way to tell the alternatives that citizens themselves would pose if they were free to frame the alternatives as they saw fit. The unrecognized loss is that there is no record of the actual words they would use to characterize these alternatives. The inevitable, if unintended, consequence is to give a sanitized impression of the real language in which many Americans talk about race. It is, accordingly, an important service of Knight to make vivid how explicit, coarse, and demeaning the public language of a significant number of white Americans remains.

In addition, by virtue of assaying the racial beliefs of whites in their own words, Knight has illuminated an important aspect of their thinking until now hidden from sight. About one-half of white Americans, she notes, "locate responsibility for the current state of affairs beyond the control of individual black people." More than one construction can be placed on this. Are they reporting a judgment they have reached themselves? Or saying not what they think but what they think they should say? Under either construction, as she remarks, it is "a finding worthy of some celebration"—worthy of celebration because what respondents say about a problem, when they are free to say (or avoid saying) whatever they wish, carries an extra measure of conviction.

A final word. The specific problem that Gilens addresses is the sources of resistance to welfare programs—that is, means-tested policies to assist the worst off. On their face, these programs are race-neutral. Being black is neither a condition for receiving assistance from welfare nor an explicit justification for it. Nonetheless, Gilens argues, the problem is deeply permeated by race. Poverty itself, he suggests, has become symbolic of race: poor Americans, in the eyes of white Americans, are overwhelmingly taken to be black Americans; and so, ostensibly offering their opinion on one subject—what government should do in behalf of those who are badly off—whites actually are expressing their views on another—how they feel about blacks who are benefiting from government assistance.

Gilens's argument, advanced on the standard fare of correlational data, would be plausible but not compelling. Whites may dislike welfare because they do not think well of blacks. But, alternatively, they may dislike welfare because they do not think well of those who have failed to make a success of their lives, whether they are black or white. Taking advantage of the power of randomization not in the measurement of the dependent variable—the customary approach—but in the assessment of the independent variable, Gilens decisively demonstrates that in the minds of whites welfare has a black face.

The studies gathered here share a concern to concentrate attention on prejudice itself, to highlight the contingency of political judgments, and to promote innovation. Because of both how, and how well, they have been done, we believe that all the studies gathered here illuminate aspects of American racial attitudes hitherto not visible.

NOTES

1. The classic study was Stouffer (1992). For follow-up studies, see especially Nunn, Crockett, and Williams (1978).
2. See especially table 3.1, on pp. 74–76.
3. The inquiries include Sniderman and Tetlock (1986a, 1986b), and Sniderman, Brody, and Kuklinski (1991).
4. This is the speculation of Schuman, Steeh, and Bobo (1984, p. 124).
5. The 1985 National Election Survey (NES) pilot study under the direction of Donald R. Kinder and David O. Sears, which focused on the politics of race, rejected recommendations to measure white attitudes toward blacks directly, choosing instead to use their symbolic-racism measure exclusively.
6. Some of these conceptual definitions we have collected ourselves, but we are especially indebted to Duckitt (1992) for his discussion.
7. For a methodological discussion, see Piazza, Sniderman, and Tetlock (1989) and Sniderman and Grob (1996).
8. One distinguished exception, we would note, is the work of John Zaller and Stanley Feldman on ambivalence. See Zaller (1992) and Zaller and Feldman (1992).

REFERENCES

Ackerman, Norman, and Marie Jahoda. 1950. *Anti-Semitism and Emotional Disorders: A Psycho-Analytic Interpretation.* New York: Harper.

Allport, Gordon W. 1954. *The Nature of Prejudice.* Reading, Mass.: Addison-Wesley.

Buss, Arnold H. 1961. *The Psychology of Aggression.* New York: Wiley.

Dovidio, John F., and Samuel L. Gaertner, eds. 1986. *Prejudice, Discrimination, and Racism.* Orlando, Fla.: Academic.

Duckitt, John. 1992. *The Social Psychology of Prejudice.* New York: Praeger.

Greeley, Andrew, and Paul Sheatsley. 1971. "Attitudes Toward Racial Integration." *Scientific American* 225:13–19.

Harding, J., Harold Proshansky, B. Kutner, and Isador Chein. 1969. "Prejudice and Ethnic Relations." In *The Handbook of Social Psychology,* vol. 5, ed. G. Lindzey and E. Aronson. Reading, Mass.: Addison-Wesley.

Hyman, Herbert H., and Paul Sheatsley. 1956. "Attitudes Toward Desegregation." *Scientific American* 195:35–39.

———. 1964. "Attitudes Toward Desegregation." *Scientific American* 211:16–23.

Jackman, Mary R. 1978. "General and Applied Tolerance: Does Education Increase Commitment to Racial Integration?" *American Journal of Political Science* 22:302–24.

———. 1981. "Education and Policy Commitment to Racial Integration." *American Journal of Political Science* 25:256–69.

Jackman, Mary, and Michael Muha. 1984. "Education and Intergroup Attitudes: Moral Enlightenment, Superficial Democratic Commitment, or Ideological Refinement?" *American Sociological Review* 49:751–69.

Jones, J. M. 1986. In *Prejudice, Discrimination, and Racism,* ed. J. F. Dovidio and S. L. Gaertner. Orlando, Fla.: Academic.

Kelman, Herbert, and Thomas Pettigrew. 1959. "How to Understand Prejudice." *Commentary* 28:436–41.

Kinder, Donald, and David O. Sears. 1981. "Prejudice and Politics: Symbolic Racism Versus Racial Threats to the Good Life." *Journal of Personality and Social Psychology* 40:414–31.

Klineberg, Otto. 1968. "Prejudice: The Concept." In *Encyclopedia of the Social Sciences,* vol. 12, ed. David Sills. New York: Macmillan.

Krech, David, Richard Crutchfield, and E. Ballachey. 1962. *Individual in Society.* New York: McGraw-Hill.

McConahay, John B., and J. C. Hough. 1976. "Symbolic Racism." *Journal of Social Issues* 32:563–79.

Milner, David. 1975. *Children and Race.* Harmondsworth, England: Penguin.

Nunn, Clyde A., Harry J. Crockett, Jr., and J. Allen Wiliams, Jr. 1978. *Tolerance for Noncomformity: A National Survey of Changing Commitment to Civil Liberties.* San Francisco: Jossey-Bass.

Piazza, Thomas, Paul M. Sniderman, and Phillip E. Tetlock. 1989. "Analysis of the Dynamics of Political Reasoning: A General Purpose Computer-Assisted Methodology." In *Political Analysis,* vol. 1, ed. James Stimson. Ann Arbor: University of Michigan Press.

Schuman, Howard, Charlotte Steeh, and Lawrence Bobo. 1985. *Racial Attitudes in America: Trends and Interpretations.* Cambridge, Mass.: Harvard University.

Sears, David O. 1988. "Symbolic Racism." In *Eliminating Racism: Profiles in Controversy,* ed. Phyllis A. Katz and Dalmas A. Taylor. New York: Plenum.

Sears, David O., and Donald R. Kinder. 1971. "Racial Tensions and Voting in Los Angeles." In *Los Angeles: Viability and Prospects for Metropolitan Leadership,* ed. W. Z. Hirsch. New York: Praeger.

Sears, David O., Carl P. Hensler, and Leslie K. Speer. 1979. "Whites' Opposition to 'Busing': Self-interest or Symbolic Politics?" *American Political Science Review* 73:369–84.

Simpson, George E., and J. Milton Yinger. 1985. *Racial and Cultural Minorities: An Analysis of Prejudice and Discrimination.* 5th ed. New York: Plenum.

Sniderman, Paul M., Richard A. Brody, and James H. Kuklinski. 1991. "The Principle-Policy Puzzle: The Paradox of American Racial Attitudes." In *Reasoning and Choice,* ed. Paul M. Sniderman, Richard Brody, and Phillip Tetlock. Cambridge: Cambridge University Press.

Sniderman, Paul M., and Edward G. Carmines. 1997. *Reaching Beyond Race.* New Haven: Yale University Press.

Sniderman, Paul M., and Douglas Grob. 1996. "Innovations in Experimental Design in General Population Attitude Surveys." *Annual Review of Sociology* 22:377–99.

Sniderman, Paul M., and Phillip E. Tetlock. 1986a. "Symbolic Racism: Problems of Motive Attribution in Political Analysis." *Journal of Social Issues* 42:129–50.

———. 1986b. "Reflections on American Racism." *Journal of Social Issues* 42:173–88.

Stouffer, Samuel A. 1992. *Communism, Conformity, and Civil Liberties.* 2d ed. New Brunswick, N.J.: Transaction.

Tajfel, Henri. 1970. "Experiments in Intergroup Discrimination." *Scientific American* 223:96–102.

Taylor, D. Garth, Paul Sheatsley, and Andrew Greeley. 1978. "Attitudes Toward Racial Integration." *Scientific American* 238:42–51.

Zaller, John R. 1992. *The Nature and Origins of Mass Opinion.* Cambridge: Cambridge University Press.

Zaller, John R., and Stanley Feldman. 1992. "A Simple Theory of the Survey Response: Answering Questions Versus Revealing Preferences." *American Journal of Political Science* 36:579–616.

Chapter 3 When White Southerners Converse About Race

James H. Kuklinski and Michael D. Cobb

Like other authors in this volume, we examine white Americans' attitudes toward African-Americans. Unlike the other chapters, this one focuses on one region of the country: the South. Whereas the other authors use time-tested, individual-level measures of prejudice and racial attitudes, we employ a new and thus untested methodology that is best suited for group comparisons such as those commonly found in psychology. We seek an answer to one question: How much racial prejudice is there in the South these days?

Others have asked the same question, of course; as we outline below, there are good reasons to pose it yet again. First, although researchers have presented considerable evidence in support of their answers, the evidence itself has been contradictory. Second, and more crucial, much of the evidence has taken the form of responses to directly asked survey questions: "Do you favor or oppose black people living next door?" "Do you favor or oppose interracial marriages?" Answering such questions, we argue, is akin to participating in a two-way conversation. Just as people anticipate what to say and what not to say in everyday conversation, so do respondents often account for what they believe to be the interviewer's expectations. The typical survey conversation, in other words, can preclude respondents from speaking openly, especially when they believe they hold views contrary to those of the person asking the question. To ensure openness requires changing the nature of the survey conversation itself.

A "NEW SOUTH"?
THE CONTRADICTORY EVIDENCE

The 1960s and early 1970s are widely viewed as the nadir of black civil rights (Sitkoff 1981). No region received more attention than the South. From the Montgomery bus boycott to sit-ins and public demonstrations, southern blacks and white civil rights workers forced the entire nation to take notice that they would no longer tolerate the elaborate set of Jim Crow laws peculiar to the South. White and black Americans watched in horror as television played and replayed images of local southern police confronting and often physically beating black protesters. Unwavering civil disobedience eventually forced the national government to intervene, and by 1965 Congress had passed and imposed strong antidiscrimination laws guaranteeing black Americans the most basic of rights: to vote, to sit at the front of a bus, to attend colleges of their choice, to sit at luncheon counters previously reserved for whites. The (often televised) scenes of federal marshals confronting local officials throughout the South symbolized the national government's resolve to implement these new dictates at all costs.

By many accounts, these highly visible activities brought about a tidal wave of change in white southerners' attitudes. Several national surveys documented dramatic declines in southern prejudice and intolerance (Greeley and Sheatsley 1974; Schuman, Steeh, and Bobo 1985; Tuch 1987), to the point that some scholars and practitioners proclaimed the emergence of a "new South" that is nearly indistinguishable from the rest of the country in its racial attitudes (Firebaugh and Davis 1988; Reed 1993). If a set of strong antidiscrimination laws is one legacy of the civil rights movement, an undeniable reduction in racial prejudice among whites, especially southern whites, is another.

But just how real is this second legacy? Another view of the political landscape raises doubt. It was during the height of the civil rights movement that George Wallace used his widespread support among white southerners to gain prominence as a national figure. Wallace did not hesitate to express hostility toward blacks and, even more, toward the intervention of the national government in the South's affairs. Soon thereafter, an all-white southern jury tellingly found Byron De La Beckwith, an avowed white supremacist, innocent of killing Medgar Evers, a black civil rights activist. More than three decades later, it took a highly visible national campaign by Evers's wife to secure a retrial; this time a mixed-race jury faced with a national audience and seemingly incontrovertible evidence found him guilty.

Each of these examples—and there are plenty more—can be interpreted as manifestations of racial prejudice. More important, it is not at all obvious why the many activities of the 1960s and 1970s, most consisting of the national government meddling in white southerners' lives, should have reduced racial animosity. Did southern whites simply concede defeat? Did the government interventions magically lead white southerners to see the light? Did cries for justice and equality so raise the discomfort level among prejudiced southern whites that they felt compelled to change their attitudes? Did white southerners unconsciously absorb the new set of racial norms that the civil rights legislation clearly articulated? If southern white adults did change their attitudes, did they also decide to socialize their children in accordance with a new set of norms orthogonal to those by which they had lived?

Or, contrary to all of the above, did the government intrusions on behalf of black Americans *increase* the level of anger and hostility? Imagine southern whites who are also prejudiced[1] watching the events of the 1960s and 1970s unfold. They see blacks walking into all-white universities, *their* universities, with the help of federal marshals. They see northerners organizing protest movements in *their* cities. They hear their own public officials condemning, if not visibly opposing, the activities. That white southerners observing such events should become less racially prejudiced is not at all obvious.[2] To be sure, the force of law, when applied, helped to prevent overt discrimination, but, ironically, it also could have exacerbated ill-will and racial resentment.

Consider, moreover, southern voting patterns, indicators of actual behavior, during the time these events took place. Carmines and Stimson (1989) and Huckfeldt and Kohfeld (1989) document the steady withdrawal of southerners from the Democratic party throughout the 1960s, 1970s, and 1980s. Not coincidentally, this withdrawal began in 1964, when Democratic officials and civil rights activists mobilized African-Americans and brought them into the fold. Also not coincidentally, it was during the 1964 presidential campaign that the Republican candidate, Barry Goldwater, sent unmistakable if not fully explicit signals that his party no longer would welcome blacks with open arms. As more and more blacks entered the Democratic coalition, more and more white southerners left it. Today the white South is heavily Republican. To be sure, a Republican white South is not prima facie evidence of a prejudiced white South (contrast Abramowitz 1994 with Carmines and Stimson 1989). It is the circumstances under which white southerners shifted their party loyalties that raises suspicions.

Finally, there is the anecdotal evidence. In his field study of changes in southern culture brought about by civil rights legislation, Wirt (1997) describes a situation that vividly illustrates how racial prejudice can exist below the surface. Wirt was invited to a private dinner party that some of the white subjects in his study hosted. These subjects were wealthy, upper-class businessmen. At some point, one of the spouses inadvertently changed the conversation to race and Martin Luther King's birthday. Some of the guests who were not subjects in the study, assuming Wirt was "one of them," soon began using unmistakably racist language to describe African-Americans. Although the dinner hosts successfully changed the topic of conversation, the change came too late. Wirt writes that the hosts' "faces promptly fell at this turn in the conversation; after much frowning, one finally reminded them that the author would quote them by name for such language. Of course, the author noted he would not, but the account is fascinating as it is evidence of a widespread black suspicion" (1997, p. 322).

The problem with anecdotal accounts, of course, is that they are not a representative sample of anything. Perhaps Wirt happened upon a rare occurrence not to be found throughout the South. However, during his field research, Dov Cohen, coauthor of a recent book on southern culture (Nisbett and Cohen 1996), found that southern whites routinely probe others, especially outsiders, to discover whether they can frankly express their racial views (personal communication). In other words, open and sincere conversation about race is conditional. Assuming for the moment that Cohen is correct, let us now consider the nature of a survey interview.

SURVEY INTERVIEWS AS CONVERSATIONS

Although not usually portrayed as such (but see Schwarz 1993), survey interviews are conversations. Granted, one person asks all the questions and the other provides the answers, unlike the give-and-take of everyday conversation. But interviews are conversations nonetheless.

When conversing with familiar others, we do not consciously ask ourselves, "Can we talk?" We know that we can. More to the point, we know what it is we can and cannot talk about, and what we can and cannot say. We have all heard the proverbial "we are good friends who don't talk politics" or, alternatively, "I never speak my mind when we talk politics." In the first instance, the individuals have concluded that they "can't talk." In the second, at least one of the individuals has determined that he or she "can't talk sincerely."

How is it that people reach such conclusions? First, those involved in conversation decide whether they share a common perspective, in this case, on politics. Second, if they believe they do not, then they consciously or unconsciously calculate the costs associated with talking sincerely, and indeed with talking at all. In both of our examples, the conversationalists recognize that they do not share similar views on politics; they also anticipate that open disagreement about politics will create conflict if not permanently damage their friendship. Consequently, the involved individuals never broach the topic, or at least one of the conversationalists eschews candor just to avoid disagreement.

So it is with respondents asked to answer survey questions. Consciously or unconsciously, they ask themselves what the other person in the conversation, the interviewer, thinks. Suppose they conclude that the interviewer shares their views. Then the respondents will openly express their sincere opinions on the relevant survey questions, much as Wirt's dinner guests did to each other. In this case, private opinions and public opinions are one and the same because respondents not only "talk" but "talk sincerely."

But suppose the respondents suspect they do not hold the same views as the interviewer, or they don't know if they do. Then they might reach any of three conclusions: (1) "we can talk sincerely," (2) "we cannot talk sincerely," or (3) "we cannot talk at all." If respondents believe that expressing their private views publicly entails no or only minimal cost, they will "talk sincerely." If they perceive a cost, however, "not talking sincerely" or "not talking at all" becomes a more probable option. In the extreme, if respondents believe that saying what they really think will land them in jail, the prudent thing to do might be to remain silent or express publicly opinions that are contrary to their private opinions.

Expressing prejudiced views does not lead to jail confinement or any other type of physical reprimand, so why would people who hold such views even ponder whether they can "talk" or, more relevant here, "talk sincerely" to the interviewer? What are the perceived costs that might preclude them from perfectly translating their private opinions about race into public ones?

Wirt's story identifies one: public exposure. Just as Wirt's subjects feared that their names would appear in print, so might prejudiced survey respondents fear that the interviewer or those in charge of the study will publicly reveal their answers. Promising anonymity will not comfort suspicious survey participants, especially if they believe the interviewer to represent a widely held norm to which they themselves do not subscribe. Some individuals might not distinguish between prejudice and discrimination, and thus believe the former to be illegal. Although academic researchers know they will use the data to conduct statistical analyses, most respondents do not. From their perspective, not talking sincerely is wise.

Immediate condemnation is another possible cost. Suppose a respondent is asked to agree or disagree with the statement "I oppose blacks living in my neighborhood." Blind to the ways of survey research, this individual might anticipate a critical reaction from the interviewer if he or she answers "agree." After all, this is precisely what happens in daily conversation. Again, social scientists know this will not happen; and again, there is no reason all others should.

Finally, for respondents who perceive their own (prejudiced) opinions as contrary to the dominant view, answering sincerely to an outsider can feel uncomfortable even when condemnation or public exposure is not expected. Scholars themselves might refrain from expressing a minority view if they sense that almost all of their colleagues strongly disagree with it.

Of course, respondents will weigh these potential costs differently (Mac-Kuen 1990). Our purpose is not to predict what weights different individuals will use. Rather, we simply have tried to show that a respondent when engaged in a survey conversation about race quickly could conclude that "we can't talk sincerely."

Figure 3.1 summarizes the preceding discussion in the form of a simple decision tree. In two of the possible situations, respondents believe they share the dominant view as represented by the interviewer or they believe otherwise but see no costs associated with expressing their true thoughts—private opinion becomes public opinion.[3] In the third case, however, where respondents believe that talking sincerely will be costly, the translation of private into public opinion takes one of two forms: either respondents refuse to express an opinion at all or they offer an insincere opinion. Private opinion does not perfectly translate into public opinion. In Kuran's words (1988, 1996), the interviewee engages in preference falsification.[4]

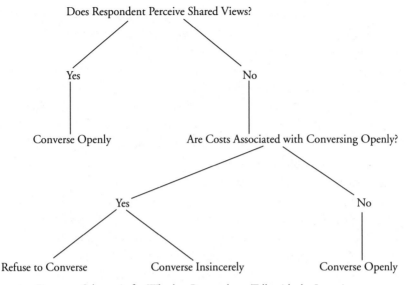

Figure 3.1 Schematic for Whether Respondents Talk with the Interviewer

ENCOURAGING SINCERE
SURVEY CONVERSATION

Method and Logic

What we seek, then, is a way to conduct surveys that encourages respondents to "talk sincerely" with the interviewer about their racial attitudes. In light of our preceding discussion, the optimal solution would be to use interviewers with whom the respondents personally know they can speak freely; for each respondent, find a trusted acquaintance who shares the respondent's views. This obviously infeasible approach (at least for a national survey)[5] would approximate the dinner setting among friends that Wirt describes. The next-best solution is to reduce if not eliminate the perceived costs of speaking freely. That is the approach we employ here. It entails encouraging respondents to "talk sincerely" about race by precluding the interviewer from knowing what they actually said.

Operationally, we randomly divided the Race and Politics Study sample of the general population into three parts. One-third were presented with a list of three items and asked to say how many of the items made them angry—not which specific items made them angry, *just how many*. The specific items were:

(1) the federal government increasing the tax on gasoline, (2) professional athletes getting million-dollar contracts, and (3) large corporations polluting the environment. The other two groups received the same list plus an additional item about race and then also indicated the number of items that made them angry. In one case the race item was "a black family moving in next door," in the other, "black leaders pushing for affirmative action." In this chapter, we focus on the former, which is our measure of racial prejudice. With the exception of the additional race items, the instructions and the wording of the items in the three conditions were identical.

How does this simple format encourage the interviewee to converse forthrightly? Suppose, for the sake of argument, that a respondent in the four-item condition takes exception to two of them, of which one is the race item. It will seem impossible to him or her that the interviewer could know that the race item is a source of anger. And indeed the interviewer cannot tell in the course of the interview if the race item angered the respondent. (As we demonstrate below, however, the data analyst can estimate afterwards the level of anger in the population as a whole and in strategic subsets of it.)

Even then, why should respondents give truthful answers? Why not simply take the safest route and not identify the race item as one that evokes anger? Kuran (1988, p. 1532) provides one answer: "Preference falsification is costly to the falsifier, in that it entails a loss of personal autonomy and a sacrifice of personal integrity." By nature, people would prefer to tell the truth, to say what they really think. When they feel they cannot, they lose something of themselves. Moreover, and in the same vein, Schwarz (1993) has demonstrated that people generally try to give interviewers the information they supposedly are looking for. Once they agree to be interviewed, respondents feel strongly inclined to cooperate. In short, prejudiced respondents likely feel torn between two opposing inclinations: "talk sincerely" and "do not talk sincerely." We designed our survey experiment to reduce the force of the latter.

Validity and Reliability

Our approach to increasing sincere conversation raises numerous validity and reliability questions. We have devoted considerable effort both to identifying the problems and to overcoming them (not always successfully), and we discuss these matters elsewhere (Kuklinski and Cobb 1997); two warrant comment here.

First, critics have questioned the wording of our instruction, which asks people to indicate the number of items that *make them angry.* This instruction sets a higher threshold than asking people, say, to indicate how many items they *oppose*. Since opposing a black family moving in next door is on its face a valid measure of racial prejudice, it therefore follows that we have underestimated the true level of racial animosity.

We plead both guilty and innocent to the charge. On the one hand, our own exploratory studies have revealed that using the term *oppose* increases the estimated percentage of prejudiced people by 10 percent or slightly more. This significant jump strengthens rather than weakens our central thesis. On the other hand, we chose the phrase "make you angry" because it more closely fits the classic conception of racial prejudice (Allport 1954), which defines white racial prejudice in affectual terms, as a strong, negative reaction to blacks. Even stereotyping, which many contemporary authors use to measure prejudice, is increasingly (and once again) seen as having a strong affective component (Mackie and Hamilton 1993).

Moreover, attitudinal measures that predict behavior have more intrinsic value to social scientists than those that do not. Stangor (1990) has shown that measures tapping the affective dimension of prejudice perform much better in this regard than those tapping the cognitive dimension.

Second, because they have not agreed on a conceptual definition of racial prejudice, researchers have not and probably will not agree on a common set of survey questions. Consequently, the choice is left to the individual's discretion. We asked respondents to react to "a black family moving in next door," which conceivably conjures a different mental image than "black people moving into your neighborhood" or "black teenagers dating white teenagers" (to take just two of many possibilities). These latter activities, one might argue, will anger prejudiced whites considerably more than the idea of a single black family moving in, which once again leaves us vulnerable to the criticism that we underestimated the level of prejudice (but see Schuman and Bobo 1988, who use a measure similar to ours).

What to do, given what currently is an almost intractable problem? Both before and after completion of the Race and Politics Survey, we undertook a series of exploratory studies to ascertain the effect of changing the wording of the race item. We included "black people moving into your neighborhood" in some of them and "black teenagers dating white teenagers" in others. Interracial dating appears to evoke the most anger, but we found little difference in the responses to the "black family" and "black people" items. All of this suggests that racial prejudice might fall along a kind of Guttman scale: everyone who negatively reacts to a black family moving in next door also becomes angry at the thought of interracial dating, although not everyone who deplores interracial dating also rejects a black family moving in. If this is indeed the character of prejudice, it raises a challenging question: are those who become angry at both thoughts more prejudiced than those who become angry at only the one? In the name of avoiding yet additional complications, we will not pursue an answer here.

RACIAL PREJUDICE IN THE WHITE SOUTH

The researcher can use analysis of variance or the equivalent regression analysis to determine what the level of prejudice among a selected group is and whether that level is statistically significant. The simplest model consists of a dependent variable—number of items named—and one independent variable—experimental condition. The regression equation takes the form

$Y = \alpha + \beta X_1 + \mu$, where
Y = number of items
X_1 = condition (1 if black family, 0 if baseline)

The intercept provides an estimate of the average number of items in the baseline condition; the intercept plus the slope of X provides the equivalent estimate in the test condition. That is, the intercept equals the baseline condition mean and the sum of the intercept and the coefficient equals the treatment condition mean. Thus, the coefficient alone $((\alpha + \beta) - \alpha)$ estimates the level of anger toward the black family item.

When applied to white southern respondents, this model provides the following parameters:

$Y = 1.95 + .42$ (condition).
$\quad$ (.08) $\quad$ (.11)

The average number of items named in the baseline condition is 1.95, out of a possible maximum of 3.00. More relevant here, the regression coefficient indicates that about 42 percent of white southerners express anger at the idea of a black family moving in next door. Merely asking about a single black family moving in elicits a strong visceral reaction from nearly half of the South's white adult population.

Ideally, the next step would be a comparison of white southerners' racial attitudes with those of whites living in the remainder of the country. The appropriate regression equation then is

$Y = \alpha + \beta_1 X_1 + \beta_2 X_2 + \beta_3 X_1 X_2 + \mu$, where
   Y = number of items
   X_1 = condition (1 if black family, 0 if baseline)
   X_2 = region (1 if South, 0 if non-South)

The interaction term, $X_1 X_2$, is especially important in this equation. If significant, it indicates an interaction between condition and region—that is, racial prejudice is greater in one region than the other. In this case, β_1 is the estimate of racial prejudice in the non-South and $\beta_1 + \beta_3$ the estimate for the South.

Unfortunately, we cannot conduct this analysis. As we have reported elsewhere (Kuklinski et al. 1997; Kuklinski, Cobb, and Gilens 1997), the baseline mean among nonsoutherners is 2.24, which indicates that many people identified all three baseline items as anger-provoking. Presumably all three baseline items angered an equal number of respondents in the test condition. If these individuals also reacted to the race item, then their sincere answer would be four items, or all of them. Thus, any incentive to "talk sincerely" that our methodology originally provided is gone; some people might still decide to talk sincerely, but others might choose only to "talk."

Therefore, we used an alternative procedure to estimate the level of prejudice among whites outside the South (see Kuklinski et al. 1997). Admittedly less desirable than the original methodology itself, this iterative procedure estimates that one in ten white nonsoutherners expresses prejudice as we measure it. Some will deem this estimate low, and we ourselves expected a higher percentage. On the other hand, our requirement for being placed in the prejudiced category—getting angry at the idea of a single black family moving in next door—is demanding, as we have already noted. Moreover, even 10 percent translates into millions of nonsouthern whites who express out-and-out hostility toward blacks.

It is in this context that the estimate of prejudice among white southerners should be interpreted. Even though we defined racial prejudice narrowly, more than four out of ten southern whites passed the test. Apparently they were willing to converse sincerely, given the opportunity to do so, and what many of them said is not unlike what the dinner guests inadvertently said in Wirt's presence. This said, it should not go unnoticed that a majority of southern whites, presumably also talking sincerely, do not express animosity toward black people (again, as we have measured it).

We must also emphasize what we are not saying here: that southern prejudice remains as intense and widespread today as it was three or four decades ago. We do not have across-time data to make such a determination. More than likely, advancing education levels and the immigration of nonsoutherners into the region have worked to reduce racial animosity. But these forces alone, our data suggest, have not produced a "new South" that stands with the rest of the country in its racial attitudes.

PINPOINTING THE PREJUDICE

Is the prejudice we have identified concentrated among certain segments of the white population or is it widespread? There are good reasons to pose this question. To find, for example, that well-educated white southerners express less prejudice than the poorly educated offers hope for the future, for average education levels in the South, as elsewhere, continue to rise. Conversely, if prejudice was concentrated, say, among a group who control the region's resources and institutions, concern rather than optimism might be the appropriate response.

To ascertain where prejudice is concentrated, if at all, we considered three demographic characteristics of the region's white population: age, gender, and education. We have already noted the relevance of education. It is especially pertinent in the context of this study, for while many scholars (Sniderman, Brody, and Kuklinski 1984) see increased education as the most effective means to reduce intolerance, others (Jackman 1978, 1981; Jackman and Muha 1984) argue that the role of education has been exaggerated. When conversing with an interviewer, the highly educated, especially, refrain from "talking sincerely" because they know the socially correct answers. Consequently, according to this view, statistical analyses of survey data overestimate the true relationship between education and prejudice.

Age has been the most prominent explanation of the supposed convergence of South and non-South attitudes about blacks. Firebaugh and Davis (1988) and Schuman and Bobo (1988) provide the strongest evidence. Using data in the General Social Surveys, the former show, first, that southern racial prejudice dropped precipitously between 1972 and 1984, and, second, that cohort replacement explains much of the decline. They use four items, separately and additively, to measure antiblack prejudice (p. 258): whether blacks are welcome for dinner, whether whites have a right to keep blacks out of their neighborhoods, whether blacks should not "push" themselves where they are not wanted, and whether there should be laws against black-white marriage. Schuman and Bobo incorporate an experimental design into their study and find that age outdis-

tances region as a correlate of support for an open-housing law. This relationship holds even when the source of enforcement—the local versus the federal
government—is controlled. As we noted earlier, however, no one has delineated the process by which this supposed generational change occurred.

Researchers have given less attention to the effect of gender on racial attitudes, which becomes especially intriguing within the context of the South. On
the one hand, men and women are equally exposed to what we identified as
still-high levels of prejudice. Moreover, they share jobs, households, and the
like, with which comes frequent and sometimes intimate interaction. All of
these imply congruent attitudes. On the other hand, historians have argued
that southern racism has its deepest roots in white males' fears about and anger
toward black men interacting with white women. To be sure, such arguments
have been largely speculative. Yet they are a commonplace among specialists in
southern history (Cash 1941; Williamson 1984). If these speculations hold true,
then the gender difference should be pronounced in the South: strong gut
reactions among men, less visceral reactions among women.

Adding the three independent variables to the original regression equation
increases its complexity. Our model now takes the form

$$Y = \alpha + \beta_1 X_1 + \beta_2 X_2 + \beta_3 X_3 + \beta_4 X_4 + \beta_5 X_1 X_2 + \beta_6 X_1 X_3 + \beta_7 X_1 X_4 + \mu, \text{ where}$$

  Y = number of items
  X_1 = condition (1 if black family, 0 if baseline)
  X_2 = age (1 if born after 1960, 0 if born before 1960)
  X_3 = gender (1 if female, 0 if male)
  X_4 = education (1 if attended college, 0 if no college)

Of particular interest are the three interactions. A statistically significant (and
positive) age by condition interaction, for example, indicates that older people
express more anger toward the idea of a black family moving in next door than
younger people do.

Table 3.1 reports the estimated coefficients. Three main effects reach statistical significance. Once again, and as expected, the average number of items in
the treatment condition exceeds the average number in the baseline condition.
In addition, women express anger toward more of the baseline items, on the
whole, than men do.[6] Similarly, the less educated are more angry, overall, than
the well educated. More important are the three interactions. Although in the
right direction, the age x condition term does not reach statistical significance.
Contrary to a widely held view, we find weak evidence at best that prejudice
increases with age among white southern adults. The story is much the same

Table 3.1. Unobtrusive Estimate of Southern Whites' Anger Over a Black Family Moving in, by Age, Education, and Gender

Variable	Coefficient
Condition	1.34***
	(.39)
Age	.02
	(.19)
Education	−.26*
	(.15)
Gender	.33**
	(.15)
Condition × Age	.21
	(.24)
Condition × Education	−.15
	(.22)
Condition × Gender	−.70***
	(.21)

Source: 1991 Race and Politics Survey
Note: $N = 285$; ***$p < .01$; **$p < .05$; *$p < .10$. Numbers in parentheses are standard errors of the regression coefficients.

with respect to education: all else being equal, the poorly educated express the most and the well educated the least anger toward a black family moving in; but, again, the interaction fails to reach statistical significance.

Prejudice is by far most strongly related to gender. Southern white men and women differ by a ratio of seven to one in their hostility toward black people. And it is men who express the markedly higher prejudice.

We must, of course, view this ratio with great caution. It is derived from a new methodology whose validity and reliability have not passed the test of time (see Kuklinski and Cobb 1997). A small sample of white southern adults is further divided into experimental conditions and demographic groupings. Also, the Race and Politics Study is designed as a representative sample of the nation, not a particular region. Ideally, our data would consist of a random sample of white southerners. All this said, we believe the gender difference to be real, although probably less than our estimate suggests. The association between gender and prejudice is too strong to be solely a function of the vagaries of sampling and unreliability. Moreover, we found nothing in the data— outliers, coding errors, and so on—to explain the relationship away.

But is it prejudice that we have identified? In their recent and provocative study, Nisbett and Cohen (1996) uncover a strong "culture of honor" among white southerners, especially men. The term *honor* refers, in this context, not to good character but to one's "strength and power to enforce his will on others" (p. 4). White southern men, the authors show, do not always express more anger or willingness to resort to violence than others; but when they believe that self-protection or social control is at stake, or when someone affronts them, they become dramatically more inclined toward anger and aggression than men elsewhere. Interestingly, the desire of southerners to convey sincerity, courtesy, and politeness, especially to outsiders, normally masks this readiness to strike out.

One plausible implication of the "culture of honor" thesis is that our measure of racial prejudice—anger over a black family moving in next door—captures white southern males' general hostility rather than their prejudice toward blacks. It is the words "make you angry," not the target group "black family," that provokes the negative response.

If males feel more anger generally, or are more inclined to respond angrily to others' actions, then their average score in the baseline condition should be higher than that of women. This is not the case. White southern women express the greater anger (mean of women = 2.12 versus mean of men = 1.76) toward the three items: government raising taxes, athletes receiving million-dollar contracts, large corporations polluting the environment. These items were not designed to tap a general dimension of anger and hostility, and we cannot say unequivocally that they do. On the other hand, the unobtrusive nature of the methodology presumably encourages people to converse sincerely about their anger rather than speak insincerely to convey a positive image to outsiders. While not a perfect measure of an overall predisposition toward anger and hostility, the three items probably approximate one.

But suppose responses to the baseline items do not accurately represent the level of general anger among southerners. Indeed, suppose that men harbor more anger than women. Would one then conclude that the "black family" item captures something other than racial prejudice? We think not.

Ideally, the Race and Politics Survey would include another treatment condition in which an otherwise equivalent nonracial item ("a family from Iowa moving in next door") replaces the racial item. We could then compare responses across the two conditions. Even in the absence of this comparison, though, it is highly unlikely that the "black family" measure is tapping more than intended. The reference to "a single black family" should not evoke a concern for self-protection; if it does, prejudice surely must underlie the response. Nor can the item be interpreted as an affront, which would be the case if it read, say, "blacks claiming that white southerners are prejudiced." In short, our race item has a tenuous and probably no link to the southern "culture of honor" as Nisbett and Cohen describe it.

Even though the data fall short of ideal, we have pushed this discussion to the limit. White men maintain a hegemonic hold on the region's institutions. They control most of the financial resources and render many of the decisions that affect people's lives. Although federal laws protect blacks from blatant racial discrimination, they fare less well at eliminating the subtle but still real effects of racial prejudice. A hidden racial animosity among those at the center of power, no matter how widespread, is a compelling reason for concern.

ANOTHER LOOK

The Survey Research Center at the University of California-Berkeley included the same methodology in its 1994 Multi-investigator Survey.[7] Three differences between the 1991 and 1994 measures warrant mention. First, whereas the original study used three items in the baseline condition and four in the test condition, the 1994 study used four and five, respectively. The additional baseline statement is: "requiring seatbelts be used when driving." Otherwise the wording of the items is identical. Second, the 1994 study included a second (randomly assigned) treatment group in which "interracial dating with black teenagers taking out white teenagers"[8] replaces the "black family" item. The latter survey, in other words, includes two measures of racial prejudice. Finally, the 1994 survey directly asked some respondents to indicate whether interracial dating and a black family moving in next door make them angry. The direct questions match the other racial items in wording.

Before turning to a summary of the results, we feel compelled to redouble our earlier cautions about the small number of respondents. In some instances, estimates are derived from fewer than thirty people; no condition contains more than sixty. Applying a new and untried methodology to such small numbers is a risky venture at best. Even if the methodology were not new, the small numbers preclude making any confident claims about the representativeness of those individuals included in our analyses. We cannot say unequivocally that they represent all white southerners in their attitudes; we doubt that they do. Compounding an already difficult problem, the small number of cases increases the probability that perfect randomness was not achieved when assigning people to one or another of the conditions. If this is the case, and we will show that it is, then the differences in demographic characteristics can influence the estimated levels of prejudice.

We face yet another problem: changing the number of items in the baseline and treatment conditions across studies introduces a potential confound whose effects we cannot determine. Especially troubling is the possibility that people cannot keep five items in short-term memory, which the 1994 study asks them to do in the two treatment (race-item-included) conditions. If they are unable to remember all five, respondents in these conditions likely will underreport the number of relevant items, which in turn will attenuate the estimated levels of prejudice.

Why, given this formidable list of concerns, even report the estimated results? This is a question we ourselves long pondered, and for which we offer two answers. First, the estimates derived from the new methodology, even if unstable and possibly biased, can be compared to the answers respondents gave to the direct questions. This comparison, as we will see, shows that respondents' "talking sincerely" cannot be taken for granted. Second, we can learn some additional lessons about the methodology itself.

The equations for "black family" and "interracial dating" are, respectively,

$$Y = 2.10 + .24 \text{ (condition) and} \qquad Y = 2.10 + .62 \text{ (condition)}$$
$$\quad (.15) \quad (.20) \qquad\qquad\qquad\quad (.14) \quad (.19)$$

where condition again is a dummy variable accounting for the difference between the baseline and relevant treatment condition.

The level of estimated anger toward the "black family" item (24 percent) falls short of that found earlier (42 percent). Indeed, the regression coefficient does not approach statistical significance, which immediately raises questions about the methodology's reliability. In a series of exploratory studies (Kuklinski and Cobb 1997), we have found that unreliability becomes a problem when the cell n's fall under 75, which is true here. Additionally, the distributions of gender, which we found earlier to be a strong predictor of prejudice, vary across the three conditions. Women are most highly concentrated in the "black family" condition (63 percent), less concentrated in the baseline condition (58 percent), and least concentrated in the interracial dating condition (48 percent). In light of our earlier finding that women hold less racial animosity than men, these distributions imply that the black family item will underestimate the level of prejudice and the interracial dating item will overestimate it.

And indeed, an estimated 63 percent of white southerners say they become angry at the thought of interracial dating among teenagers. This highly significant figure is astounding, and comports with the results of other studies (Kuklinski and Cobb 1997) that consistently generate higher estimates with the interracial dating item than with the black family item. But, again, these data must be interpreted with great caution. In this case, the markedly higher proportion of (older)[9] men could bias the estimate in an upward direction.

Let us summarize and try to interpret what we have uncovered thus far. The 1991 data reveal that 42 percent of white southerners express anger at a black family moving in next door. A replication of this study, based on a smaller number of cases and a revised methodology that includes more items, provides a lower estimate that does not reach statistical significance. Finally, the 1994 data also indicate that more than 60 percent of white southerners included in the study react negatively to interracial dating among teenagers. The 1994 estimates, we noted, are more problematic both because of the smaller number of cases within the conditions and because of the lack of completely random assignment of respondents to these conditions.

All in all, we deem our original portrayal of white southern prejudice to be near the mark. If there is one estimate in the first study that warrants skepticism, it is the gender difference. Not that the substantive conclusion is wrong; but it would be prudent to assume that we have overestimated the magnitude of the gap. That the 1994 replication does not produce similar results is, frankly, disappointing. We do not know why the coefficient falls so far short of statistical significance. On the other hand, the estimate of anger toward interracial dating appears solid. We repeated the analysis three times, each time randomly removing older men so that the demographic distributions in the treatment condition mirrored those in the baseline condition. Of course, this elimination lowers the cell size even more. Yet, in all three instances the estimate remained above 50 percent and was highly significant.

There is yet another way to put these findings into perspective: examine the responses people give when conversing directly with the interviewer. When asked to say directly if a black family moving in next door would anger them, only 7 percent answer in the affirmative; this figure is significantly lower than the estimates provided by the unobtrusive measure.

Interracial dating is more complex. Nearly 40 percent, when asked directly, say that interracial dating angers them. This figure is surprising; indeed, we do not know another publicly reported percentage that approaches it. What is going on here? Do direct measures work well after all?

First, we must remember that the very small numbers of cases precludes any confident statement about the nature of white southerners' attitudes. We are not in a position to generalize. More significant, the wording of the question—"black teenagers taking out white teenagers"—conjures an image of black teenage men taking out white teenage women. It apparently evokes an unusual level of anger. We are not suggesting that this wording is not a good measure of racial prejudice; to the contrary, it might be the most valuable measure yet used. In any case, it produces numbers that direct measures heretofore have not produced in modern times.

As revealing as this direct measure might be, note that our alternative measure estimates an even higher percentage—63—who express anger at the idea of interracial dating. Even on an item that apparently incenses many people and prompts them to say what they really think, an additional 25 percent refrain. The difference between the two estimates is worth knowing.

Clearly, some white southerners will publicly express their hostility toward blacks, especially on matters involving close interpersonal relations.[10] Far more critical, it appears that many others, when involved in a fully open conversation with the interviewer, choose to "talk" rather than "talk sincerely." And so they tell a story they think the interviewer wants to hear.[11]

Methodologically, the preceding exercises demonstrate that proper random assignment of respondents to conditions is crucial to the technique's success. Variation in the distributions of relevant characteristics across conditions can skew the estimates. The larger the number of respondents, of course, the more likely that this problem will not be severe. In any event, we urge researchers who use the methodology to compare the distributions well before undertaking an analysis. Randomness cannot be taken for granted.

That the methodology we used here identified markedly higher levels of prejudice than the direct questions raises concerns about the validity of the latter. On the other hand, we readily admit the need to conduct more research into the reliability of our own technique. The journey to a near-perfect measure of racial prejudice is far from over.

Surveys provide most of what we know about racial attitudes. And we know a lot. Some of the most visible works in political science (Carmines and Stimson 1989; Kinder and Sanders 1996; Sears and Kinder 1981; Sniderman and Piazza 1993; Schuman, Steeh, and Bobo 1985) analyze survey data on race.

We began with the premise that interviews function as conversations between interviewer and interviewee. Just as people do in their daily lives, interviewees consciously or unconsciously ask themselves whether the other person involved in the conversation is "one of us."[12] Does the interviewer share our views of the world? If the answer is no, then interviewees choose between "talk sincerely," "do not talk sincerely," and "do not talk at all." If respondents perceive the costs of "talking sincerely" to be high, they likely will not choose that option.

The methodology we developed to encourage sincere conversation is by no means a panacea for the study of racial attitudes. We have devoted considerable space to the problems that accompany it, at least as it has been used to date. On the other hand, more than any other approach we know, ours provides the opportunity for respondents to speak their minds. When given this opportunity, they apparently do.

We chose to talk with white southerners. Both the region's legacy and conflicting evidence about white southerners' true attitudes toward black people served as motivations. So did our conclusion that no one had proffered a compelling reason why a tidal wave of attitudinal change should have occurred. What would compel white southerners to change their attitudes just when the national government and people from "the North" intruded into their affairs?

We have not argued that change has been nonexistent in the South. Forty years ago most southern whites spoke openly and unhesitatingly about their prejudice. Today, most do not. Whether that itself represents progress is, of course, debatable; that it represents a departure from the past is not. More significant, many white southerners today do not express racial animosity, even when given the chance to say what they really think. Indeed, it would be a grave injustice to those living in the South ever to lose sight of this fact.

But sizable numbers of white southerners say that they continue to feel animosity toward blacks. Many get angry at the idea of a black family moving in next door; even more react negatively to interracial dating among teenagers. As best we can ascertain, the percentages reach their peak among white southern men, the group that maintains most of the economic and political power in the region.

We do not wish to indict anyone. But these findings underline more than ever the need to construct new survey techniques that facilitate sincere conversation. Until we do, we must choose between anecdotes, such as Wirt's, that provide a true but possibly unrepresentative portrayal and survey items that provide a representative but possibly not altogether true portrayal. Getting the best of both worlds is a worthwhile goal.

NOTES

We thank the Research Board of the University of Illinois for financial support. Mark Peffley and Paul Quirk provided invaluable comments on earlier drafts.

1. We have chosen our words carefully. To be a white southerner is not necessarily to be prejudiced. In fact, many whites in the South have participated in black civil rights activities.

2. We are *not* arguing that different types of causal factors, such as increased education and the immigration of nonsouthern whites into the region, failed to reduce the level of southern prejudice.

3. A more elaborate schematic would include probabilities.

4. Kuran proffers two provocative claims that relate to race. First, preference falsification has grossly exaggerated the support for affirmative action. Second, it has portrayed the general citizenry as considerably less prejudiced than it is.

5. Gough and Bradley (1993) come close to this approach in their small-scale study of racial attitudes. They use assessments of close acquaintances to measure attitudes, rather than have the acquaintances actually conduct interviews.

6. We tested for ceiling effects but found none.

7. Paul Sniderman, Thomas Piazza, and Henry Brady are the principal investigators.

8. Ideally, the item would have been written "interracial dating among black and white teenagers."

9. The interracial dating condition contains proportionately more men *and* more people born before 1960.

10. More than likely, people see reacting negatively to interracial dating as more legitimate than reacting to a black family moving in. Thus the perceived costs of talking sincerely should be less.

11. We are *not* implying that direct questions about race have no value. Although they might underestimate the overall level of prejudice, much of the evidence indicates that they still work when analyzing relationships. The stereotype measures, for example, relate as expected to a set of policy preferences.

12. Race-of-interviewer effects represent one instance of people asking whether they and the interviewer are "one." Students of survey research have found these effects to be pervasive. In an early study, Hatchett and Schuman (1976) found that whites give more pro-black responses to black than to white interviewers. Several years later, Groves and Kahn (1979) compared face-to-face with over-the-telephone responses on attitudes toward integration. Thirteen percent more southern respondents favored an all-white neighborhood and 11 percent fewer favored a mixed neighborhood when a fellow southerner conducted a face-to-face interview than when a nonsoutherner anonymously completed the interview over the telephone. This pattern did not exist among nonsoutherners. More recently, Anderson, Silver, and Abramson (1988a, b) showed that black respondents report more favorable attitudes toward whites to white interviewers than to black ones (see also Kinder and Sanders 1996). Finally, Finkel, Guterbock, and Borg (1991) used statewide poll data to estimate that white respondents were 8–11 percent more likely to express support for Douglas Wilder, a black candidate for governor, when a black conducted the interview.

REFERENCES

Abramowitz, Alan I. 1994. "Issue Evolution Reconsidered: Racial Attitudes and Partisanship in the U.S. Electorate." *American Journal of Political Science* 38:1–24.

Allport, G. W. 1954. *The Nature of Prejudice.* Reading, Mass.: Addison-Wesley.

Anderson, Barbara A., Brian D. Silver, and Paul R. Abramson. 1988a. "Interviewer Race and Black Voter Participation." *Public Opinion Quarterly* 52:53–83.

———. 1988b. "Interviewer Race and Attitudes of Blacks." *Public Opinion Quarterly* 52:289–324.

Carmines, Edward, and James Stimson. 1989. *Issue Evolution: Race and the Transformation of American Politics.* Princeton, N.J.: Princeton University Press.

Cash, W. J. 1941. *The Mind of the South.* New York: Alfred A. Knopf.

Finkel, Steven, Thomas Guterbock, and Marian Borg. 1991. "Race-of-Interviewer Effects in a Preelection Poll: Virginia, 1989." *Public Opinion Quarterly* 55:313–30.

Firebaugh, Glenn, and Kenneth Davis. 1988. "Trends in Antiblack Prejudice, 1972–1984: Region and Cohort Effects." *American Journal of Sociology* 94:251–72.

Gough, Harrison G., and Pamela Bradley. 1993. "Personal Attributes of People Described by Others as Intolerant." In *Prejudice, Politics, and the American Dilemma,* ed. Paul M. Sniderman, Philip E. Tetlock, and Edward G. Carmines. Stanford, Calif.: Stanford University Press.

Greeley, Andrew, and Paul Sheatsley. 1974. "Attitudes Toward Racial Integration." In *Inequality and Justice,* ed. Lee Rainwater. Chicago: Aldine.

Groves, Robert, and Robert Kahn. 1979. *Surveys by Telephone: A National Comparison with Personal Interviews.* New York: Academic.

Hatchett, Shirley, and Howard Schuman. 1976. "White Respondents and Race-of-Interviewer Effects." *Public Opinion Quarterly* 39:523–28.

Huckfeldt, Robert, and Carol Kohfeld. 1989. *Race and the Decline of Class in American Politics.* Chicago: University of Illinois Press.

Jackman, Mary. 1978. "General and Applied Tolerance: Does Education Increase Commitment to Racial Integration?" *American Journal of Political Science* 22:302–24.

Jackman, Mary. 1981. "Education and Policy Commitment to Racial Integration." *American Journal of Political Science* 25:256–69.

Jackman, Mary, and Michael J. Muha. 1984. "Education and Inter-Group Attitudes: Moral Enlightenment, Superficial Democratic Commitment, or Ideological Refinement?" *American Sociological Review* 49:751–69.

Kinder, Donald, and Lynn Sanders. 1996. *Divided by Color: Racial Politics and Democratic Ideals in the American Republic.* Chicago: University of Chicago Press.

Kinder, Donald and David O. Sears. 1981. "Prejudice and Politics: Symbolic Racism Versus Threats to the Good Life." *Journal of Personality and Social Psychology* 40:414–31.

Kuklinski, James H., and Michael Cobb. 1997. "Toward Unobtrusive Survey Measures of Sensitive Attitudes." Paper presented at the annual meeting of the Midwest Political Science Association, Chicago.

Kuklinski, James H., Michael D. Cobb, and Martin Gilens. 1997. "Racial Attitudes and the 'New South.'" *Journal of Politics* 55:323–49.

Kuklinski, James H., Paul M. Sniderman, Kathleen Knight, Thomas Piazza, Philip Tetlock, Gordon Lawrence, and Barbara Mellers. 1997. "The Politics of Affirmative Action." *American Journal of Political Science* 41:402–19.

Kuran, Timur. 1995. *Private Truths, Public Lies: The Social Consequences of Preference Falsification.* Cambridge, Mass.: Harvard University Press.

Kuran, Timur. 1988. "The Inevitability of Future Revolutionary Surprises." *American Journal of Sociology* 100:1528–51.

Mackie, Diane, and David Hamilton, eds. 1993. *Affect, Cognition, and Stereotyping: Interactive Processes in Group Perception.* New York: Academic.

MacKuen, Michael. 1990. "Speaking of Politics: Individual Choice, Public Opinion, and the Prospects for Deliberative Democracy." In *Information and Democratic Processes,* ed. John A. Ferejohn and James H. Kuklinski. Chicago: University of Illinois Press.

Nisbett, Richard E., and Dov Cohen. 1996. *Culture of Honor: The Psychology of Violence in the South.* Boulder, Colo.: Westview.

Reed, John Shelton. 1993. *Surveying the South: Studies in Regional Sociology.* Columbia: University of Missouri Press.

Schuman, Howard, Charlotte Steeh, and Lawrence Bobo. 1985. *Racial Attitudes in America: Trends and Interpretations.* Cambridge, Mass.: Harvard University Press.

Schuman, Howard, and Lawrence Bobo. 1988. "Survey-based Experiments on White Racial Attitudes Toward Residential Integration." *American Journal of Sociology* 94:273–99.

Schwarz, Norbert. 1993. "Judgment in a Social Context: Biases, Shortcomings, and the Logic of Conversation." In *Advances in Experimental Social Psychology,* vol. 26, ed. Mark Zanna. San Diego, Calif.: Academic.

Sitkoff, Harvard. 1981. *The Struggle for Black Equality, 1954–1980.* New York: Hill and Wang.

Sniderman, Paul M., and Thomas Piazza. 1993. *The Scar of Race.* Cambridge, Mass.: Harvard University Press.

Sniderman, Paul M., Richard Brody, and James H. Kuklinski. 1984. "Policy Reasoning on Political Issues: The Problem of Racial Equality." *American Journal of Political Science* 28:75–94.

Stangor, C. 1990. "Arousal Accessibility of Trait Constructs and Person Perception." *Journal of Experimental Social Psychology* 26:305–21.

Tuch, Steven. 1987. "Urbanism, Region, and Tolerance Revisited: The Case of Racial Prejudice." *American Sociological Review* 52:504–10.

Williamson, Joel. 1984. *The Crucible of Race.* New York: Oxford University Press.

Wirt, Fredrick. 1997. *We Ain't What We Used to Be.* Durham, N.C.: Duke University Press.

Chapter 4 Whites' Stereotypes of Blacks: Sources and Political Consequences

Mark Peffley and Jon Hurwitz

Race continues to be a powerfully divisive force in American politics. For the last several decades, racial issues (such as segregation, busing, and affirmative action) have remained on the front burner of the political agenda, polarizing the American electorate and, as a consequence, dramatically affecting voting patterns, partisan alignments, and trust in government (Carmines and Stimson 1989). It seems likely, however, that the power of race to divide Americans is not confined to explicitly racial issues, but extends to other prominent "hot-button" issues like crime and welfare. Although neither issue is explicitly racial in the same fashion as affirmative action or busing, both become linked to race inasmuch as white Americans (inaccurately) tend to see the typical welfare recipient and criminal as being African-American. While a variety of forces are likely to drive whites' attitudes on such issues, few would deny that perceptions of African-Americans are an important contributing factor. Whites, we may assume, who continue to negatively stereotype blacks—perceiving them to be "lazy" or "violent"—may be substantially more likely to oppose welfare payments or to support "get tough" policies on crime, especially when blacks are the targets of such policies.

Our purpose in this chapter is to conduct a systematic analysis of racial stereotyping, or the images that white Americans hold of blacks, by examining the *content* of such beliefs as well as their *antecedents* and political *consequences*. Our purpose in exploring the *content* of whites' images of blacks is to determine the extent to which whites subscribe to a jaundiced view of blacks as lazy and violent. To what extent have blacks become associated with a hostile "underclass" of the undeserving poor in the minds of whites? The problems of contemporary urban poverty are among the most troubling of our time: skyrocketing joblessness, a disintegrating social structure, violent crime, and more. It is doubtless tempting for some whites to link such problems to the perceived shortcomings of African-Americans, for such linkages become a ready-made, albeit faulty, explanation for the quintessential problems of the underclass— welfare and crime. Because respondents in the Race and Politics Survey were asked an extensive battery of stereotypic traits along a variety of trait dimensions, we are in a particularly advantageous position to evaluate the extent to which white society has shorn its historically negative views of blacks as well as to make a rough assessment of one likely source of opposition to improved race relations.

A second goal is to gain an appreciation of the major social and political *antecedents* of contemporary racial stereotypes to better understand the dynamics of racial prejudice and to identify types of individuals most likely to subscribe to such negative beliefs about blacks. Does the contemporary stereotype of blacks as a hostile underclass have essentially the same roots as racial prejudice in an earlier age? To what extent are such individuals likely to be found in particular regions of the country (the South, for example) and segments of society (among the least educated)? Even more important, to what extent are whites' images of blacks embedded in a wider belief system of social and political orientations such as ethnocentrism and individualism? By drawing on the wide variety of sociodemographic and attitudinal variables assessed in the national survey, we are able to heed, to some degree, Gordon Allport's (1954) admonition against looking for the roots of prejudice and stereotyping in a "single sovereign explanation."

Our principal purpose, however, is to explore the powerful *consequences* of racial stereotypes in shaping whites' political judgments about blacks in the context of the explosive issues of crime and welfare. In this portion of the analysis, we make use of a number of survey experiments to investigate more precisely the conditions under which racial stereotypes do and do *not* affect political judgments. Specifically, by experimentally varying the race and socioeconomic status of the target individual (or group) in various questions about welfare mothers, police searches, and assistance programs, we are able to determine the extent to which whites' political evaluations of blacks in the areas of welfare and crime are biased by race, as well as the degree to which this bias is driven by racial stereotypes.

Our investigation departs from much of the extant research on racial stereotypes, which focuses on how whites feel about generic blacks and the policies—such as welfare and affirmative action—that affect minorities. Although the insights from this work are invaluable, our survey experiments allow us to present whites with counterstereotypical black targets to answer questions such as the following: What happens when whites who *embrace* negative stereotypes of blacks are confronted with scenarios in which blacks do not fit the pejorative impression? Does positive individuating information have any impact on their political judgments of blacks? Is it possible to inhibit the impact of negative stereotypes on hot-button issues like crime and welfare? And, conversely, how do whites who *reject* such stereotypes respond in the presence of blacks who are stigmatized and who correspond to quite negative images? Are their more positive views of blacks in the abstract mere window dressing that they quickly abandon when confronted with stigmatized blacks?

THE CONTENT OF RACIAL STEREOTYPING

One of the first treatments of stereotypes appears in Walter Lippmann's *Public Opinion* (1922, p. 16), where he argued that the "pictures in the head" which individuals form of other groups are functionally necessary for imposing order on an "environment [that is] altogether too big and complex, and too fleeting. . . . We are not equipped to deal with so much subtlety, so much variety and so many permutations and combinations. And although we have to act in that environment, we have to reconstruct it on a simpler model before we can manage with it." This assumption that stereotyping results from limitations in human capacities for processing information squares nicely with the more contemporary social cognition perspective, which treats stereotypes as "generalizations about social groups that are not necessarily more or less inaccurate, biased, or logically faulty than any other kinds of cognitive generalizations" (Taylor 1981, 84).[1]

A serious problem with this research is that an exclusive focus on cognitive forces is unable to account adequately for the ethnocentric bias of much social stereotyping (Stroebe and Insko 1989). The fact that images of outgroups tend to be quite negative suggests that stereotypes are used not just to simplify the world but to justify discrimination and hostility toward the outgroup. This bias is emphasized in theoretical traditions as diverse as *The Authoritarian Personality* (Adorno et al. 1950; Altemeyer 1988) and "realistic conflict theory" (Campbell 1965; Bobo 1988), and more recently by Social Identity Theory (Tajfel 1982; Tajfel and Turner 1979), which holds that stereotyping is prompted, in part, by a universal ethnocentric bias to enhance one's own group and to disparage outgroups. This research makes plain that some group stereotypes are not simply heuristic devices to simplify experience but are destructive forces that historically have evoked punitive and discriminatory responses to ethnic, racial, and religious groups.[2]

Just how negative are the images which white Americans hold of blacks? And to what degree do stereotypes of blacks conform to an image of a hostile, undeserving underclass? Until very recently, the survey evidence with which to answer these questions was, at best, ambiguous and incomplete. Many of the "classic" studies of racial stereotypes used small, unrepresentative samples of college students (for instance, Katz and Braly 1933; and the replication by Karlins et al. 1969), while others have provided only a very selective glimpse at a handful of attributes (Schuman et al. 1988). Fortunately, in the last few years several national surveys have sought to provide a more complete and contemporary portraiture of whites' views of blacks, including the Race and Politics Survey, a principal objective of which was to assess the political impact of whites' stereotypes of African-Americans.

Data and Measures

Respondents (N = 2,223) in the survey were asked a battery of questions designed to elicit their beliefs about the personal attributes of "most blacks." Guided by the testing framework of Rothbart and Oliver (1993), as modified by repeated pretesting, respondents were asked to rate the degree to which various words or phrases accurately described "most blacks" on a scale from 0 (very good description) to 10 (very inaccurate description). The reference to "most" blacks in the question is designed to elicit "global" impressions of prototypical blacks. (See the Appendix for further details and a discussion of various measurement issues.)

Whites' Responses to Stereotype Items

Two central dimensions of whites' (N = 1,841) African-American stereotypes are of obvious relevance here: "black work ethic" (consisting of the traits "lazy," "determined to succeed," "dependable," "hard-working," and "lack discipline") and "black hostility" ("aggressive or violent"). To gauge the pervasiveness of negative impressions of blacks along these two dimensions, responses to the stereotype items are presented in table 4.1, where to simplify the interpretation answers are recoded from 11-point scales to 3-point scales indicating whether the direction of the response was "negative" (above the midpoint of 5 for negatively worded traits, below the midpoint for positively worded traits), "positive" (less than 5 for negative traits, greater than 5 for positive traits), or "neutral" (equal to 5).

Even though positive and neutral responses outnumber negative responses for five of the seven traits, we still find a substantial proportion of whites agreeing that most blacks are lazy (31 percent), not determined to succeed (22

Table 4.1. Percentage of Whites Giving Negative, Neutral, and Positive Responses to Racial Stereotype Items

Stereotype Item	Negative Response	Neutral Response	Positive Response
Black Work Ethic			
Lazy*	31.1%	30.6%	38.3%
Determined to Succeed*	22.0	29.0	49.0
Hard-working*	16.8	26.1	57.1
Dependable*	13.0	31.6	55.4
Lack Discipline**	59.7	0.0	40.3
Black Hostility			
Aggressive or Violent*	50.0	27.4	22.6

Source: 1991 Race and Politics Survey
Note: Percentages are based on N's that range from 1,767 to 1,780.
*Responses to the positively worded items were first reflected so that higher values on all the scales indicate more negative assessments. To simplify the display of responses for this table, the 11-point scales were collapsed into three categories, such that a score of 5 at the mid-point of the original scale is considered a neutral response, while negative responses are scores above the midpoint (6–10) and positive responses are scores below the midpoint (0–4) of the original scale.
**Responses are based in the Likert item, "Most black parents don't teach their children the self-discipline and skills it takes to get ahead in America." Negative responses are those which agree (either strongly or somewhat) with the statement, while positive responses are those which disagree (either strongly or somewhat).

percent), aggressive (50 percent), and lacking in discipline (60 percent). In short, although whites with positive images of blacks constitute a plurality of the larger American public, a very sizable number of whites—as many as one in two—openly endorses frankly negative characterizations of "most" blacks. We note that this distribution of whites' responses to our stereotype measures is similar to that found in other recent national surveys, such as the 1992 American National Election Study.[3]

Antecedents of Whites' Stereotypes of Blacks

The next logical question is, what types of individuals are more likely to subscribe to such negative stereotypes of blacks and what social and political antecedents help to explain the dynamics of racial stereotyping? Two classes of explanations of prejudice and stereotyping have been investigated in survey studies: sociodemographic variables and core beliefs and values.

Social Background Characteristics

Sociological explorations of the demographic correlates of prejudice and stereotyping (such as Schuman, Steeh, and Bobo 1988) tend to assume that racial animus stems from an individual's social background and early socialization experiences. Consequently, important demographic variables such as education, income, gender, age, and region are the focus of our investigation of the social bases of racial stereotyping (see Appendix for measures). Two variables, in particular, are key in our analysis of contemporary stereotypes of blacks: education and region. Traditionally, declining prejudice toward blacks, Jews, and other minorities has been associated with increasing levels of formal education (Page and Shapiro 1992; Selznick and Steinberg 1969), although Schuman et al. (1988) found differences in racial attitudes across educational groups to be shrinking over time. More recently, Sniderman and Piazza's (1993) San Francisco Bay Area study found education to be pivotal in predicting negative racial stereotyping among whites, at least as indicated by the simple correlation between education and agreement with negative stereotypes. Regional differences in racial attitudes have also been found to be narrowing: socioeconomic changes in the South as well as the migration of whites from the "rustbelt" to the "sunbelt" have tempered the traditionally high levels of racial prejudice evinced by southern whites (Black and Black 1986; Schuman et al. 1988). Thus, interest in both social antecedents will receive careful scrutiny in the analysis below.

Core Beliefs and Values

Another tradition of research in political psychology has investigated the extent to which prejudice and other attitudes toward specific groups are embedded in the individual's wider belief system, emanating from such general orientations as liberalism, individualism, ethnocentrism, and a variety of other core values and beliefs. The value receiving the most attention in the racial attitudes literature is individualism (Appendix, III.A and B), or a support for the components of the Protestant ethic such as individual achievement, self-reliance, obedience, discipline, and the work ethic. According to Kinder and Sears (1981), Lipset and Schneider (1979), Kluegel and Smith (1986), and others, individualists oppose government policies such as affirmative action because they are alleged to undermine the work ethic. By extension, because rugged individualists tend to attribute poverty to lack of effort versus structural forces (for example, discrimination, not enough jobs), they may also tend to view blacks, who suffer more from poverty than whites, as lazy. Although empirical support for the impact of individualism on racial policy attitudes and stereotypes is limited (see Sears 1988 for a review), the value continues to occupy a central place in studies of racial attitudes.

Additionally, racial stereotypes may be related to several explicitly political orientations (Appendix, II) such as partisanship and ideology, if, for example, conservatives who oppose government assistance to blacks do so because they view them as lazy. Another political orientation, political sophistication or awareness, may also be a useful predictor of racial stereotyping if individuals who are less attentive to political life are also less sensitive to the elite consensus against more open forms of prejudice and bigotry in American politics (such as the condemnation that former Ku Klux Klan member David Duke received from both major parties when he ran for higher office in Louisiana).

An important tradition in the study of racism assumes that racial prejudice and stereotyping stem from more generalized forms of ethnocentrism. Studies from Adorno et al. (1950) to the present (Altemeyer 1988; Bierly 1985; Sidanius 1992; Snyder and Ickes 1985) find that stereotyping and prejudice toward different outgroups—blacks, Jews, Hispanics, homosexuals, and others—tend to coexist in the same individuals. Accordingly, we incorporate three different aspects of ethnocentrism into our analysis of racial stereotyping: social intolerance, conformity, and anti-Semitism.

Social intolerance (Appendix, III.B.1), or an unwillingness to accept or "put up with" individuals or groups with different values, appearances, and behaviors, has been found to be an important predictor of both racial policy attitudes and stereotypes (Hurwitz and Peffley 1992), most likely because blacks represent a distinct outgroup often perceived to be outside the mainstream of white, middle-class society.

A related value, *conformity* (Appendix, III.B.2), has, to this point, received less empirical support as a determinant of stereotyping (Hurwitz and Peffley 1992) but has long been linked to the rejection of social and political outgroups (see, for instance, Kohn 1977; Feldman 1989), suggesting that further analysis is warranted. Conformity is defined as a desire for an orderly and structured world in which people obey authority and adhere to convention and externally imposed rules. Those placing a premium on conformity are expected to view unconventional outgroups (such as minorities) as a threat to the established order, leading such persons to negative views of blacks.

Finally, in an attempt to include a more direct form of at least one form of misanthropy, we focus on *anti-Semitism* (Appendix, III.B.3). The logic behind focusing on linkages between stereotypes of Jews and blacks was established by Sniderman and Piazza (1993). If we find that negative stereotypes toward two very different groups are highly correlated, we have strong evidence that a wider sort of ethnocentrism and prejudice underlies both sets of beliefs.

Prior to the analysis, we constructed an index of black work ethic by summing responses to the several indicators presented in table 4.1 (Cronbach's α = .765 for the items lazy, determined to succeed, dependable, hard-working, and lack discipline). Black hostility is measured with a single indicator (aggressive and violent). In the analysis below, we begin by regressing the two stereotyping measures (see Appendix, I) on the set of demographic variables to identify which groups are more and less prone to adopt stereotypic attitudes toward blacks. Subsequently, more endogenous predictors (values and political predisposition variables) will be added in an attempt to determine the relative explanatory power of the various constructs.

Sociodemographic Correlates of Racial Stereotyping

In the left-hand side of table 4.2, the two stereotype dimensions are regressed on the demographic indicators identified previously. Perhaps the most obvious conclusion to be drawn from the equations is that the demographic variables (such as formal education, age, gender, income, and living in the deep South) offer only a very partial explanation of stereotyping; in neither equation do the variables, in combination, explain more than 5 percent of the variance.

Nonetheless, the results reveal some important demographic patterns in

Table 4.2. Predicting Racial Stereotypes from Demographic, Value, and Ethnocentrism Variables

	Demographic Model				Full Model			
	Black Work Ethic		Black Hostility		Black Work Ethic		Black Hostility	
	b (se)	Beta	b (se)	Beta	b (se)	Beta	b (se)	Beta
Demographic								
Education	-.683** (.148)	-.121	-.34** (.05)	-.176	.093 (.148)	.016	-.135* (.053)	-.070
South	2.06** (.393)	.126	.593** (.133)	.106	1.68** (.367)	.103	.510** (.132)	.091
Age	.031** (.01)	.073	.00 (.004)	.001	.017 (.010)	.040	-.002 (.004)	-.016
Gender	-.832* (.340)	-.059	-.01 (.005)	-.021	.053 (.324)	.004	.058 (.116)	.012
Income	.003 (.05)	.016	-.02 (.017)	-.031	.067 (.047)	.035	-.013 (.017)	-.020
Values, Predispositions								
Ideology	—	—	—	—	.054 (.111)	.013	-.019 (.040)	-.013

Party ID	—	—	—	—	-.043	-.012	.021	.017
					(.089)		(.032)	
Pol. Sophistication	—	—	—	—	.009	.002	-.122*	-.056
					(.154)		(.005)	
Social Tolerance	—	—	—	—	-.300**	-.174	-.042**	-.070
					(.042)		(.015)	
Individualism	—	—	—	—	-.136*	-.048	-.072**	-.075
					(.065)		(.023)	
Anti-Semitism	—	—	—	—	-.417**	-.343	-.109**	-.262
					(.030)		(.011)	
Conformity	—	—	—	—	-.140*	-.050	-.019	-.020
					(.071)		(.025)	
R^2/Adj R^2	.040	.037	.048	.045	.216	.210	.140	.135
Number of cases	1,637	1,693			1,592		1,592	

Source: 1991 Race and Politics Survey

Note: Entries in left-hand columns are unstandardized regression coefficients with standard errors in parentheses; standardized coefficient in right-hand columns. Lower values on the above variables indicate: rejection of negative stereotypes, lower education, not living in the deep South, younger, male, lower income, conservative, Republican, low political sophistication, social intolerance, individualism, anti-Semitism, and conformity.

*$p < .05$; **$p < .01$

whites' perceptions of blacks, for, although income emerges as irrelevant in both models, the other variables are at least selectively important determinants. Southern respondents, for example, are more likely to perceive blacks as violent and lazy than are those from outside of the region; and these regional differences are independent of any differences in education and income that may distinguish the South from the rest of the country. Clearly, despite large-scale changes in the South over the last several decades, this area of the country remains distinct in engendering disparaging views of African-Americans (see also Chapter 3 in this volume).[4]

Education is also a significant predictor of negative stereotyping, even if its effects are not particularly powerful. Despite a much-publicized upsurge of racial incidents on college campuses in the last two decades, education continues to shape more racially tolerant views. In keeping with previous studies, pejorative views of blacks are held disproportionately among the less-educated segment of the population: less-educated individuals are substantially more likely than others to see blacks as hostile and lazy. Additional clues about the likely process by which education promotes racial tolerance can be gleaned from the analysis below, where we examine the impact of values and ethnocentrism.

Before addressing more fully specified models of stereotyping, we note the significant though small effects of gender and age in the black work ethic equation: older respondents and males are more likely to views blacks as lazy than are younger female respondents. Although numerous explanations of the effects of the demographic variables may be offered, it will be seen below that, with the exception of the South, the impact of the demographic variables is reduced to mere trace effects once value orientations are added to the equations.

Ethnocentrism and Racial Stereotyping

In the right-hand side of table 4.2 appear the estimates of the full model regressing the two stereotype variables on political predispositions (ideology, partisanship, and political information), values (individualism) and ethnocentrism variables (social intolerance, conformity, and anti-Semitism) along with the demographic predictors. Clearly, these additional factors contribute to our understanding of stereotyping beyond the explanation provided by demographic variables; on average, we explain three to four times as much variance in these equations as in those employing the demographics factors alone.

With the inclusion of the new variables, the effects of all the demographic variables except region are reduced to mere trace effects. Thus, much of the impact of these social background variables is mediated by values—namely, ethnocentrism. Apparently, one reason why the less educated are less racially tolerant is that they are also more ethnocentric in general. In other words, the benefits for education in reducing racial intolerance are evidently registered through a more pervasive tempering of ethnocentrism, which in turn discourages pejorative views of African-Americans.

Of the variables tapping ethnocentric orientations, anti-Semitism (negative stereotypes of Jews) stands out as far and away the strongest predictor of negative racial stereotyping, which suggests several conclusions. First—as if one needed affirmation of this fact—racial stereotyping among whites is most aptly characterized as prejudice. How else could one explain the substantial overlap between animus toward two very different groups (the zero-order correlations between anti-Semitism and the stereotype variables are .41 and .33, respectively, for black work ethic and hostility)? Second, the fact that much of the covariation between anti-Semitism and racial stereotypes remains even after including social intolerance and conformity (beta coefficients for anti-Semitism shrink to .34 and .26, respectively, in the work ethic and hostility models) indicates that we were only partially successful in our attempts explicitly to capture different sources of ethnocentrism that have appeared in the literature. In the work ethic model, social intolerance makes a respectable showing and conformity is at least statistically significant, but the effect of neither variable is impressive in the hostility equation. The important point, however, is that we have uncovered a more sweeping form of ethnocentrism that indiscriminately targets both blacks and Jews. Generally speaking, our results are certainly reminiscent of Adorno et al.'s (1950) finding that antagonistic attitudes toward members of various outgroups (defined along ethnic, racial, nationalistic, political, and religious lines) are tightly clustered together.

CONSEQUENCES OF STEREOTYPES

The foregoing analysis of the content and antecedents of racial stereotypes would seem much less important if we were unable to demonstrate that these beliefs also have important consequences for political behavior. Accordingly, we now turn to our principal concern, which is to determine when and how racial stereotypes influence whites' political judgments about blacks in the areas of welfare and crime policy. More specifically, we ask: To what degree, and under what circumstances, do racial stereotypes "bias" whites' political judgments about blacks in the areas of welfare and crime policy? The suspicion is that the biasing effects of race are substantial—that, for example, individuals who endorse negative stereotypes will tend to adopt harsher views of black welfare recipients and, furthermore, will express greater opposition to government assistance when the intended recipients are black than when they are described as being white.

A wealth of research on social stereotyping in cognitive psychology provides a strong theoretical basis for expecting such biasing effects. As "pictures in the head," stereotypes tend to put their imprint on data in the very process of acquiring it. The social cognition literature uses the term *theory-driven processing* to refer to this strategy whereby cognitive misers develop expectations based on their impressions (or theories) of others to direct their attention to information that is consistent with the theory; information that is inconsistent, on the other hand, may tend to be ignored, discounted, or somehow interpreted so that it becomes confirmatory of the initial impression (see, for example, Hamilton and Sherman 1994). In this fashion, stereotypes are believed to be remarkably perseverent and strongly determinative of judgments that are related to the stereotype (racial policy judgments, for instance).

Empirically speaking, however, the connection between stereotypes and policy attitudes is considerably more complex (Bobo and Kluegel 1993; Carmines and Sniderman 1992; Terkildsen 1993), appearing under some conditions but not others. These findings are perfectly consistent with data-driven models of processing, where even individuals with crystallized stereotypes will attend to, and be influenced by, information that is discrepant from the impression (for example, Locksley et al. 1980). Even one who believes blacks to be dangerous criminals would have a hard time ignoring the reality of, say, Colin Powell. Continuum or dual process models (such as Fiske and Pavelchak 1986; Fiske and Neuberg 1990) integrate these models of stereotypic processing by specifying the conditions under which people tend to rely on categorical (theory-driven) or piecemeal (data-driven) processing strategies. Continuum models regard individuals as generally theory-driven, but with the flexibility to engage in more cognitively taxing data-driven processing when, for example, information about the target is clearly inconsistent with the stereotypical expectations. These models therefore predict that stereotype and policy judgment will be less closely linked when individuals are presented with information that clearly runs counter to the stereotype (see Rahn 1993).

It is precisely for this reason that we intensively analyze two subpopulations—those who endorse and those who reject negative racial stereotypes—both of which are confronted with counterstereotypical data of a kind often found in the real world. Although much of the extant research focuses on correlational linkages between stereotypes of generic blacks and policy attitudes, in the survey experiments below we manipulate the attributes of blacks to examine how whites react when confronted with counterstereotypical black targets in the explosive context of welfare and crime.

We find the questions posed above intriguing because, in the real world, they represent everyday confrontations between data and theory. Those with intensely negative images of blacks—who see them as lazy and unmotivated, for instance—doubtless often work alongside African-Americans who, by their presence in the factory or office, have demonstrated that they can, and do, conform to the work ethic. And whites who reject such negative stereotypes must regularly consume media coverage of issues such as welfare and crime in which the dominant images in such coverage strongly suggest that welfare recipients and violent criminals are disproportionately black (Entman 1990, 1992).

Methodology

In exploring the relationship between race and welfare/crime, one could begin by assessing individuals' judgments of welfare and crime policies (as well as of welfare recipient and criminal) and then methodically regressing such judgments on measures of racial stereotypes. There are, however, several difficulties with such an approach. First, it does not provide us with a way of estimating racial bias, since the race of the target has not been manipulated. Second, such a strategy does not allow us to separate the impact of the race versus the class of the target. For many whites, stigmatizing characteristics associated with the "underclass" (for example, being unproductive or aggressive) have become commingled with race (Franklin 1991; W. J. Wilson 1987). Thus, it is necessary to manipulate other stigmatizing characteristics to disentangle the biasing effects of race on whites' political judgments from the biasing effects of class-related attributes. Finally, the aforementioned strategy does not permit us, in any systematic way, to confront respondents with counterstereotypical information.

Consequently, we systematically vary both the race and other characteristics of the target. In the series of experiments which follow, utilizing computer-assisted telephone interviewing (CATI) technology, we ask respondents about both black and white welfare recipients and criminal suspects, randomly varying the potentially stigmatizing information about the targets (work history, educational background, aggressiveness, and so on) to enable us to separate the effects of race from those of the associated social characteristics. In this way, our design benefits from not only the control and internal validity gained from experiments but also the generalizability and external validity gained from cross-sectional surveys, an important consideration in the study of racial attitudes (see, for example, Sigelman et al. 1995 and Terkildsen 1993).

Our first set of experiments explores the linkage between whites' racial stereotypes and their attitudes toward welfare, an ostensibly race-neutral program that has, for many, become charged with racial connotations. How do racial stereotypes affect perceptions of black versus white welfare mothers? Are black welfare mothers more subject to stigmatizing myths of welfare recipients than similarly described whites? To what extent do racial stereotypes account for this racial bias? And how do individuals who accept and reject negative stereotypes respond when confronted with welfare mothers who confirm and challenge their more general impressions of African-Americans?

The "Welfare Mother" Experiment

To answer these questions, we constructed a set of survey experiments that asked respondents to form impressions of "welfare mothers," variously described in the following pair of survey questions:

1. Now think about a [black woman, white woman] in her early twenties. She is a [high school dropout, high school graduate] with a ten-year-old child and she has been on welfare for the past year. How likely do you think it is that she will try hard to find a job in the next year—very likely (coded 1), somewhat likely (2), somewhat unlikely (3), or not at all likely (4)?
2. How likely is it that she will have more children in order to get a bigger welfare check—very likely (1), somewhat likely (2), somewhat unlikely (3), or not at all likely (4)?

The rationale of the experiment is to determine whether respondents are more likely to subscribe to popular myths about welfare recipients if the mother is black, and to what extent racial stereotypes are responsible for any such bias. In addition, by independently manipulating the educational status of the mother, we hope to better understand the power of stereotypes to shape impressions in the face of mildly inconsistent individuating information. Having completed high school signifies an effort to improve one's lot in life (contrary to the lazy stereotype), while dropping out indicates a lack of effort (contrary to the belief that blacks are hard-working). However, the manipulation of individuating information in this case is not so strong as to be clearly inconsistent with prior expectations. The mother, after all, is described as being on welfare, and for many Americans this fact alone is indicative of a lack of effort. Furthermore, there is nothing inherently contradictory about being a high school graduate and simultaneously being on welfare. Thus, we characterize this experiment as one that provides respondents with mildly inconsistent, or mixed, individuating information.

The top panel (A) of figure 1 displays whites' responses to the two questions across different descriptions of the welfare mother. Consistent with several survey studies (such as Kluegel and Smith 1986), respondents are pessimistic: 45–63 percent think she is unlikely even to try to find a job, and 58–68 percent expect her to have another child to get bigger welfare checks. But although varying the mother's educational status generates different assessments (with more negative judgments for the dropout than for the graduate), the differences across racial treatments are small and statistically insignificant. Moreover, as the rest of figure 1 makes clear, the virtual absence of any racial differences is a persistent finding for the remaining experiments as well. There is little evidence in panels B and C of figure 1 that the race of the target affects whites' support for welfare programs (fig. 4.1.B) or evaluations of a police search of drug suspects (fig. 4.1.C).

This result, precisely because of the absence of a difference, merits the closest attention. Is the absence of a difference evidence that race has lost its stigmatizing power? More to the point, to what degree are whites' judgments of black versus white welfare mothers in the current experiment shaped by more global racial stereotypes, vis-à-vis a variety of other considerations? To answer these questions, assessments of the welfare mother (for each question) were regressed on the two racial stereotypes (black work ethic and black hostility) and a variety of "control" variables, including core beliefs and values (social intolerance, conformity, individualism, and anti-Semitism), political predispositions (ideology, party ID, political sophistication), and several sociodemographic variables (education, gender, age, income, and living in the deep South), the measurement of which is described in the Appendix.[5] These OLS results are reported in table 4.3.

In both tables, the noteworthy findings are the substantial coefficients for the black work ethic stereotype when the mother is a black dropout (upper left-hand cells of both tables). Thus, whites who question the commitment of most blacks to the work ethic are much less likely to think that the black dropout will try to find a job in the next year (b = .034, beta = .257 in table 4.3.A) and are more likely to expect her to have another child to get a bigger welfare check

A. *Welfare Mother Experiments:* Assessments of welfare mother described as: [black; white], [high school dropout; high school graduate].

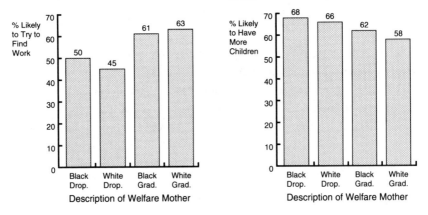

Likely to try hard to find a job?

Likely to have kids to get bigger welfare check?

B. *Welfare Policy Experiment:* Favor welfare programs to help [blacks; new immigrants from Europe] [who are in trouble; who want to work]?

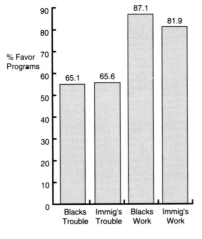

Source: 1991 Race and Politics Survey

Note: Percentages are based on the first two response categories of 4-point scales (e.g., very likely + somewhat likely, etc.). None of the percentage differences across similarly described blacks vs. whites are significant at the .05 level.

Figure 4.1 Marginal Responses to Survey Experiments (Whites Only)

C. Police Search Experiment: Drug search is reasonable for suspects described as two young [black; white] men [using foul language; well dressed and well behaved]?

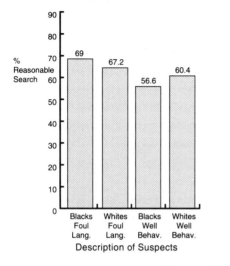

Figure 4.1 (*Continued*)

(b = -.037, beta = -.287 in table 4.3.B). Although other variables such as individualism, anti-Semitism, education, and age are selectively significant, none is as powerful as the work ethic variable in shaping judgments.

Clearly, the relationship between racial stereotypes and perceptions of welfare mothers is a conditional one, appearing selectively for some stereotypes and experimental conditions but not others.[6] First, racial stereotypes are important only when making assessments of black, not white, welfare mothers. Moreover, people tend to rely on stereotype dimensions that are most relevant to the task at hand: assessments of welfare mothers are closely tied to beliefs concerning blacks' commitment to the work ethic, but rarely—and never strongly—to a less relevant trait like hostility.

Plainly, racial stereotypes shape impressions of welfare mothers in theoretically explicable ways, even in the face of stringent controls for a variety of other variables. But what light do these results throw on the puzzle with which we began—the absence of a difference in judgments of black and white welfare mothers? Why do racial stereotypes shape responses to the question when black high school dropouts are mentioned (table 4.3), but, overall, there is little (percentage) difference in the way whites respond to black versus white welfare mothers (fig. 4.1.A)? More important, how do whites who accept negative racial

Table 4.3. Regression Analysis of Assessments of Welfare Mother on Racial Stereotypes Across Different Descriptions of Target

A. Likely to try hard to find a job?

	DESCRIPTION OF WELFARE MOTHER							
	Black Dropout		Black Graduate		White Dropout		White Graduate	
Racial Stereotypes	b (se)	Beta	b (se)	Beta	b (se)	Beta	b (se)	Beta
Black Work Ethic	.034**	.257	.006	.052	.013	.102	.003	.023
	(.009)		(.008)		(.008)		(.009)	
Black Hostility	.019	.098	.021	.109	.006	.032	−.013	−.067
	(.013)		(.013)		(.012)		(.013)	
R^2/Adj R^2	.149	.118	.160	.129	.092	.062	.069	.035
Number of Cases	395		395		450		398	

B. Likely to have another child to get a bigger welfare check?

DESCRIPTION OF WELFARE MOTHER

Racial Stereotypes	Black Dropout		Black Graduate		White Dropout		White Graduate	
	b (se)	Beta	b (se)	Beta	b (se)	Beta	b (se)	Beta
Black Work Ethic	-.037**	.287	-.015	-.114	-.014	-.103	-.005	-.041
	(.008)		(.010)		(.008)		(.010)	
Black Hostility	.009	.047	-.016	-.08	-.026*	-.135	.006	.031
	(.012)		(.013)		(.012)		(.013)	
R^2/Adj R^2	.235		.159		.152		.120	
Number of Cases	391		403		446		395	

Source: 1991 Race and Politics Survey

Note: Entries in left-hand columns are unstandardized regression coefficients with standard errors in parentheses; standardized coefficient in right-hand column. Lower values on the above variables indicate: predict welfare mother is likely to try to find a job, likely to have more children to get a bigger welfare check, and rejection of negative stereotypes. Coefficients are also controlled for various political predispositions (social intolerance, conformity, anit-Semitism, partisan and ideological identifications, and political sophistication) and sociodemographic characteristics (education, gender, age, income, and residing in the deep South).

$*p < .05; **p < .01.$

stereotypes differ from those who reject them in the way they respond to individuating information that is consistent with or departs from stereotypical expectations?

The answers to these questions lie in the different ways that whites with varying expectations of blacks react to the race (and the educational status) of the welfare mother. Accordingly, we now analyze how whites who accept and reject negative racial stereotypes respond to individuating information that either confirms or contradicts the stereotype. Table 4.4 displays the differences in whites' assessments of the welfare mother depending on their placement on the work ethic scale, showing the mean and percentage responses to the items for whites who *accept* the negative stereotype (that is, scored in the top third of the scale) versus those who *reject* the negative characterization of blacks as lazy (bottom third of the work ethic scale). Treatment differences across the race and the educational status of the welfare mothers are presented in the bottom rows of the table for each of the two groups of respondents.

Why does manipulating the race of the welfare mother make no difference overall (fig. 4.1.A), while it appears to be very important in activating the use of stereotypes in the regression analysis (table 4.3)? Comparing table 4.4.A across alternative targets of judgment, the answer to the puzzle is clear. Those with negative characterizations of blacks judge black targets more *harshly* than white targets, while those who *reject* negative characterizations of blacks tend to judge blacks more *positively* than they judge whites. Thus, the reason there are no treatment differences for the full sample (fig. 4.1.A) is that these two diverging biases cancel out overall.

More interesting, for our purposes, is the substantive interpretation given to the responses of these two groups. Among whites who see blacks as lazy, we find that black welfare mothers are consistently judged more harshly than whites with a similar educational background. Blacks, more than whites, are not expected to look for a job and are expected to "have another child to get a bigger welfare check." Although the impact of the mother's educational status plays a slightly larger role in affecting such judgments, the important finding is that even when individuating information runs counter to the negative stereotype—when the mother completes high school—negative expectations continue to affect judgments. For negative stereotypers, the impact of race and the individuating information (educational status) on evaluations is clearly additive: the discriminatory bias against the black welfare mother is roughly the same whether the mother completes high school or not.

Thus, black welfare mothers who are high school dropouts have two strikes against them—being black and failing high school. Those who finish high school, according to whites who assume blacks are lazy, still have an important character deficit—being black. For by virtue of being black, welfare mothers are more likely to be treated to an assortment of stigmatizing myths about welfare recipients. In short, when mildly discrepant individuating information is presented to negative stereotypers, their stereotypes are not interrupted or undercut; rather, their tendency to hold black welfare mothers to a racially discriminatory double standard is roughly the same even in the face of positive information about the target.

The contrast with whites who reject negative stereotypes is striking, for their dominant pattern is the consistency of their reactions even in quite different settings. Whites are just as likely to say that a black high school dropout will really try to get off welfare by looking for a job as a black high school graduate.

How should this consistency be interpreted? Do whites with a more positive image of blacks simply attach no importance to graduation as a predictor of social behavior? Plainly not. As the second cell of table 4.4.A documents, it matters whether a white woman on welfare has graduated from high school: 62.1 percent of them believe that a white graduate will try to get off welfare, as compared to 49.6 percent who believe the same about a white dropout. This differential reaction—assigning a weight to graduating for white, but not black, women—is evidence, we suggest, of the sensitivity of whites who reject negative stereotypes to the continuing danger of stigmatizing blacks. Even in circumstances that would permit a negative response to a black, they give no evidence of "taking the bait." In other words, whites who reject negative stereotypes in the abstract also respond more positively to blacks in a specific setting, regardless of whether the blacks in question exhibit socially desirable characteristics (completing high school, presumably while raising a child) or socially stigmatizing characteristics (dropping out of high school). The more positive view they express of blacks in the abstract does not appear to be mere window dressing.

The "Welfare Policy" Experiment

Conceptually, racial stereotypes may be regarded as a readily accessible summary of the prototypical black: if negative, a picture of the flaws of blacks; if positive, a picture of their virtues. From a public policy perspective, though, what counts is not the pictures people carry in their minds but the impact of such beliefs on support for policies that affect blacks. And, as we shall show, this impact hinges heavily on whether targets are consistent with stereotypical

Table 4.4. Responses to Different Descriptions of Welfare Mother Among Whites Accepting and Rejecting Negative Racial Stereotypes

A. Welfare mother [description] is likely to . . . try really hard to find a job in the next year?

Description of Welfare Mother	Accept Neg. Stereotype			Reject Neg. Stereotype		
	% Likely	Mean	N	% Likely	Mean	N
Black Dropout	32.3%	2.976	(127)	67.1%	2.179	(140)
Black Graduate	51.1	2.610	(141)	70.1	2.150	(127)
White Dropout	40.1	2.841	(157)	49.6	2.558	(129)
White Graduate	60.9	2.397	(151)	62.1	2.207	(116)
Diff. Bl–Wh Drop	−7.8%	.135*		17.5%	−.379*	
Diff. Bl–Wh Grad	−9.8	.213*		8.0	−.057	
Diff. Bl drop–Bl Grad	18.8	.366*		3.0	.029	
Diff. Wh drop–Wh Grad	20.8	.444*		12.5	.351*	

B. Welfare mother [description] is likely to . . . have another child to get a bigger welfare check?

Description of Welfare Mother	Accept Neg. Stereotype				Reject Neg. Stereotype			
	% Likely	Mean	N		% Likely	Mean	N	
Black Dropout	81.9%	1.748	(127)		52.9%	2.529	(136)	
Black Graduate	74.3	1.986	(140)		44.4	2.595	(126)	
White Dropout	82.1	1.949	(156)		50.8	2.460	(126)	
White Graduate	60.3	2.265	(151)		51.3	2.522	(115)	
Diff. Bl–Wh Drop	−.20%[a]	−.201*			2.1%[a]	.069		
Diff. Bl–Wh Grad	14.0	−.279*			−6.9	.073		
Diff. Bl drop–Bl Grad	7.6	−.238*			8.5	−.066		
Diff. Wh drop–Wh Grad	21.8	−.316*			1.5	−.062		

Source: 1991 Race and Politics Survey

Note: Means are computed on 4-point scales ranging from likely (1) to very unlikely (4); percentages based on first two categories (i.e., very likely + somewhat likely), with those accepting negative stereotypes offering more positive evaluations of black than white targets.

[a]Indicated differences run in unexpected direction.

*Indicates means are significantly different from one another ($p < .05$) using ANOVA contrast analysis.

expectations. Our next experiment accordingly focuses on support for welfare programs. Our primary aim in the welfare policy experiment is to determine what difference both the race and the work history of the recipient make. The design is similar to the previous experiment, involving two randomized variations in question wording. Specifically, half of the respondents were asked their opinion of a welfare program "specially designed to help blacks," whereas the other half were asked their view of exactly the same program but instead directed to help "new immigrants from Europe," who are presumably white. In addition, and quite independently, half of the respondents were told that the beneficiaries of the program were "people who have shown that they want to work their way out of their problems"; in contrast, the other half of respondents were told that they were "people who have had trouble hanging onto their jobs." All respondents, after hearing different descriptions of the program, were asked whether they were strongly in favor of (coded 1), somewhat in favor of (2), somewhat opposed to (3), or strongly opposed to (4) a welfare program in the described circumstances.

Not only do we change the attitude object (from welfare recipient to welfare policy) in this experiment, but we also increase the level of discrepancy between stereotype and individuating information. For although the information in the welfare mother experiment is only modestly discrepant with the perception of laziness, "wanting to work their way out of their problems" is more unambiguously at odds with the trait of laziness. By increasing the level of discrepancy, we expect the impact of individuating information to be more pronounced, relative to the moderately discrepant condition found in the welfare mother experiment.

As indicated earlier, figure 1.B suggests that support for welfare among whites is essentially "color-blind," since welfare support is affected by the work history of the recipient (with higher support for those wanting to work than for those with trouble holding onto a job) but not by their race. A substantially different interpretation is suggested by table 4.5.A, which displays the OLS results generated from regressing the welfare support attitudes in the four experimental conditions on the same stereotype, attitudinal, and demographic variables used to predict responses to the welfare mother experiment in table 4.3. Clearly, when whites evaluate welfare for black—but not immigrant—recipients, their decision to support welfare is heavily colored by racial stereotypes. Even in the face of stringent controls for a variety of other variables, the work ethic stereotype measures are consistently strong predictors of welfare support for black recipients.

The analysis also indicates that stereotypic expectations interact with information about past work experience in shaping welfare policy support. When black recipients have a poor work record, the work ethic variable is strongly positive, indicating that those perceiving blacks as lazy are substantially less supportive of welfare. The relationship is reversed, however, when blacks are described as wanting "to work their way out of their own problems": now whites who regard blacks as lazy are far more supportive of welfare.[7]

To analyze the interaction between stereotypic expectations and individuating information in influencing welfare support, table 4.5.B contrasts the reactions of whites who see blacks as lazy (that is, score in the upper third of the work ethic scale) with those who reject such a characterization (score in the bottom third of the scale). Among whites with a negative image of blacks, support for welfare hinges heavily on the beneficiary. When the target fits their stereotypical expectations (blacks with a troubled work history), they are substantially less likely to favor welfare programs for blacks (46.8 percent are in favor) than for immigrants who have the same troubled history (61.7 percent)—a clear-cut instance of a racially discriminatory double standard. But when blacks are at odds with these stereotypes, whites' support shoots up to 92.8 percent, as compared to 71.9 percent for European immigrants who are similarly described as "people who have shown they want to work." From the perspective of whites with a disparaging view of blacks, then, blacks who try hard are an exception, and in consequence deserve to be treated exceptionally well.[8]

Should we celebrate the fact that individuals with a jaundiced view of African-Americans can be persuaded to "go overboard" in their support of welfare for "hard-working" blacks? Certainly not. For although we might take heart in finding that negative stereotypes are discounted in the face of clearly inconsistent individuating information, we must remember that the dominant "picture in the head" of stereotyping whites is of blacks who have problems keeping jobs. And, as revealed in the welfare mother experiment, unless the individuating information presented about blacks clearly contradicts the negative stereotype (mildly discrepant individuating information did not undermine the negative stereotype in the welfare mother experiment), blacks are subject to a punitive or discriminatory response. On the other hand, these results do suggest that it is possible to *inhibit* negative stereotypes from affecting political judgments. Since negative stereotypes have proven remarkably tenacious in resisting change, inhibition may be one of the few practical means of interrupting stereotypical reasoning from biasing political judgments in the explosive context of welfare policy.

Table 4.5. Welfare Policy Experiment

A. Regression analysis of support for welfare program on racial stereotypes across difference descriptions of recipients

	RECIPIENTS							
	Blacks with Trouble		Blacks Who Work		Immigrants with Trouble		Immigrants Who Work	
Racial Stereotypes	b (se)	Beta	b (se)	Beta	b (se)	Beta	b (se)	Beta
Black Work Ethic	.029**	.210	−.025*	−.227	.007	.066	−.010	−.087
	(.013)		(.011)		(.012)		(.012)	
Black Hostility	.005	.024	.024	.144	.023	.134	.031	.175
	(.019)		(.017)		(.017)		(.018)	
R²/Adj R²	.253	.197	.114	.041	.165	.088	.161	.088
Number of cases	199		185		176		177	

Note: Entries in left-hand columns are understandardized regression coefficients with standard errors in parentheses; standardized coefficients in right-hand columns. Lower values on the above variables indicate: favor welfare programs and rejection of negative stereoypes. Coefficients are also controlled for various political predispositions (social intolerance, conformity, anti-Semitism, partisan and ideological identification, and political sophistication) and sociodemographic characteristics (education, gender, age, income, residing in the deep South).

*p < .05; **p < .01.

B. Favor welfare policy across whites who accept and reject negative racial stereotypes

Description of Group	Accept Neg. Stereotype			Reject Neg. Stereotype		
	% Favor	Mean	N	% Favor	Mean	N
Blacks with Trouble	46.8%	2.684	(79)	82.3%	1.952	(62)
Blacks Who Work	92.8	1.536	(69)	84.9	1.604	(53)
Immigrants with Trouble	61.7	2.426	(47)	78.3	2.083	(60)
Immigrants Who Work	71.9	2.078	(64)	87.9	1.707	(58)
Diff. Bl–Im. Trouble	–14.9%	.258*		4.0%	–.131	
Diff. Bl–Im. Work	20.9[a]	–.542*[a]		–3.0	–.103	
Diff. Bl trouble–Bl Work	46.0	1.148*		2.6	.348*	
Diff. Im trouble–Im Work	10.2	.348*		.96	.376*	

Source: 1991 Race and Politics Survey

Note: Means are computed on a 4-point scale ranging from strongly favor (1) to strongly oppose (4); percentages based on first two categories (i.e., strongly favor + somewhat favor).

[a]Indicates differences run in unexpected direction, with those accepting negative stereotypes offering more positive evaluations of black than white targets.

*Indicates means are significantly different (*p* < .05) using ANOVA contrast analysis.

The implications of this important result will be explored more fully in our conclusions. For now, we focus on a very different pattern displayed by whites who *reject* negative characterizations of blacks (right side of table 4.5.B). As in the welfare mother experiment, there is a slight (though statistically insignificant) tendency for these individuals to favor blacks over similarly described immigrants. The dominant pattern, however, is one of support for government assistance, regardless of the beneficiary. Those rejecting stereotypes are, for example, as likely to favor assistance for blacks as for new European immigrants. Even more impressive, they are as likely to back assistance for blacks with a troubled work history (82.3 percent favor) as for blacks wanting to work out their problems (84.9 percent favor). This pattern of findings is consistent with those uncovered in the welfare mother experiment: whites who reject negative stereotypes in the abstract respond more positively to blacks in a specific setting, even in circumstances that would permit a negative response to a black.

The Drug Search Experiment

The crucial result of the welfare policy experiment is that whites with a negative image of blacks react very differently to black targets depending on whether individuating information runs contrary to, or is consistent with, their stereotypical expectations of blacks. But confidence and dependability go hand in hand: a result obtained with different measures in different settings bolsters faith in the results.

The drug search experiment is constructed to replicate the welfare policy experiment, now focusing on the role of stereotypes in the domain of criminal justice. Several researchers have made the forceful argument that crime in the United States has become a racially charged issue, due to statistics showing violent crime to be a greater problem in black neighborhoods, to the exaggerated media portrayals of blacks as violent criminals (Entman 1992; Peffley, Shields, and Williams 1994), and to the political rhetoric of politicians who often talk about crime in racially coded language (Edsall and Edsall 1991; Jamieson 1992). How does the apparently widespread belief that blacks are "aggressive or violent" bias judgments of blacks in the criminal justice domain, and how does stereotypic knowledge interact with inconsistent individuating information?

We investigated these and other questions by examining whites' responses to the drug search experiment, where respondents were asked the following question:

Now consider an instance where the police see two young [black, white] men about 20 years old. They are [using foul language, well dressed and well behaved] and walking very near a house where the police know drugs are being sold. The police search them and find that they are carrying drugs. Do you think this is definitely a reasonable search (coded 1), probably a reasonable search (2), probably not a reasonable search (3), or definitely not a reasonable search (4)?

Because the race and the behavior of the men are independently randomized, one quarter of the time the two men are black and using foul language—obviously the deliberately inflammatory condition—and so on. Recall from figure 4.1.C that, consistent with the other experiments, the race of the men does not have a major impact on judgments of whether the search was reasonable or not. However, as before, the regression results displayed in table 4.6.A tell a different story.

As seen in the first row of coefficients, although the influence of racial stereotypes is not quite as strong here as in the welfare mother or welfare policy experiments, we find that individuals endorsing the hostility stereotype are more likely to approve of the police search when the suspects are black and using foul language. Thus, in a different content domain we find results paralleling those from prior experiments: the more relevant stereotype dimension (in this case, black hostility) is used to shape political judgments.[9]

Table 4.6.B presents the reactions of whites who accept and reject the perception of blacks as hostile. How does individuating information interact with the hostility stereotype for whites who negatively view blacks (that is, score in the top third of the hostility scale)? Plainly, being "well dressed and well behaved" is incompatible with the picture of criminality; the discrepancy between stereotype and individuation is comparable in this case to that of the prior (welfare policy) experiment. Predictably, then, the police search experiment strikingly corroborates the welfare policy experiment: whites with a negative image of blacks, when confronted with blacks who confirm their stereotype, utilize a discriminatory double standard in judging the police search more favorably for blacks than for similarly described whites. And when blacks depart from expectations, these same whites are now more disapproving of the police search for "well-dressed and well-behaved" blacks than for whites described in exactly the same manner. Once again, individuating information that clearly contradicts the negative stereotype prompts such individuals to "bend over backwards" in departing from a stereotyped response.

Also in keeping with the previous two experiments are the responses of whites who reject the negative stereotype. As table 4.6.B shows, their response is

Table 4.6. Analysis of Police Search Experiment

A. Regression analysis of evaluations of police search on racial stereotypes across different descriptions of suspects

SUSPECTS

Racial Stereotypes	Blacks Using Foul Language		Blacks Well Behaved		Whites Using Foul Language		Whites Well Behaved	
	b (se)	Beta	b (se)	Beta	b (se)	Beta	b (se)	Beta
Black Work Ethic	−.006	−.044	−.005	−.034	−.001	−.007	−.004	−.030
	(.007)		(.007)		(.006)		(.008)	
Black Hostility	−.051**	−.151	−.004	−.011	−.021	−.057	−.015	−.037
	(.019)		(.019)		(.019)		(.021)	
R²/Adj R²	.282	.256	.187	.157	.209	.181	.176	.147
Number of Cases	412		411		413		414	

Note: Entries in left-hand columns are unstandardized regression coefficients with standard errors in parentheses; standardized coefficients in right-hand columns. Lower values on the above variables indicate: police search reasonable and rejection of negative stereotypes. Coefficients are also controlled for various political predispositions (social intolerance, conformity, anti-Semitism, partisan and ideological identifications, and political sophistication) and sociodemographic characteristics (education, gender, age, income, residing in deep South).

*p < .05; **p < .01.

B. Evaluations of police search across whites who accept and reject negative stereotypes

Description of Suspects	Accept Neg. Stereotype			Reject Neg. Stereotype		
	% Reason	Mean	N	% Reason	Mean	N
Black Using Foul Language	86.0%	1.710	(100)	50.6%	2.556	(89)
Blacks Well Behaved	62.0	2.304	(92)	47.0	2.610	(100)
Whites Using Foul Language	73.5	2.041	(98)	56.6	2.425	(106)
Whites Well Behaved	72.9	2.104	(96)	53.2	2.587	(109)
Diff. Bl–Wh Foul Lang.	12.5%	−.333*		−6.6%	.131	
Diff. Bl–Wh Well Beh.	−10.9[a]	.200*[a]		−6.2	.023	
Diff. Bl Foul–Bl Beh.	24.0	−.594*		3.6	−.054	
Diff. Wh Foul–Wh Beh.	.6	−.186		3.4	−.162	

Source: 1991 Race and Politics Survey

Note: Means are computed on a 4-point scale ranging from search definitely reasonable (1) to definitely not reasonable (4); percentages based on first two categories (i.e., definitely + possibly reasonable).

[a]Indicates differences run in unexpected direction, with those accepting negative stereotypes offering more positive evaluations of black than white targets.

*Indicates means are significantly different ($p < .05$) using ANOVA contrast analysis.

very nearly invariant regardless of the race or the behavior of the "suspects." Thus, 50.6 percent of whites with a positive image of blacks feel that the police search was reasonable when the blacks were using foul language—the deliberately inflammatory condition—as compared to 47 percent when the black men were "well dressed and well behaved."

CONCLUSIONS

What light do our specific findings throw on the role of racial stereotypes in shaping the contemporary thinking of whites about issues of race in America? To begin with, how pervasive are negative impressions of blacks among whites today, approximately three decades after the high-water mark of the civil rights movement and the passage of historic civil rights legislation? As other studies have shown, a majority of whites now rejects blatantly racist beliefs (such as the genetic inferiority of blacks) that were popular in the 1940s (Page and Shapiro 1992; Schuman, Steeh, and Bobo 1988). Judging from the results of the Race and Politics Survey, however, it is clear that although many whites reject negative characterizations of blacks, many others continue to hold negative stereotypes of African-Americans. In fact, from a third to half of the white population now views "most" blacks as "lazy" and "violent." Assuming that there may be a slight tendency for whites to underreport negative sentiments toward blacks, these percentages are disturbing, to say the least. They strongly suggest that a substantial minority of whites views blacks as a hostile underclass of the undeserving poor.

Our analysis of the antecedents of these beliefs clearly demonstrates that a purely demographic explanation of the phenomenon is inadequate. For, even though stereotyping is more prevalent among southerners and those with less education, our analysis of social background factors provided only a very incomplete accounting of the phenomenon. A more sufficient explanation requires an examination of the core beliefs and values of citizens, particularly those falling under the rubric of ethnocentrism. Social intolerance and, particularly, anti-Semitism were, by a wide margin, consistently the strongest predictors of whites' acceptance of negative racial stereotypes. In one sense, the fact that stereotypes of Jews and blacks are so highly correlated—even after controlling for a variety of social characteristics and value orientations—provides additional testimony that such beliefs should be treated as prejudice. Many (though not all) whites who endorse negative views of blacks have bigoted views of other minorities. Our results are certainly reminiscent of Adorno et al.'s

(1950) finding that different types of prejudice tend to go together in the same ethnocentric individuals. On the other hand, these same results indicate that more work needs to be done to identify the sources of this covariation between anti-Semitism and racial prejudice. For neither of the two orientations included in the analysis to account for ethnocentrism (social intolerance and conformity) adequately explains the strong tendency for different types of prejudice to covary in the same individual.

Even at this point one might argue that negative racial stereotypes do not constitute "true" prejudice if, for example, whites come by their erroneous beliefs through negative media portrayals of blacks. In our view, however, this argument overlooks the conceptual overlap between negative stereotyping and prejudice underlined in Chapters 1 and 2 of this volume: negative stereotypes are clearly evaluative, overgeneralizations, and highly resistant to change, regardless of their source (Hamilton and Sherman 1996). More important, the pernicious effects of stereotyping in biasing political evaluations of blacks are likely to be the same irrespective of how such beliefs are formed.

On this score, our results clearly demonstrate that racial stereotypes play a powerful role in shaping whites' political views of blacks in the highly charged contexts of welfare and crime. But in contrast to previous studies that have looked at the association between whites' views of generic blacks and various policy attitudes, we have taken a different tack. Specifically, through the use of computer-assisted survey technology, we manipulated both the race and other attributes of welfare recipients and drug suspects to (1) assess the power of racial stereotypes to bias political judgments of black (versus white) targets, and (2) examine how two groups of whites—those who embrace and those who reject negative racial stereotypes—respond to particular blacks who confirm and challenge their more general impressions of African-Americans.

Whites who embrace negative stereotypes provide some of the more theoretically interesting but morally distressing results. Under most circumstances, their judgments are clearly theory-driven. When responding to scenarios of blacks who confirm (or only mildly disconfirm) their negative expectations—welfare mothers, welfare recipients with poor work histories, or drug suspects using foul language—such respondents consistently display a discriminatory double standard in judging black targets more harshly than similarly described white targets. Significantly, our experiments were designed as conservative tests of racial bias. Inasmuch as the experiments manipulate both the race and stigmatizing "class"-related characteristics of the targets, the racial bias of negative stereotypers is clearly independent of (or in addition to) any class bias displayed by these respondents. Plainly, cultural conservatives will find sympathetic audiences among this group, as long as they frame their antiwelfare and law-and-order policies as essential for regulating undeserving and lawless minorities.

The responses of the negative stereotypers confronted with counterstereotypical individuating information clearly depends on the degree of the discrepancy between information about the target and negative expectations about blacks. Modest discrepancies, as in the welfare mother experiment, failed to inhibit the impact of negative stereotypes. In the welfare policy and police search experiments, however, where the level of discrepancy between information and stereotype is more pronounced, favorably described blacks are judged far more approvingly than the white counterparts, with almost consensual support of welfare for blacks who "work their way out of their problems" among negative stereotypers. In short, even whites with strongly negative perceptions of blacks respond quite favorably to them when confronted with individuating information that clearly contradicts their stereotype.

Why do these whites seem to "bend over backwards" on behalf of nonstigmatized blacks? This tendency toward overcorrection is consistent with a veritable grab-bag of models in psychology designed to explain contrast effects (for example, Manis, Biernat, and Nelson 1991; Martin, Seta, and Crelia 1990; and Schwartz and Bless 1992) that arise when people are confronted with targets who diverge from their prior expectancies (for two excellent studies of racial bias in the selection of political candidates, see Sigelman et al. 1995, and Terkildsen 1993).[10] A more politically compelling explanation, for our purposes, however, draws on models of impression formation by Fiske and associates (for example, Fiske and Neuberg 1990), which assume that perceivers often rely on category subtypes to evaluate individuals who do not fit more global categories. Positive racial subtypes of especially hard-working or well-behaved blacks (such as the businessman black) may exist alongside negative global categories (for instance, lazy or violent), with subtypes being reserved for the few exceptions that "prove the rule." Such subtyping may also allow negative stereotypers to deny, in a sense, their own prejudice by being able to conceptualize "good" blacks while simultaneously disparaging most others.

Clearly, the architects of the Republican campaign to sell Clarence Thomas to the country during his Senate confirmation hearings understood this tendency toward overcompensation well and employed it for purposes of political manipulation, with powerful results. Realizing that focusing on Thomas's conservative ideology would ignite the liberal opposition, the strategists in the White House emphasized his "biography"—how he was born in Pin Point, Georgia, pulled himself up by his bootstraps, worked extremely hard, and so on. Despite the fact that the story was greatly exaggerated (even mythical), this "pin-point strategy" was extremely effective in selling Thomas to socially conservative whites, who continue to hold Thomas up as an atypical model while at the same time disparaging most blacks for failing to measure up (Mayer and Abramson 1994).

By way of contrast, respondents who reject negative stereotypes of African-Americans display a remarkable consistency in their responses across both the race and the individuating information of the target. Although there is a slight (though rarely significant) tendency for these whites to respond more generously toward black welfare recipients or criminal suspects than toward similarly described whites, the dominant pattern is the consistency of their responses, regardless of whether the blacks in question exhibit socially desirable attributes (are high school graduates, are well behaved and well dressed, are working hard to improve their lives) or display socially undesirable attributes (are high school dropouts, use foul language, have trouble hanging on to their jobs).[11]

It is important that this consistency does not appear to be due to social desirability pressures of impression management. In fact, the randomized experiments are designed in part to "smoke out" the prejudices even of self-proclaimed racially tolerant subjects. And we found that a substantial number of such whites, even when given the ammunition that blacks are "dropouts" or use "foul language" or have a history of work problems, do not take advantage of the opportunity to respond negatively.[12]

Another, more likely possibility, in our view, is that people who reject negative racial stereotypes genuinely do not want to disparage blacks. This position is consistent with the experimental work of Devine and her colleagues (1989, 1991), which indicates that "those who report being low in prejudice actually are low in prejudice" (1989, p. 195). Neither we nor Devine, however, suggest that whites who reject racial stereotypes never engage in prejudicial responses toward blacks. Rather, the responses of such individuals are likely to depend on whether they are able consciously to control their responses. According to Devine, when people who reject negative stereotypes are unconsciously "primed" to think about negative cultural stereotypes of blacks, they are as susceptible to racially intolerant responses as are individuals who accept negative stereotypes. The important point is that under most circumstances, such individuals are likely to avoid prejudice and even actively reject stigmatizing responses (for example, when race becomes an issue in a political campaign). Yet there are many circumstances under which negative cultural stereotypes may be unconsciously activated (for instance, when crime and welfare are discussed in racially coded language), and these are equally worrisome. Quite likely, the producers of the infamous Willie Horton ad employed against Democratic candidate Michael Dukakis in 1988 understood this principle fully (see, for example, Jamieson 1992).

Our results also have important implications for the power of individuating information to inhibit the racial beliefs of negative stereotypers. Given the dim chances of actually changing such stereotypes (see Rothbart and Evans 1993), individuating information that clearly contradicts extant beliefs may be one of the few feasible means for "decoupling" racial stereotypes from welfare and crime policy judgments, as was demonstrated in the welfare policy and police search experiments. Clearly, vivid anecdotes that deviate from our general beliefs can go a long way toward mitigating the power of stereotypes and other sources of base-rate information (Nisbett and Ross 1980). Just as President Reagan excelled at using "Horatio Alger" anecdotes to demonstrate that poverty and drug abuse were not the problems of the federal government (Pratkanis and Aranson 1991, pp. 131–33), President Clinton has often used vivid personal anecdotes of successful (black) welfare mothers being helped by the federal government to get off the public dole. In this respect, then, our results are consistent with studies that show that popular support for a given policy depends on the way that policy is framed. Just as income-targeted policies engender more support than race-targeted policies, in part because they suppress the activation of negative racial stereotypes (Bobo and Kluegel 1993; Sniderman and Piazza 1993), personal vivid anecdotes that are counter to stereotype may also suppress (or even reverse) racial biases in evaluating policies that benefit African-Americans.

The likelihood of this happening in the current environment, however, is slight, given political discourse that discusses welfare and crime in racially coded terms and media coverage that portrays welfare recipients and criminal suspects as black. Stereotype inhibition requires sufficiently powerful and plentiful contrary examples so that whites do not automatically associate problems such as welfare and crime with African-Americans. Regrettably, however, blacks face a double problem in this regard. Welfare recipients and criminals are far too often portrayed as black in the media and, the media focus far more often on atypical blacks in a stigmatizing context. Thus, although stereotypes can be, and doubtless are, often inhibited by information that undercuts the stereotype, this type of information is far from abundant in our culture. Given the manner in which race is linked with welfare and crime in the current political environment, it is likely that public attitudes on these issues will continue to be biased by the racial stereotypes prevalent in the culture.

NOTES

1. By studying stereotypes as the products of normal, everyday cognitive processes, this perspective has successfully documented the pervasive impact that such beliefs have on all stages of information processing, biasing what information is perceived, how that information is interpreted and stored in memory, and hence how that information is used to form appraisals of individual group members (for reviews see Stephan 1985; Bar-Tal et al. 1989; and Hamilton and Trolier 1986).

2. As Hamilton and Trolier (1986, p. 153) point out, social cognition theorists do not *deny* the importance of motivational and other noncognitive variables in the stereotyping process but push the cognitive analysis as far as it can go—exploring the extent to which cognitive factors *alone* can produce stereotyping and its effects.

3. The postelection interview of the 1992 National Election Survey (ANES) asked respondents to rate "blacks in general" on two 7-point semantic differential scales (i.e., "lazy" vs. "hard-working" and "prone to violence" vs. "peaceful"), which are comparable to the "lazy" and "aggressive/violent" scales in the Race and Politics Survey. The percentage of white respondents falling into negative (1–3), neutral (4) and positive (5–7) categories on the two ANES scales are as follows: lazy to hard-working (36.5, 40.4, and 23.1%); violent to peaceful (50.5, 33.3, and 15.9%). While the wording and format of our stereotype items differ from those used by the NES, it is reassuring that responses appear robust and comparable across the two measures.

4. To examine the possibility that regional differences in socialization patterns have faded over recent years, South/non-South comparisons were analyzed across age cohorts. If region and generation interact, we would find that regional differences would diminish among younger respondents. We found, however, that regional comparisons are essentially constant across cohorts.

5. The regression model implicitly assumes, consistent with the prevailing wisdom in the area (e.g., Bobo and Kluegel 1993), that racial stereotypes are causally prior to political judgments—an assumption consistent with findings that such general beliefs are acquired in early childhood, whereas political attitudes are formed in late adolescence and early adulthood (e.g., Sears 1975). We also consider global racial stereotypes, which are general dispositions, to be logically prior to more specific political judgments. On the other hand, causal assumptions are not absolutely crucial to our analysis, which is designed to show the conditions under which stereotypes are, and are not, connected to political judgments.

6. The coefficients for the black work ethic variable are significantly different from one another at the .05 level or less across the race of the welfare mother (columns 1 and 2 versus 3 and 4) and between black dropout and black high school graduate conditions (column 1 versus 2). Significance tests were conducted by pooling the data for all four experimental

conditions and including appropriate interaction terms representing black work ethic times the race and educational status dummy variables. We report the separate regressions (instead of the interactive models estimated with pooled data) in table 4.2 because they are more informative and allow the effects for all the variables to vary across experimental conditions (not just black work ethic).

7. The coefficient for black work ethic varies significantly (at the .05 level or less) across both the race and the work history of the proposed welfare recipient (i.e., across columns 1 and 2 versus 3 and 4 and across columns 1 versus 2), as indicated by a regression analysis of the pooled data including appropriate interaction terms for black work ethic times the race and work history dummies.

8. Possible explanations for this result, which recurs in the drug search experiment discussed below, are explored in the conclusions.

9. The coefficient for black hostility varies significantly (at the .05 level or less) across both the race and the behavior of the men (i.e., across columns 1 and 2 versus 3 and 4 and across column 1 versus 2), as indicated by a regression analysis of the pooled data including appropriate interaction terms for black hostility times the race and behavior dummies.

10. Although our data do not allow us to choose between contrast and subtyping explanations, one advantage of the subtyping explanation, in our judgment, is that it views overcompensation as a habitual response on the part of negative stereotypers (similar to the familiar refrain "I'm not prejudiced, but . . . "), whereas contrast effects tend to resemble transitory and artifactual response biases.

11. As a barometer of their consistency, these respondents evidence an average percentage difference (across the four experiments) of only 4.3% between judgments of stigmatized versus nonstigmatized black targets. Among those holding negative stereotypes, the average difference between stigmatization groups is 24.1%.

12. Moreover, we sought to control for social desirability biases in another way. Regardless of how whites rejecting negative stereotypes score on the eight-item Crowne-Marlowe Social Desirability Index (Crowne and Marlowe 1964), their responses were consistent across the experimental conditions.

REFERENCES

Adorno, T. W., E. Frenkel-Brunswik, D. J. Levinson, and N. Sanford. 1950. *The Authoritarian Personality.* New York: Harper.

Altemeyer, Bob. 1988. *Enemies of Freedom.* San Francisco: Jossey-Bass.

Bobo, Lawrence. 1988. "Group Conflict, Prejudice, and the Paradox of Contemporary Racial Attitudes." In *Eliminating Racism: Profiles in Controversy,* ed. Phyllis A. Katz and Dalmas A. Taylor. New York: Plenum.

Bobo, Lawrence, and James Kluegel. 1993. "Opposition to Race-targeting: Self-interest, Stratification, Ideology, or Racial Attitudes?" *American Sociological Review* 58:443–64.

Bodenhausen, Galen V. 1988. "Stereotypic Biases in Social Decision Making and Memory: Testing Process Models of Stereotype Use." *Journal of Personality and Social Psychology* 55:726–37.

Carmines, Edward G., and Paul M. Sniderman. 1992. "The Asymmetry of Race as a Political

Issue: Prejudice, Political Ideology, and the Structure of Conflict in American Politics." Paper presented at the annual meeting of the American Political Science Association, Chicago.

Crowne, D. P., and Marlowe, D. 1964. *The Approval Motive.* New York: Wiley.

Devine, Patricia G. 1989. "Automatic and Controlled Processes in Prejudice: The Role of Stereotypes and Personal Beliefs." In *Attitude Structure and Function,* ed. Anthony Pratkanis, Steven Breckler, and Anthony Greenwald. Hillsdale, N.J.: Lawrence Erlbaum Associates.

Devine, Patricia G., and Sara M. Baker. 1991. "Measurement of Racial Stereotype Subtyping." *Personality and Social Psychology Bulletin* 17:44–50.

Devine, Patricia G., Margo J. Monteith, Julia R Zuwerink, and Andrew J. Elliot. 1991. "Prejudice Without Compunction." *Journal of Personality and Social Psychology* 60:817–30.

Edsall, Thomas B., and Mary D. Edsall. 1992. *Chain Reaction: The Impact of Race, Rights, and Taxes on American Politics.* New York: W. W. Norton.

Entman, Robert. 1990. "Modern Racism and the Images of Blacks in Local Television News." *Critical Studies in Mass Communication* 7:332–45.

———. 1992. "Blacks in the News: Television, Modern Racism, and Cultural Change." *Journalism Quarterly* 69:341–61.

Feldman, Stanley. 1989. "The Roots of Moral Conservatism." Paper presented at the annual meeting of the International Political Psychology Association, Tel Aviv, Israel.

Fiske, Susan T., and S. L. Neuberg. 1990. "A Continuum of Impression Formation, from Category-based to Individuating Processes: Influences of Information and Motivation on Attention and Interpretation." In *Advances in Experimental Social Psychology,* vol. 23, ed. M. P. Zanna. New York: Academic.

Fiske, Susan T., and Mark A. Pavelcheck. 1986. "Category-based Versus Piecemeal-based Affective Responses: Developments in Schema-triggered Affect." In *The Handbook of Motivation and Cognition: Foundations of Social Behavior,* ed. R. M. Sorenti and E. T. Higgins. New York: Guilford.

Franklin, Raymond S. 1991. *Shadows of Race and Class.* Minneapolis: University of Minnesota Press.

Hamilton, David, and Jeffrey W. Sherman. 1994. "Stereotypes." In *Handbook of Social Cognition,* 2d ed., ed. R. S. Wyer, Jr., and T. K. Srul. Hillsdale, N.J.: Lawrence Erlbaum Associates.

Hamilton, David, and Trolier, T. K. 1986. "Stereotypes and Stereotyping: An Overview of the Cognitive Approach." In *Prejudice, Discrimination, and Racism,* ed. J. Dovidio and S. L. Gaertner. New York: Academic.

Hurwitz, Jon, and Mark Peffley. 1992. "Traditional Versus Social Values as Antecedents of Racial Stereotyping and Policy Conservatism." *Political Behavior* 14:395–421.

Jamieson, Kathleen Hall. 1992. *Dirty Politics: Deception, Distraction, and Democracy.* New York: Oxford University Press.

Kinder, Donald R., and David O. Sears. 1981. "Prejudice and Politics: Symbolic Racism Versus Racial Threats to the Good Life." *Journal of Personality and Social Psychology* 40:414–31.

Kluegel, James R., and Elliot R. Smith. 1986. *Beliefs About Inequality.* New York: Aldine.

Kohn, M. L. 1977. *Class and Conformity.* Chicago: University of Chicago Press.

Lippmann, Walter. 1922. *Public Opinion.* New York: Free Press.

Lipset, Seymour M., and William Schneider. 1978. "The Bakke Case: How Would It Be Decided at the Bar of Public Opinion?" *Public Opinion* 1:38–44.

Locksley, Anne, Eugene Borgida, Nancy Brekke, and Christine Hepburn. 1980. "Sex Stereotypes and Social Judgments." *Journal of Personality and Social Psychology* 39:821–31.

Lodge, Milton, Kathleen M. McGraw, and Patrick Stroh. 1989. "An Impression-driven Model of Candidate Evaluation." *American Political Science Review* 83:399–419.

Manis, Melvin, Monica Biernat, and Thomas F. Nelson. 1991. "Comparison and Expectancy Processes in Human Judgment." *Journal of Personality and Social Psychology* 61:203–11.

Martin, Leonard L., Jon Seta, and Rick A. Crelia. 1990. "Assimilation and Contrast as a Function of People's Willingness and Ability to Expend Effort in Forming an Impression." *Journal of Personality and Social Psychology* 59:27–37.

Mayer, Jane, and Jill Abramson. 1994. *Strange Justice: The Selling of Clarence Thomas.* Boston: Houghton Mifflin.

Nisbett, Richard, and Lee Ross. 1980. *Strategies and Shortcomings of Social Judgment.* Englewood Cliffs, N.J.: Prentice Hall.

Peffley, Mark, Todd Shields, and Bruce Williams. 1994. "The Intersection of Race and Crime in Television News Stories: An Experimental Study." Paper presented at the annual meeting of the Midwestern Political Science Association, Chicago.

Pratkanis, Anthony, and Elliot Aronson. 1991. *Age of Propaganda: The Everyday Use and Abuse of Persuasion.* New York: Freeman.

Rahn, Wendy M. 1993. "The Role of Partisan Stereotypes in Information Processing about Political Candidates." *American Journal of Political Science* 37:472–96.

Rothbart, Myron and John Oliver. 1993. "Race, Politics, and the American Dilemma." In *Prejudice, Politics, and the American Dilemma,* ed. Paul Sniderman, Philip Tetlock, and Edward Carmines. Stanford, Calif.: Stanford University Press.

Schuman, Howard, Charlotte Steeh, and Lawrence Bobo. 1988. *Racial Attitudes in America.* Cambridge, Mass.: Harvard University Press.

Schwartz, Norbert, and Herbert Bless. 1992. "Constructing Reality and Its Alternatives: An Inclusion/Exclusion Model of Assimilation and Contrast Effects in Social Judgment." In *The Construction of Social Judgments,* ed. Leonard L. Martin and Abraham Tesser. Hillsdale, N.J.: Lawrence Erlbaum Associates.

Sears, David O. 1975. *Political socialization.* In *Handbook of Political Science,* vol. 4, ed. Fred I. Greenstein and Nelson W. Polsby. Reading, Mass.: Addison-Wesley.

Selznick, Gertrude J., and Stephen Steinberg. 1969. *The Tenacity of Prejudice: Anti-Semitism in Contemporary America.* New York: Harper and Row.

Sidanius, James. 1992. "A Comparison of Symbolic Racism Theory and Social Dominance Theory: Explanations for Racial Policy Attitudes." *Journal of Social Psychology* 132:377–95.

Sigelman, Carol K., Lee Sigelman, Barbara J. Walkosz, and Michael Nitz. 1995. "Black Candidates, White Voters: Understanding Racial Bias in Political Perceptions." *American Journal of Political Science* 39:243–65.

Sniderman, Paul M., and Thomas Piazza. 1993. *The Scar of Race.* Cambridge, Mass.: Harvard University Press.

Snyder, Mark, and William J. Ickes. 1985. "Personality." In *The Handbook of Social Psychology,* 3rd ed., ed. Gardner Lindzey and Elliot Aronson. New York: Random House.

Terkildsen, Nadya. 1993. "When White Voters Evaluate Black Candidates: The Processing Implications of Candidate Skin Color, Prejudice and Self-monitoring." *American Journal of Political Science* 37:1032–53.

Wilson, William Julius. 1987. *The Truly Disadvantaged: The Inner City, the Underclass and Public Policy.* Chicago: University of Chicago Press.

Chapter 5 When Prejudice Matters: The Impact of Racial Stereotypes on the Racial Policy Preferences of Democrats and Republicans

Edward G. Carmines and Geoffrey C. Layman

More than any other issue, race has divided the modern Democratic party. Franklin D. Roosevelt's original New Deal Democratic coalition was successful largely because it brought together large groups of voters—workers, recent European immigrants to the North, and southerners—who had been most adversely affected by the Great Depression and looked to the national government for relief. When substantial numbers of equally desperate but hopeful blacks began voting for Roosevelt in the 1936 presidential election, the party had assembled a truly impressive cross-race, class-oriented electoral coalition (Weiss 1983; Sitkoff 1976; Kirby 1980). But this coalition was inherently unstable because it included two groups, blacks and southern whites, that had diametrically opposed preferences on civil rights. Roosevelt was able to hold the coalition together because the country was focused on economic and class issues during the 1930s and because he assiduously avoided dealing directly with racial issues, including not taking a stand on the federal antilynching bill before the Congress (Brinkley 1995).

Subsequent Democratic administrations, however, have not been so fortunate. The first rupture occurred in the 1948 presidential election campaign, when a group of southern segregationist delegates bolted the Democratic convention and formed a third party, the States' Rights Democrats, in response to a relatively mild civil rights plank adopted by the convention's delegates. After simmering during the 1950s—at least as far as Democrats were concerned—the divisive effects of race came to a boil with a vengeance during the early 1960s. During the latter part of the Kennedy administration, as race rose to the top of the political agenda, open warfare between white racial liberals and blacks on the one side and southern conservatives and segregationists on the others side became the focal point of internal Democratic party conflict (Carmines and Stimson 1989). In time, this stage in the struggle for the racial soul of the party was resolved; the national Democratic party became firmly committed to equal rights for African-Americans. As a result, blacks became the most loyal group in the Democratic coalition, while the most conservative southern whites turned to the GOP (Carmines and Stanley 1990; Black and Black 1987).

Guaranteeing equal rights for African-Americans did not, however, eliminate racial differences from American society. On the contrary, it merely shifted the focus from political and legal rights to social and economic conditions. For it almost immediately became clear that in spite of the great civil rights victories embodied in the passage of the 1964 Civil Rights Act and the Voting Rights Act of 1965, large and persistent differences in the socioeconomic circumstances of blacks and whites would continue, in effect, relegating many of the former to the bottom of the American economic order.

Two different racial policy agendas emerged in response to this situation (Sniderman and Piazza 1993). The first, initiated during Johnson's Great Society War on Poverty, was intended to improve the condition of the worst-off blacks by improving the situation of the worst-off, black or white. Job training programs, improved medical care for children, and increased educational opportunities were designed to aid those from disadvantaged economic backgrounds, whether they were black or white. Yet it was clear that these programs would disproportionately benefit African-Americans, so they were quickly seen as social welfare for blacks. The second, and more controversial, post–civil rights policy agenda focused explicitly on race-conscious programs designed to aid only blacks and other minorities. These policies, collectively often referred to as affirmative action, encourage and sometimes force government, business, industry, and professions to include qualified minorities in their workforce. In addition, affirmative action programs also apply to admission to public institutions of higher education.

PREJUDICE, PARTISANSHIP, AND
RACIAL POLICY PREFERENCES

The emergence of these two new racial policy agendas poses a severe challenge to the Democratic party. Both sets of policies are widely supported by blacks and white racial liberals but lack broad white support. Affirmative action is especially unpopular among whites, often disparagingly characterized as racial quotas for minorities. Thus, the question we pursue in this chapter is whether Democrats are now divided over these new racial issues, just as they were divided earlier over the issue of equal rights for black Americans. We posit that racial prejudice does indeed have a much more powerful influence on the racial policy preferences of white Democrats than it does among white Republicans. Prejudice, we argue, shapes the political thinking of ordinary Democrats to a much greater extent than it does that of Republicans. It is not that white Democrats are more racially prejudiced than white Republicans. By our measure, the correlation between partisan identification and racial prejudice is less than .01, and the mean scores of white Democrats and Republicans are less than half a point apart on a 50-point scale. In other words, there is virtually no difference in the frequency with which prejudice is found among white Democrats and Republicans.

Although racial prejudice is no more frequent on one side of the partisan divide than the other, it should affect the racial policy preferences of Democrats to a far greater extent than it affects those of Republicans. The reason for this differential impact is not difficult to understand, once the different political perspectives of Republicans and Democrats are taken into account. Whether Republicans are prejudiced or not, they are united by a commitment to the principle of limited government—at least when it comes to the social welfare and economic role of the national government. As a consequence, precisely because they are simply being good Republicans, even unprejudiced Republicans should see no compelling reason why blacks should receive any special treatment or even significant welfare assistance from the government. After all, Republicans oppose a major role for the national government in providing for the general welfare of the citizenry, and this opposition ought to apply to blacks and other minorities just as it does to whites. Thus, in following long-accepted and -practiced Republican ideology, unprejudiced Republicans, just like their more prejudiced fellow partisans, should oppose government aid to minorities. Moreover, this decision ought to be relatively easy for Republicans, even unprejudiced Republicans, because it derives so directly and straightforwardly from their deeply held Republican ideology (Carmines and Stimson 1980).

The situation should be very different among Democrats. Given their general support for activist government and the increased contribution that blacks have made to the Democratic electoral coalition in recent presidential elections, their natural inclination should be to support government aid to various groups, including most especially African-Americans. But, of course, racially prejudiced Democrats should not share this outlook. Instead, they should take exactly the opposite position—opposing government assistance and special treatment for blacks. In other words, racial issues should be hard issues for racially prejudiced white Democrats because they are vulnerable to being pulled in opposing directions depending on their feelings toward blacks— inclined to support government programs to assist blacks because of their commitment to New Deal government activism but tempted to oppose them because of their dislike of blacks. In other words, some white Democrats are susceptible to cross-pressures in a way that Republicans are not. Their big-government philosophy flies in the face of their racial prejudice. Thus, our contention is not that racial prejudice is more rampant among white Democrats than Republicans but that it is more consequential for them. It has the capacity to shape their racial policy preferences to a much greater extent than those of Republicans. In sum, prejudice should play a major role in shaping the political thinking of Democrats, a minor one in shaping the thinking of Republicans.

THE IMPACT OF PREJUDICE AMONG
DEMOCRATS AND REPUBLICANS

Our central concern is the comparative impact of racial prejudice in shaping the political thinking of Democrats and Republicans, and our principal hypothesis—that contemporary racial policies are less divisive and tend to represent an easier choice for Republicans than for Democrats—suggests that prejudice will have a greater impact on the racial policy preferences of Democrats than on those of Republicans. In order to examine this possibility, we employ the battery of questions about racial stereotypes contained in the Race and

Politics Survey. The survey covered five negative stereotypes (in addition to those utilized in other chapters of this volume) commonly attributed to blacks: "aggressive or violent," "lazy," "boastful," "irresponsible," and "complaining." Given the desirability of avoiding either-or choices that require unconditional acceptance or rejection of a stereotype, respondents were instead asked to indicate how good a description of blacks each of these characterizations was; the higher the score, which could range from 0 to 10, the more accurate they believed the negative characterization to be. Responses to the five negative stereotypes have been summed to form our measure of prejudice: the Index of Negative Stereotypes (INS).[1]

Table 5.1 presents the results of an initial test of the hypothesis of differential impact. It shows the correlations between racial prejudice—the Index of Negative Stereotypes—and positions on five racial policy issues—government spending for jobs for blacks, fighting discrimination against blacks in jobs, welfare spending, racial employment quotas for companies that have discriminated in the past, and preferential admissions to universities for black students—for (self-identified) Democrats, independents, and Republicans. Welfare spending is a three-category variable with a score of 0 indicating "decrease," a score of .5 indicating "keep about the same," and a score of 1 indicating

Table 5.1. Correlation of Index of Negative Stereotypes and Racial Policy Preferences, by Party Identification (Whites)

	Party Identification		
Racial Policies	Democrat	Independent	Republican
Government Spending for Programs to Help Blacks Get More Jobs	.34**	.13**	.13**
Fighting Discrimination Against Blacks in Jobs	.29**	.19*	−.01
Welfare Spending	.28**	.06*	.04
Job Quotas for Blacks	.11	.26	−.14
Preferential Admissions to Universities for Blacks	.22**	−.04*	.005

**p < .01; *p < .05.
Source: Race and Politics Survey
Note: The index of negative stereotypes ranges from most to least prejudiced. All racial policies range from most conservative to most liberal. Entries are product moment correlation coefficients. The number of observations ranges from 167 to 488 for Democrats, from 200 to 549 for independents, and from 183 to 596 for Republicans. The exact coding of each variable is presented in the Appendix.

"increase." The other four policy variables are dichotomous, with a score of 0 indicating opposition and a score of 1 indicating support.

As an examination of the results makes plain, it is flatly wrong to conclude that prejudice has been reduced to a minor force in shaping the views of ordinary Americans about contemporary issues of race merely because the *zero order* correlation between prejudice and racial policy preference is so low (the mean correlation for these five policies is .12). If prejudice plays only a minor role in the public as a whole, it is a major factor in shaping the thinking of white Democrats. On the issue of government spending for black jobs, for example, the correlation between issue positions and prejudice is .34 for Democrats. Indeed, across most of these racial issues, including fighting racial discrimination in employment ($r = .29$), welfare spending ($r = .28$), and preferential treatment for blacks in university admissions ($r = .22$), the role of prejudice in shaping the political thinking of Democrats is striking. Not only are these correlations substantial—the mean correlation for these four policies is .28— they are also highly statistically significant ($p < .01$). In contrast, the comparable correlations between issue positions and prejudice among white Republicans are for all intents and purposes negligible. The largest is .13, the mean is .04, and only one of these correlations is statistically significant. The evidence clearly indicates that prejudice plays little or no role in shaping the racial policy preferences of Republicans. Not surprisingly, the correlations for independents tend to fall between those for Democrats and Republicans, but it is the striking differences between the latter two groups that is impressive.

This asymmetry between prejudice and partisanship suggests that it is the interaction between these variables that affects support for racial policies. Table 5.2 undertakes a more rigorous test of this hypothesis. It shows the results of a series of logistic regressions (ordered logit for the three-category welfare variable) in which each of the racial policies is a function of party identification (a seven-point scale ranging from strong Republican to strong Democrat), prejudice (the Index of Negative Stereotypes ranging from most to least prejudiced), and their interaction created by multiplying partisanship and prejudice: Policy Liberalism $= b_0 + b_1$Partisanship $+ b_2$Prejudice $+ b_3$(Partisanship $\times$ Prejudice). The table shows that there is indeed a noticeable interaction between prejudice and party identification in determining support for racial policies. This interaction term has a statistically significant ($p < .05$, and in most cases $p < .01$) effect on support for all five of the racial policies. In short, it is the interaction of greater attachment to the Democratic party *and* less prejudice that is associated with more liberal positions on racial policy issues.

Table 5.2. Logits and Ordered Logit of Racial Policy Positions on Party Identification, Prejudice, and Their Interaction (Whites)

Racial Policies	Independent Variable		
	Party Identification	Prejudice	Interaction (Prejudice by Party Identification)
Goverment Spending for Programs to Help Blacks Get More Jobs[a]	−.11 (−.96)	.002 (.08)	.01 (2.31**)
Fighting Discrimination Against Blacks in Jobs[a]	−.30 (2.77*)	−.02 (−1.26)	.01 (3.43**)
Welfare Spending[b]	−.20 (−2.92*)	−.03 (−2.28*)	.01 (4.78**)
Job Quotas for Blacks[a]	−.18 (−1.38)	−.04 (−1.69)	.01 (2.71*)
Preferential Admissions to Universities for Blacks[a]	−.15 (−1.24)	−.03 (−1.52)	.01 (2.42*)

**p < .001; *p < .05
[a]Dichotomous dependent variable—binomial logit was used.
[b]Three category dependent variable—ordered logit was used.
Source: Race and Politics Survey
Note: Party identification is a 7-point scale ranging from strong Republican to strong Democrat. Prejudice is the index of negative stereotypes, which here ranges from most prejudiced to least prejudiced. Entries are either binomial logit coefficients or ordered logit coefficients. *T*-scores are in parentheses. Dependent variables are coded so that higher scores indicate more liberal positions. *N*-sizes range from 545 to 1,620.

Because the logit model is nonlinear, the effect of any explanatory variable is specific to a particular point on the probability distribution of the dependent variable. This means, in turn, that the coefficients for explanatory variables must be evaluated with respect to the dependent variable's distribution as well. In order to demonstrate the substantive effect of the coefficients from the logistic regressions in table 5.2, figure 5.1 shows the probabilities (predicted across the full range of the Index of Negative Stereotypes by these logit models) of taking the liberal position on each of the five racial issues for those at the extremes of the partisan continuum—strong Republicans and strong Democrats. The figures clearly show the asymmetrical effects of prejudice on the racial policy attitudes of these two groups of committed partisans. For Republicans, the lines depicting the predicted probabilities are relatively flat and are always below .50, indicating that Republicans tend to oppose these racial policies regardless of their level of prejudice. Conversely, the lines depicting the predicted probabilities of strong Democrats reveal a marked steepness; their degree of support for these liberal racial policies is strongly affected by prejudice. When prejudice is high, strong Democrats display no more support for these policies than do strong Republicans. But as prejudice declines, Democrats show an increasing tendency to support these policies, and this support reaches its highest level for those expressing no racial prejudice. In sum, the figures show graphically the much greater impact that prejudice has on the racial policy preferences of Democrats than on those of Republicans.

The political implications of the greater impact of prejudice among Democrats than among Republicans are important to underscore. Thus, table 5.3 examines not only the differential impact of prejudice for Democrats and Republicans, but also the changes in the actual levels of support of both parties' supporters that result as a function of increasing prejudice. It shows the mean level of support for each racial policy by the combined effects of party identification (divided here into only the three categories) and racial prejudice (divided here into equal thirds).[2] Again, the asymmetrical effects of prejudice are evident. Among Democrats, prejudice has a marked effect on support for these racial policies. For example, whereas 70 percent of white Democrats who are low in prejudice (the bottom third of the Index of Negative Stereotypes) support an increase in government spending to promote black employment, only 32 percent of Democrats with high levels of prejudice (the top third of the Index of Negative Stereotypes) do so.[3] Similarly, although 65 percent of low-prejudiced Democrats favor government efforts to fight discrimination against blacks in employment, only 37 percent of high-prejudiced Democrats support such efforts.

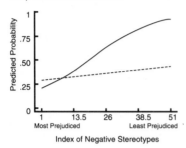

A. Government Spending for Programs to
   Help Blacks Get More Jobs

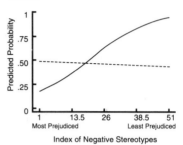

B. Fighting Discrimination Against Blacks
   in Jobs

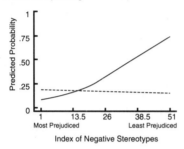

C. Welfare Spending

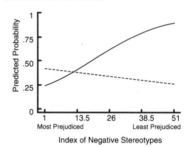

D. Job Quotas for Blacks

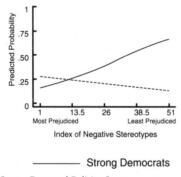

E. Preferential Admissions to Universities
   for Blacks

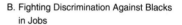

——————— Strong Democrats   ------------ Strong Republicans

Source: Race and Politics Survey

Figure 5.1 Predicted Probabilities of Taking the Most Liberal Position on Racial Policies
for White Democrats and White Republicans, by Prejudice

Table 5.3. Mean Support for Racial Policies by Negative Stereotypes and
Party Identification (Whites)

	Low	Middle	High	T-Test
	Index of Negative Stereotype			
Government Spending for Programs to Help Black Get More Jobs				
Democrat	.70	.49	.32	4.96**
Independent	.49	.46	.42	
Republican	.46	.39	.31	1.61
Fight Discrimination Against Blacks in Jobs				
Democrat	.65	.45	.37	3.55**
Independent	.64	.43	.40	
Republican	.48	.44	.46	.26
Welfare Spending				
Democrat	.54	.35	.28	5.95**
Independent	.37	.35	.31	
Republican	.30	.31	.26	1.04
Jobs Quotas for Blacks				
Democrat	.50	.51	.42	.76
Independent	.53	.37	.25	
Republican	.26	.35	.37	−1.05
Preferential Admissions to Universities for Blacks				
Democrat	.42	.32	.21	2.83*
Independent	.23	.28	.34	
Republican	.21	.18	.23	−.32

**$p < .001$; *$p < .05$.
Source: Race and Politics Survey
Note: T-tests are between Democrats (Republicans) who are low on prejudice and Democrats
(Republicans) who are high on prejudice. Higher scores on policies indicate more liberal posi-
tions. Since all racial policies are on a 0–1 scale, these means can also be read as percentages
supporting these policies. N-sizes range from 40 to 199 for mean scores in the table.

In contrast, the differences are much smaller among Republicans. For example, 48 percent of Republicans who are low in prejudice support efforts to fight
discrimination against blacks in jobs, while 46 percent of Republicans who are
high in prejudice do so. Although the differences between Democrats who are
racially prejudiced and those who are not are highly significant ($p < .01$) on all
of the policies except job quotas, the differences among Republicans do not
reach statistical significance for any of the issues.

This has clear consequences for both racial policy programs and electoral politics. The division of the Democratic coalition and the unity of the Republican coalition mean that majority support for ameliorative racial policies may be impossible to garner. On issues of race, the Republican party enjoys its own undivided support plus a portion of the Democratic party's. This also means that focusing on racial issues should be a very successful electoral strategy for Republican candidates. Although racial matters have long been employed in the South to hinder the development of left-leaning electoral coalitions (Key 1949; Havard 1972; Huckfeldt and Kohfeld 1989), Republican candidates throughout the country now may find it advantageous to stress conservative racial themes. They do not appear to risk losing any of their own partisan support from this strategy and they may attract a significant portion of the Democratic coalition. Since blacks play a central role in the Democratic coalition (Huckfeldt and Kohfeld 1989), Democratic candidates are severely constrained in their ability to maintain the support of prejudiced Democrats when racial issues move to the forefront of a campaign.

Due to the divisive political nature of prejudice within the Democratic coalition, the rest of this chapter will be largely devoted to the political consequences of race prejudice for the Democratic party. First, however, we will examine a bit more closely the lack of a cleavage in the Republican party along the lines of racial prejudice. The finding that prejudice has little political importance for Republicans contradicts the commonly held view that prejudice plays its largest role on the political right, with contemporary racial politics being defined by the "conjunction" of conservatism and antiblack affect (Kinder and Sears 1981). Given the divergence of this finding from the conventional wisdom, it seems appropriate to subject it to a rigorous counterargument: that the lack of cleavage among white Republicans may be illusory. It may be illusory because Republicans who take conservative positions on racial issues even though they claim to be unprejudiced may not be so. Their seeming lack of prejudice may be misleading, created by a mere veneer of racial sympathy.

UNITY AMONG REPUBLICANS:
SINCERE OR SUPERFICIAL?

The questions we seek to answer here regard what can and should be said about Republicans who say they feel positively about blacks, or at least display no overt racial prejudice. Are they only saying what they think they ought to say, or is there reason to believe that they are being sincere? For that matter, may

Republicans with positive feelings conform to a Republican line on racial issues, not because their positive feelings toward blacks are a sham, but because their feelings are superficial and lack the power to influence their behavior? The "government dependency" experiment was designed to determine whether Republicans who say they have a positive regard for blacks in fact respond positively if they are provided with a socially acceptable excuse to respond negatively. It comprises three experimental conditions. In the first—or "poverty"—condition, a (randomly selected) set of respondents is asked to respond to the following statement: "Most *poor people* these days would rather take assistance from the government than make it on their own through hard work." In the second—or "race"—condition, one-third of respondents is asked to respond to the statement: "Most *blacks* these days would rather take assistance from the government than make it on their own through hard work." In the third—or "combined"—condition, the final third of respondents is asked to respond to the statement:"Most *poor blacks* these days would rather take assistance from the government than make it on their own through hard work." It should be emphasized that the three statements are exactly alike but for the variation in the description of recipients.

It is not, we have suggested, that Republicans who report positive feelings toward blacks are insincere but rather that, insofar as they are committed Republicans, their feelings are largely irrelevant to the positions they take on racial policy issues. After all, from the perspective of a person on the right, the social welfare role of government *should* be narrow whether the group to benefit is blacks or women or whoever. But if this reasoning is correct, then even though Republicans with positive attitudes toward blacks should not deviate on issues of public policy from a Republican line, they should respond markedly more positively to blacks outside of the context of the government's agenda than their fellow Republicans who dislike blacks. In terms of the "government dependency" experiment, the prediction then follows that Republicans with relatively positive feelings toward blacks should be *less* likely than those with relatively negative feelings toward blacks to agree that blacks "these days would rather take assistance from the government than make it on their own through hard work." For if they are not less likely to stigmatize blacks in this manner, it must be accepted that they do not mean what they say when they say they are unprejudiced toward them. In addition, and more subtly, if Republicans who have seemingly more positive feelings toward blacks are opposing government assistance for blacks out of political conviction and have not merely simulated a positive regard for blacks, then they should manifest these convictions by characterizing the "poor" who avail themselves of government services as people who "would rather take assistance from the government than make it on their own through hard work"; and, indeed, in the identical circumstances, they should respond *more negatively to a person who is poor than to one who is black.*

Figure 5.2 graphically displays white Republicans' levels of agreement with

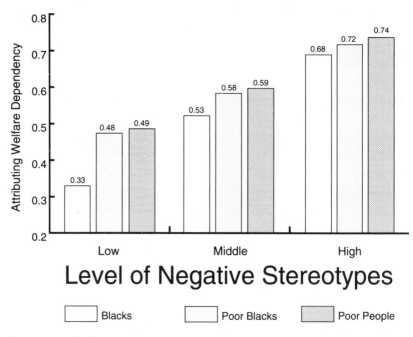

Level of Negative Stereotypes

☐ Blacks   ☐ Poor Blacks   ▨ Poor People

Source: Race and Politics Survey
Note: Higher scores represent agreement with the statement that "[poor people; blacks; poor blacks] would rather take government assistance than work." Since the variable has been placed on a 0–1 scale, mean scores can be read as the percentage agreeing with such a statement.

T-Tests Between the Least Prejudiced Republicans and the Most Prejudiced Republicans on Different Versions of the Question:
    Poor People: $t = -4.09$, $p < .001$
    Blacks: $t = -6.72$, $p < .001$
    Poor Blacks: $t = -4.30$, $p < .001$

T-Test Between the Least Prejudiced Republicans on the "Poor People" Version of the Question and the Least Prejudiced Republicans on the "Blacks" Version of the Question:
    $t = 2.70$, $p < .01$

Figure 5.2 Mean Score on Statement Attributing Welfare Dependency to Contrasting (and Randomized) Groups by Level of Negative Stereotypes (White Republicans)

attributions of welfare dependency to blacks, poor blacks, and poor people, depending on whether their feelings toward blacks are positive (the bloc of columns to the left), in the middle (the bloc of columns in the middle), or negative (the bloc of columns on the right). The higher the bar, the greater the agreement with the attribution of welfare dependency.

Two aspects of the results deserve to be underlined. First, Republicans whom we have scored as having positive attitudes toward blacks are indeed less likely to respond negatively to blacks than are Republicans whom we have scored as having negative attitudes toward them. That is, Republicans classified as having a positive regard for blacks in general are significantly ($p < .001$) less likely to say that blacks would "rather take assistance from the government . . . than make it on their own." Second, as we predicted, Republicans who say they like blacks do respond more positively to blacks than to people who are poor. Republicans scoring low in prejudice are significantly ($p < .01$) more likely to believe that the poor take advantage of government assistance than that blacks do so.

Even so, it could be argued that the results of the government dependency experiment show not that Republicans who say they like blacks should be taken at their word, but rather that such Republicans are sensitive to social desirability pressures. They are indeed consistent: they express a positive view of blacks when asked to describe what blacks are like, and they are less inclined to endorse a negative one. But perhaps they do both of these things to present a socially desirable image of themselves.

Arguments invoking considerations of social desirability are notoriously difficult to assess empirically, but the government dependency experiment was designed to provide an honest check on impression management. It contrasts *three* conditions—the beneficiaries of government help are described as "poor people," "blacks," and "poor blacks," respectively. It is therefore crucial to notice that, in figure 5.2, unprejudiced Republicans are *as likely* to say that poor blacks take advantage of government assistance as they are to say that poor people do. They are thus not unwilling to express negative reactions to blacks. As Republicans, they identify with a party that is apprehensive about the abuse of government assistance and they express this apprehension as readily when blacks are involved as when they are not—as long as they are poor. In short, the trigger that leads to increased apprehension among unprejudiced Republicans is "poor," not "black."

A final line of argument merits attention. According to our argument, Republicans who have a positive attitude toward blacks nonetheless oppose an array of racial policies to assist blacks because to do otherwise would conflict with their partisan and ideological commitments. But if this is indeed so, then we should expect that these same Republicans, presented with a policy that is intended to help blacks and that does not conflict with their own and their party's views, would support it.

The integration experiment, by presenting unprejudiced Republicans with an opportunity to help blacks that does not involve government activism, is designed to assess whether this expectation is valid or not. In the experiment, three different (and randomly selected) sets of respondents were asked three different questions about programs to encourage blacks to buy houses in white suburbs. One set was asked how it felt about "programs set up by religious and business groups that encourage blacks to buy homes in white suburbs." Another set was asked how it felt about "the government putting its weight behind programs to encourage blacks to buy homes in white suburbs." A final set was asked how it felt about "government-subsidized housing to encourage blacks to buy homes in white suburbs." Table 5.4 reports mean white responses to the housing question broken down in three ways: by respondents' partisan identification, by their positions on the trichotomized Index of Negative Stereotypes, and by the framing of the issue.

The crucial distinction among the three forms of the integration proposal is that the first specifies the involvement of only private organizations, while the second and third specify government involvement. If unprejudiced Republicans really do have positive attitudes toward blacks and oppose government programs to assist them not because of well-hidden negative racial feelings but because of their ideologically motivated aversion to government involvement in private affairs, and particularly to government spending, then they should give significantly greater approval to a program to help blacks that involves only private organizations than to ones that involve the government. In other words, if unprejudiced Republicans really do like blacks, then given an opportunity to help them that does not run counter to their partisan and ideological bearings, they should take it.

Table 5.4 shows that, in fact, they do. First, Republicans with positive attitudes toward blacks are significantly ($p < .05$) more likely to support integration under the aegis of religious and business groups than are Republicans with negative attitudes toward blacks. In contrast, the differences between the levels of support for prejudiced and unprejudiced Republicans on either of the two versions of the policy involving government are not statistically significant ($p > .10$). Second, although unprejudiced Republicans are no less likely

Table 5.4. Mean Support for Black Housing in White Suburbs by the Nature of the Program, Party Identification, and the Index of Negative Stereotypes (Whites)

| Nature of the Program | Index of Negative Stereotypes | | | |
	Low	Middle	High	T-Test[a]
Set up by Religious and Business Groups				
Republican	.58	.51	.45	2.12*
Independent	.65	.57	.56	
Democrat	.47	.52	.41	
T-Test (Party Identification)[b]	1.79			
Government Puts Its Weight Behind				
Republican	.39	.43	.36	.46
Independent	.48	.44	.46	
Democrat	.53	.46	.38	
T-Test (Party Identification)[b]	−1.95			
Goverment-Subsidized Housing				
Republican	.35	.38	.38	−.54
Independent	.41	.44	.45	
Democrat	.51	.46	.44	
T-Test (Party Identification)[b]	−2.72**			
T-Test (Policy Type)[c]	2.73**			
T-Test (Policy Type)[d]	3.84**			

**p < .01; *p < .05
Source: Race and Politics Survey
Note: Higher scores represent greater support.
[a] T-test between the mean support for a particular version of the policy of Republicans who are low on prejudice and the mean support of Republicans who are high on prejudice.
[b] T-test between the mean support for a particular version of the policy of Republicans who are low on prejudice and the mean support of Democrats low on prejudice.
[c] T-test between the mean support of Republicans who are low on prejudice for programs set up by religious and business groups that encourage blacks to buy homes in white suburbs and the mean support of Republicans who are low on prejudice for the government putting its weight behind such programs.
[d] T-test between the mean support of Republicans who are low on prejudice for programs set up by religious and business groups that encourage blacks to buy homes in white suburbs and the mean support of Republicans who are low on prejudice for government-subsidized housing.

than unprejudiced Democrats to support housing programs set up by religious and business groups, they are significantly (p < .01) less supportive than unprejudiced Democrats of government-subsidized housing. Moreover, Republicans who like blacks are less supportive than Democrats who like blacks to support even the much milder form of government involvement indicated by "government putting its weight behind it," and the difference comes very close to standard levels of statistical significance ($p < .06$). Finally, and perhaps most important, unprejudiced Republicans are significantly ($p < .01$) more likely to favor housing programs set up by religious and business groups than they are to favor either of the programs in which the government is involved.

In short, unprejudiced Republicans respond exactly as they should if they really have positive attitudes toward blacks but are committed Republicans. They support efforts to help blacks when the government is not involved, displaying levels of support no lower than those of unprejudiced Democrats, but do not support such efforts when they are directed by the government, showing levels of support indistinguishable from those of prejudiced Republicans. All the various lines of evidence, then, converge. All run against the suggestion that Republicans who score low on the Index of Negative Stereotypes are saying not what they think but what they think they should say.

DIVISION AMONG DEMOCRATS: POLITICAL AND ELECTORAL CONSEQUENCES

The policy and electoral consequences of the divisive role played by racial prejudice in the Democratic coalition are closely connected. Advocates of government programs directed toward blacks may find it quite difficult to build majority support for these policies. Since Republican identifiers are opposed to these programs regardless of their feelings toward blacks, Republican legislators are likely to be united in opposition to ameliorative racial policies. The enthusiasm of Democratic legislators for such programs also may be less than overwhelming. Although blacks are an integral part of Democratic electoral coalitions, Democratic elected officials may stand to lose a significant portion of their white support if they promote liberal racial policies. The remainder of this chapter thus examines the electoral implications of the division of the Democratic coalition along the lines of racial prejudice. First, we assess the extent to which the Democratic party stands to lose electorally because of prejudice. Second, we attempt to denote the groups in the Democratic coalition from which this electoral loss is most likely to come. Finally, we consider the possibility that the potential electoral losses accruing to the Democratic party because of its racial liberalism may in fact be overstated. Prejudiced Democrats may, in fact, be Democrats in name only: identifying themselves as Democrats due to traditional group ties but opposing the party's ideology on a whole range of issues, both racial and nonracial.

Racial Prejudice and the Potential
for Democratic Electoral Loss

Although prejudiced Democrats may be as strongly attached to the Democratic party as nonprejudiced Democrats,[4] they may be less likely to support the party's candidates at the polls, particularly when racial issues are a salient issue in the campaign. Unfortunately, the timing of the Race and Politics Study— during a year, 1991, in which no federal elections and only a few statewide elections were held—did not allow for many questions regarding electoral choice. However, the survey did ask respondents to rate the incumbent president, George Bush, on a feeling thermometer ranging from 0 (least warm) to 10 (most warm), and these ratings of Bush may provide some indication of whether racial prejudice divides the Democratic electoral coalition. Although Bush was not involved in an electoral campaign in 1991, he clearly aligned himself with conservative stances on racial issues in his 1988 campaign and during his presidency. Previous research indicates that such affective evaluations of presidential candidates are a very strong predictor of individual voting behavior (Page and Jones 1984).

Figure 5.3 shows the mean thermometer ratings given to President Bush by white Democrats, independents, and Republicans in all three categories of the trichotomized Index of Negative Stereotypes. Not surprising, since Bush's approval ratings were at record highs during the time period of the survey, is the fact that whites in all three partisan categories and in all three prejudice categories give relatively favorable ratings to Bush. More interesting is the differential impact of prejudice on the ratings given to Bush by white Republicans and white Democrats. Just as prejudice has little effect on the racial policy attitudes of Republicans, there is no difference ($p > .10$) between the most prejudiced Republicans and the least prejudiced Republicans in their evaluations of Bush. Both groups rate the ex-president very highly. In contrast, prejudice divides the Democratic coalition here just as it does with regard to racial policies. Prejudiced Democrats are significantly ($p < .01$) more supportive of Bush than are nonprejudiced Democrats.

Racial prejudice does appear to have some electoral costs for the Democratic party. As is evidenced by the near unanimous support of Republicans across the range of the Index of Negative Stereotypes for George Bush, Republican candidates can stake out conservative positions on racial issues without much risk of losing the support of white Republicans—even those who feel positively toward blacks. At the same time, these conservative racial stances may allow the

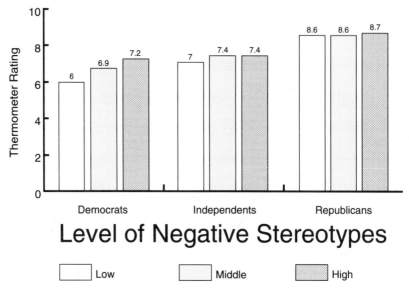

Level of Negative Stereotypes

Low   Middle   High

Source: Race and Politics Survey

T-Tests Between the Most Prejudiced Whites and the Least Prejudiced Whites:
Democrats: t = 3.61, p = .0004
Republicans: t = .73, p = .46

Figure 5.3 Mean Feeling Thermometer Ratings of George Bush by Party Identification and Level of Negative Stereotypes (Whites)

Republican to seize a portion of the Democratic coalition—racially conservative Democrats—particularly if the Democratic candidate espouses liberal positions on matters of race.

The Locus of Democratic Electoral Loss:
Levels and Impact of Prejudice Among
Groups in the Democratic Electoral Coalition

Since racial prejudice has a deleterious effect not only on the support of the Democratic coalition for liberal racial policies but also on Democratic electoral support, the logical next question is, where is this race-based loss in support likely to be greatest? In other words, where in the Democratic party can Democratic candidates expect to lose and Republican candidates expect to gain when race moves to the forefront of a campaign? Answering this question involves asking two more specific questions. First, what types of white Democrats are more prejudiced toward blacks and are thus in greater conflict with their party? Second, where in the Democratic party are divisions among whites most severe? Does prejudice have more of an impact on policy preferences among some groups in the Democratic coalition than among others?

In order to ascertain where prejudice is greatest in the Democratic party, table 5.5 shows whites' mean scores on the Index of Negative Stereotypes by party identification and four different demographic traits: region (southern and border states versus nonsouthern states), yearly income ($0–$30,000, $30,000–$50,000, and $50,000 and greater), education (no college, some college but no degree, and bachelor's and advanced degrees), and religion

Table 5.5. Mean Levels of Prejudice by Party Identification and Sociodemographic Group (Whites)

Group	Party Identification		
	Democrat	Independent	Republican
All Identifiers	27.3	25.0	26.9
Region			
South/Border	26.4	24.6	26.5
Non-South	28.8	26.1	27.7
T-Test (South vs. Non-South)	2.58*	1.54	1.46
Income			
$0–30,000	28.2	26.6	27.7
$30,000–50,000	27.3	24.5	26.4
$50,000 +	25.1	23.3	26.6
T-Test (Lowest vs. Highest)	2.92**	3.25**	1.19
Education			
No College	28.5	26.2	28.6
Some College	25.7	25.1	25.6
College Graduate	23.6	21.5	24.8
T-Test (No College vs. College Grad.)	4.04**	4.86**	4.38**
Religion			
Protestant	27.2	24.8	26.6
Catholic	28.6	25.4	27.8
Secularist	22.1	23.9	25.2
T-Test (Protestant vs. Catholic)	−1.59	−.63	−1.37
T-Test (Secularist vs. Nonsecular)	−3.64**	−1.17	−1.17

$**p < .01$; $*p < .05$

Source: Race and Politics Survey

Note: Prejudice is the index of negative stereotypes, which here range from 0 (least prejudiced) to 50 (most prejudiced). The number of observations ranges from 37 to 490 for Democrats, from 67 to 552 for independents, and from 26 to 602 for Republicans.

(Protestants, Catholics, and those who have no religious ties [other denominations were excluded because of insufficient numbers]). The table shows that prejudice is greater among southern Democrats than among Democrats in the non-South, greater among Democrats with relatively low incomes than among Democrats with high incomes, and greater among Democrats with no college than among college graduates. Catholic Democrats are also slightly more prejudiced than Democratic Protestants, but the difference is not statistically significant. In other words, racial prejudice, and thus the potential for conflict within the Democratic party, is greatest among those groups that, in addition to racial minorities, traditionally have formed the core of the Democratic coalition (Axelrod 1972). It is thus no wonder that race and racial attitudes have played a principal role in bringing about the disintegration of that coalition (Huckfeldt and Kohfeld 1989; Carmines and Stimson 1989).

At the same time, an agenda of racial liberalism may appeal to those without religious ties who are coming to constitute an increasing proportion of the Democratic coalition (Green, Guth, and Fraser 1991). Democratic secularists have significantly ($p < .01$) more positive attitudes toward blacks than do nonsecular Democrats. Such an agenda may also attract those independents with high education and income levels, as these groups appear to be quite likely to reject negative stereotypes of blacks. However, it is quite unlikely that Democratic gains from secularists and upper-status independents will offset the loss of key portions of its traditional coalition.

Racial prejudice is thus highly damaging to the Democratic party. Not only does it lead white Democrats to diverge from their party's policy stances and to support Republican political figures, it is also most prevalent among those groups that traditionally have constituted the core of the Democratic electoral coalition. However, prejudice may be more damaging among some groups than among others. Certain groups of white Democrats may be more likely to defect from the party's policy and electoral coalitions not only because they have higher levels of prejudice but also because prejudice has more of an impact on their political decisions than on those of other groups of Democrats. This is likely to be particularly true in comparisons between white Democrats in the South and in the non-South. Due to the heavier concentration of blacks in the South and the related tendency of conservative politicians in the South to appeal to the racial prejudices of southern whites, race traditionally has been a more salient issue in the South than in the states outside of the South, and in fact has been the overriding issue in all of southern politics (Key 1949; Havard 1972; Black and Black 1987; Bartley and Graham 1975; Huckfeldt and Kohfeld

1989). Because southern whites are more likely to come into contact with blacks than are whites outside of the South and because they long have been encouraged by conservative southern politicians to act on these prejudices, how white Democrats feel about blacks may have more impact on their evaluations of racial policies in the South than in the non-South. Southern Democrats who dislike blacks may be even more opposed to policies directed toward blacks than are prejudiced whites outside of the South.

In order to assess whether racial prejudice has more of an impact on the racial policy preferences of some groups in the Democratic coalition than on those of others, table 5.6 shows the correlation between whites' positions on the five racial issues and their levels of prejudice by their party identification and their traits on several demographic variables. Although there are a few exceptions, the table demonstrates that the key finding of this chapter largely holds across demographic categories. For the most part, prejudice has more of an impact on the policy preferences of Democrats than on those of Republicans regardless of demographic traits. Table 5.6 also shows that there is a clear distinction between the impact of prejudice on the racial policy attitudes of white Democrats in the South and the non-South. On all five of the racial issues, prejudice is more highly correlated with the policy preferences of southern Democrats than with those of nonsouthern Democrats. Racial prejudice is more important politically in the South than in the states outside of the South.

There are some distinctions with regard to other demographic variables. For instance, with regard to attitudes toward government spending for programs to help blacks get more jobs, prejudice has more of an impact for those Democrats with high income levels than for those with low income levels, and prejudice has more of an impact for Democratic Catholics than for Democratic Protestants. Prejudice has more of an impact on the attitudes toward welfare spending of low-income Democrats than on those of high-income Democrats. Prejudice has more of an effect on the attitudes toward preferential admissions to universities for blacks of Protestant Democrats than on those of Catholic Democrats. However, none of these differences are consistent across the range of racial policy issues.

The finding of a greater impact of prejudice on the policy preferences of southern Democrats than on those of nonsouthern Democrats deserves more attention, particularly with regard to its political consequences. The cause of the higher correlation in the South has clear political implications. If the correlation is higher in the South because nonprejudiced Democrats are more supportive of liberal racial policies in the South than in the non-South, the

Table 5.6. Correlation of Index of Negative Sterotypes and Racial Policy Preferences, by Party Identification and Sociodemographic Categories (Whites)

| | Sociodemographic Category | | | | | | | |
| | Region | | Education | | Income | | Religion | |
	Non-South	South	No College	Some College	0–30K	50K+	Prot.	Cath.
Spending for Jobs for Blacks								
Democrats	.28	.41	.31	.28	.30	.39	.31	.34
Independents	.18	.03	.10	.14	.23	−.18	.36	−.22
Republicans	.16	.05	.08	.21	.26	.09	.13	.04
Fighting Discrimination in Jobs								
Democrats	.26	.31	.24	.34	.16	.42	.23	.41
Independents	.22	.13	.15	.29	.11	.15	.15	.40
Republicans	−.05	.02	−.02	−.05	−.004	.05	.04	−.26

Welfare Spending

Democrats	.24	.32	.22	.35	.29	.18	.28	.26
Independents	.08	−.002	−.04	.25	.09	−.005	.15	−.02
Republicans	.02	.06	.07	.05	.04	.06	.04	.02

Job Quotas

Democrats	.01	.26	.17	.07	.10	.16	.29	−.14
Independents	.31	.17	.32	.19	.38	.01	.36	.34
Republicans	−.10	−.26	−.24	.13	−.16	−.01	−.12	−.41

Preferential Admissions

Democrats	.17	.33	.14	.66	.29	.26	.28	.07
Independents	.01	−.16	−.14	.10	−.09	.01	−.06	−.12
Republicans	.02	−.03	−.001	.05	.03	.21	−.02	.06

Source: Race and Politics Survey

Note: The index of negative stereotypes ranges from most to least prejudiced. All racial policies range from most conservative to most liberal. Entries are product moment correlation coefficients. The number of observations range from 44 to 332 for Democrats, from 49 to 404 for independents, and from 38 to 386 for Republicans.

Democratic party actually may find it easier to build coalitions for these racial programs in the South and, especially given the larger black population in the South, may find it more advantageous electorally to advance an agenda of racial liberalism in the South than in the non-South. If, as is more likely, the correlation is higher among southern Democrats because prejudiced Democrats are more opposed to liberal racial policies in the South than in the non-South, the Democratic party may find it more difficult to garner support for these programs in the South and may find the electoral risks to stressing racially liberal themes greater in the South than in the non-South.

In order to determine which of these two scenarios is a better explanation of the higher correlation between racial prejudice and racial policy attitudes in the South than in the non-South, table 5.7 shows whites' mean levels of support for the five racial policies by their region, their party identification, and their position on the trichotomized Index of Negative Stereotypes. The table shows that nonprejudiced Democrats in the South are more supportive of the two affirmative action programs—job quotas for blacks and preferential admissions for blacks—than are nonsouthern Democrats who like blacks. It may be that the greater contact southern whites have with blacks causes those Democrats who like blacks to be more supportive of efforts to promote their climb up the social and economic ladder. However, on the other racial issues, there is no difference between the levels of support of nonprejudiced southern Democrats and nonprejudiced Democrats outside of the South. Both groups are unusual in their overall support for these liberal racial policies. Instead, the higher correlation between prejudice and racial policy preferences among southern Democrats is due to the fact that prejudiced southern Democrats are considerably less supportive of ameliorative racial programs than are prejudiced nonsouthern Democrats. Indeed, prejudiced southern Democrats tend to be the most racially conservative group in the electorate—even more conservative than prejudiced Republicans and independents in the South or non-South. Perhaps because of the greater concentration of blacks in the South or the important role of racial attitudes in southern political culture, racial prejudice is most strongly associated with opposition to liberal racial policies among southern Democrats.

This has clear implications for Republican candidates in the South. Republicans in both regions can espouse an agenda of racial conservatism with little risk of losing much support from white Republicans. However, because both racial prejudice and the antipathy of prejudiced Democrats toward liberal racial policies are greater in the South than in the non-South, Republicans should find it even more advantageous to emphasize conservative racial themes in the South than in the other parts of the country. The large black population in the South should offer little constraint on the tendency of Republicans to focus on race in the region, since only a small percentage of blacks votes for Republican candidates anyway.

The implications are less clear for Democratic leaders and candidates in the South. Democrats advocating liberal racial policy programs should find greater opposition from whites in the South than in the non-South. However, the heavier concentration of blacks in the South may encourage Democrats to pursue these programs despite strong opposition from whites in their own party. Democratic candidates may emphasize liberal racial themes and these polices may be enacted in southern states or localities in which blacks and nonprejudiced white Democrats constitute a majority. Although white opposition may be somewhat less in southern states or localities with fewer blacks (compare Key 1949; Wright 1977; Huckfeldt and Kohfeld 1989), Democratic candidates and officials may be less likely to pursue liberal racial policies since there may not be enough blacks to form a majority coalition in favor of these policies.[5]

Division Among Democrats: Race-Based
or More Broadly Ideological?

It is possible that we have placed too much emphasis on the Democratic electoral loss related to intraparty divisions along the lines of race prejudice (Abramowitz 1994). It may be that prejudiced Democratic identifiers are not really a group upon whom the party can count for any degree of electoral support. They may oppose not only Democratic racial policies but also the party's whole orientation with regard to the role of government in society. In other words, the divisions between Democrats who like blacks and Democrats who dislike blacks on racial issues may be part of a broader ideological division within the Democratic party. As recent election results indicate, a large portion of the American electorate is becoming increasingly disenchanted with government activism, and this is particularly true among key groups in the Democratic coalition, such as blue-collar workers and southern whites (Ladd and Hadley 1975; Carmines and Stanley 1991). Although many white Democrats may have become disillusioned with their party's commitment to liberal ameliorative programs, the forces of tradition and loyalty may continue to connect them to the Democratic label (Campbell et al. 1960). As a consequence, the intraparty cleavage we have denoted may be less a function of attitudes toward

Table 5.7. Mean Support for Racial Policies by Region, Party Identification, and Negative Stereotypes (Whites)

	Non-South				South			
	Index of Negative Stereotypes				Index of Negative Stereotypes			
Policy and Party	Low	Middle	High	T-Test	Low	Middle	High	T-Test
Spending for Jobs for Blacks								
Democrats	.70	.53	.40	3.00**	.71	.41	.22	4.00**
Independents	.59	.45	.44	2.17*	.28	.51	.39	
Republicans	.49	.38	.28		.38	.40	.40	−.14
Fighting Discrimination in Jobs								
Democrats	.64	.48	.43	2.10*	.67	.37	.30	2.82**
Independents	.61	.45	.35		.76	.39	.52	
Republicans	.48	.50	.48	−.01	.48	.34	.43	.38

Welfare Spending								
Democrats	.52	.35	.30	4.04**	.58	.33	.24	4.53**
Independents	.40	.36	.32		.35	.32	.29	
Republicans	.28	.33	.25	.64	.34	.25	.28	.87
Job Quotas for Blacks								
Democrats	.47	.60	.54	−.49	.56	.27	.30	1.66
Independents	.54	.35	.24		.47	.44	.27	
Republicans	.25	.31	.29	−.39	.29	.44	.56	−1.62
Preferential Admissions								
Democrats	.37	.30	.21	1.84	.67	.36	.22	2.91*
Independents	.27	.21	.32		.15	.39	.38	
Republicans	.23	.19	.23	−.05	.19	.15	.23	−.40

$**p < .01; *p < .05$

Source: Race and Politics Survey

Note: Higher scores on policies indicate more liberal positions. *N-sizes* range from 15 to 153. *T-tests* are between Democrats (Republicans) who are low on prejudice and Democrats (Republicans) who are high on prejudice.

blacks as we have argued and more a function of support for and opposition to government activism more generally. In other words, Democrats who dislike blacks may be Democrats in name only, opposed not only to policies designed to help blacks but to the whole philosophy of social welfare liberalism favored by the Democratic party at least since the New Deal.

In order to examine this possibility, we compare the positions of more and less prejudiced Democrats on mainstream social welfare issues. Table 5.8 shows the mean position of whites on four social welfare issues—providing medical insurance for the unemployed, repealing tax breaks for the rich, government spending to reduce unemployment, and narrowing the gap between rich and poor—depending on their feelings toward blacks and their party identifications, and it shows this separately for the South and the non-South. The results are striking and consistent. In both regions, there are no systematic differences on any of these issues between the positions of the most prejudiced Democrats and those of the least prejudiced Democrats. Democrats who dislike blacks are as likely as Democrats who like blacks to believe that government should increase spending to reduce unemployment, to favor narrowing the gap between rich and poor, and to get angry over special benefits like tax breaks going to the richest people and biggest businesses and the lack of affordable medical care for people who do not have jobs. In short, on bread-and-butter social welfare issues, Democrats who dislike blacks are just as liberal as Democrats who like blacks; they are not Democrats in name only. At the same time, in both regions, prejudiced as well as unprejudiced Democrats are more supportive of these social welfare policies than their Republican counterparts.

This creates a substantial dilemma for Democratic leaders. When the focus is on traditional social welfare issues, the party's activist agenda receives substantial support from all segments of the Democratic coalition. However, when the focus moves to social welfare and affirmative action programs on behalf of blacks—a group crucial to Democratic electoral hopes—a notable cleavage along the lines of race prejudice emerges among white Democrats. In other words, it is racial attitudes—not social welfare liberalism generally—that drive a wedge through the Democratic coalition.

CONCLUSION

Our findings indicate that racial prejudice remains a politically powerful force, but its influence is now most pronounced exactly where it is least expected. It is not in the Republican party—the new home of racial conservatism—where prejudice finds its most consequential expression. Republicans, whatever their level of prejudice, are committed to a limited role for the national government in the social welfare domain. This leads unprejudiced Republicans—who we show have a genuinely positive regard for African-Americans—to be virtually as limited in their support for government aid to minorities and special treatment for blacks as more prejudiced Republicans. In the contest between subjective personal attitudes and political party philosophy, unprejudiced Republicans have no trouble following the latter rather than the former. Presumably, the reason why racially tolerant Republicans do not translate these sentiments into support for government activism is because they believe that the national government is an inappropriate vehicle for this purpose. For, at the same time, they are significantly more likely to support private initiatives in civil rights than their more prejudiced copartisans.

Prejudice has its most powerful influence on white Democrats. Prejudiced Democrats are not only more conservative in their racial policy preferences than unprejudiced Democrats but are virtually indistinguishable from Republicans. Unlike the attitudes of nonprejudiced Republicans, the attitudes these Democrats hold toward blacks are translated directly into racial policy preferences, into opposition to government efforts to overcome racial inequality. As we have seen, these prejudiced Democrats are committed to an activist role for the national government in social welfare generally; they are not Democrats in name only. But this commitment does not extend to providing government aid and support to African-Americans. They are social welfare liberals but racial conservatives—a mix that has significant electoral as well as policy implications.

Racial prejudice among ordinary Democrats divides the Democratic coalition not only with regard to racial policy preferences but also with regard to electoral choice. Whereas Republican support for George Bush did not vary along the lines of racial prejudice, white Democrats who dislike blacks were significantly more supportive of Bush than their less prejudiced fellow partisans. This indicates that, by espousing conservative racial themes, Republican candidates may be able to attract a significant number of Democratic votes with relatively little risk of losing support from Republican identifiers. Republican gains from racial conservatism are most likely to come in the South. Contributing to a large body of literature denoting the important role of racial attitudes in the South (Key 1949; Black and Black 1987; Havard 1972), this chapter has shown not only that white Democrats are more prejudiced in the South than in the non-South, but that race prejudice also has more of an impact on the racial

Table 5.8. Mean Liberalism on Social Welfare Concerns by Region, Party Identification, and Level of Negative Stereotypes (Whites)

	Non-South				South			
	Index of Negative Stereotypes				Index of Negative Stereotypes			
Policy and Party	Low	Middle	High	T-Test	Low	Middle	High	T-Test
No Medical Insurance for Unemployed[a]								
Democrats	.86	.90	.91	−1.31	.86	.89	.84	.42
Independents	.82	.77	.89		.80	.91	.79	
Republicans	.72	.77	.79		.66	.77	.81	
Tax Breaks for Rich[a]								
Democrats	.79	.88	.84	−1.34	.84	.84	.78	1.04
Independents	.86	.81	.86		.80	.76	.80	
Republicans	.73	.83	.80		.86	.83	.79	

Spend More to Reduce Unemployment[b]

Democrats	.70	.74	.70	−.03	.76	.68	.72	.73
Independents	.68	.71	.72		.65	.68	.69	
Republicans	.60	.61	.63		.61	.59	.58	

Narrow Gap Between Rich and Poor[b]

Democrats	.77	.75	.80	−.71	.71	.74	.75	−.70
Independents	.71	.70	.78		.66	.70	.68	
Republicans	.56	.61	.60		.50	.51	.60	

Source: Race and Politics Survey

Note: All policy positions range from 0 (most conservative) to 1 (most liberal). *T*-tests are between Democrats who are low on prejudice and Democrats who are high on prejudice.

[a]Degree of anger over "no medical insurance for the unemployed" and "tax breaks for the rich."

[b]Degree of support for "spend more to reduce unemployment" and "narrow the gap between rich and poor."

policy preferences of Democrats in the South than in the non-South. Prejudiced Democrats in the South are considerably less supportive of ameliorative racial programs than are prejudiced Democrats outside of the South.

The political implications of the differential impact of prejudice on the political thinking of Democrats and Republicans are clear and profound. Republicans stand mostly united in their opposition to major government responsibility for the social welfare of the citizenry, including that of black Americans. White Democrats, however, are sharply divided in their racial policy preferences, with a sizable number favoring limited government activity. Thus, Republicans have not only their own political support but that of some Democrats as well. It is not surprising, then, that when it comes to race, not only do Democrats continue to be divided against themselves, but the nation itself also lacks the will and capacity to resolve this most long-lasting American dilemma.

NOTES

1. The construction of the Index of Negative Stereotypes, in addition to that of all other variables used in this analysis, is discussed in the Appendix. A principal-component-factor analysis of the five items provides strong evidence that they form a single dimension. The first factor has an eigenvalue of 2.7 and explains 54.7 percent of the variance in the items; the second factor is well below 1.0 (.72) and explains only 14 percent of the variance. The reliability of the scale is .79 (alpha), and its validity is indicated by a significant correlation with an Index of Anti-Semitism (.39).

2. The cut-points were established, of course, taking into account the distribution of whites as a whole regardless of their ideological orientation.

3. Since, with the exception of welfare spending, the measures of racial policies are dichotomous and scored 0 for opposition and 1 for support, these means can be interpreted as percentages from 0 to 100 percent. Thus, for example, a mean of .79 can be interpreted as 79 percent of the given category supporting that particular policy.

4. In fact, evidence from the Race and Politics Study shows that prejudiced Democrats are only slightly less attached to the party than are nonprejudiced Democrats. The correlation between prejudice and the strength of attachment to the Democratic party is −.10 among white Democrats.

5. In fact, the relationship between black population density and policy responsiveness to black interests in the South may be curvilinear (Keech 1969; Black 1976). When black concentration is low, white opposition to liberal racial policies may be relatively small, so that increases in black density are associated with increases in the responsiveness to blacks by Democratic candidates and policymakers. However, white opposition to political and social gains for blacks also rises along with increases in the black share of the electorate (Keech 1969; Key 1949). At a certain point, the opposition of prejudiced Democrats may be great enough to outweigh further electoral gains from blacks in the minds of Democratic candidates and officials. At this point, further increases in black density may be

associated with less responsiveness. As black density becomes large enough that a coalition of blacks and nonprejudiced white Democrats approaches majority status, the interests of blacks may begin to outweigh the protests of prejudiced white Democrats. At this point, further increases in black density may be associated with increases in the responsiveness of Democratic candidates and policymakers to black interests.

REFERENCES

Abramowitz, Alan I. 1994. "Issue Evolution Reconsidered: Racial Attitudes and Partisanship in the U.S. Electorate." *American Journal of Political Science* 38:1–24.

Axelrod, Robert. 1972. "Where the Votes Come from: An Analysis of Electoral Coalitions." *American Political Science Review* 66:11–20.

Bartley, Numan V., and Hugh D. Graham. 1975. *Southern Politics and the Second Reconstruction.* Baltimore: Johns Hopkins University Press.

Black, Earl. 1976. *Southern Governors and Civil Rights: Racial Segregation as a Campaign Issue in the Second Reconstruction.* Cambridge, Mass.: Harvard University Press.

Black, Earl, and Merle Black. 1987. *Politics and Society in the South.* Cambridge, Mass.: Harvard University Press.

Brinkley, Alan. 1995. *The End of Reform: New Deal Liberalism in Recession and War.* New York: Knopf.

Campbell, Angus, Philip E. Converse, Warren E. Miller, and Donald E. Stokes. 1960. *The American Voter.* Chicago: University of Chicago Press.

Carmines, Edward G., and Harold W. Stanley. 1990. "Ideological Realignment in the Contemporary South: Where Have All the Conservatives Gone?" In *The Disappearing South?: Studies in Regional Change and Continuity,* ed. Robert P. Steed, Lawrence W. Moreland, and Tod A. Baker. Tuscaloosa: University of Alabama Press.

Carmines, Edward G., and James A. Stimson. 1980. "The Two Faces of Issue Voting." *American Political Science Review* 74:78–91.

———. 1989. *Issue Evolution: Race and the Transformation of American Politics.* Princeton, N.J.: Princeton University Press.

Green, John C., James L. Guth, and Cleveland R. Fraser. 1991. "Apostles and Apostates? Religion and Politics Among Party Activists." In *The Bible and the Ballot Box: Religion and Politics in the 1988 Election,* ed. James L. Guth and John C. Green. Boulder, Colo.: Westview.

Havard, William C., ed. 1972. *The Changing Politics of the South.* Baton Rouge: Louisiana State University Press.

Huckfeldt, Robert, and Carol Weitzel Kohfeld. 1989. *Race and the Decline of Class in American Politics.* Urbana: University of Illinois Press.

Keech, William R. 1969. *The Impact of Negro Voting: The Role of the Vote in the Quest for Equality.* Chicago: Rand McNally.

Key, V. O., Jr. 1949. *Southern Politics in State and Nation.* New York: Alfred A. Knopf.

Kinder, Donald R., and David O. Sears. 1981. "Prejudice and Politics: Symbolic Racism Versus Racial Threats to the Good Life." *Journal of Personality and Social Psychology* 40:414–31.

Kirby, John B. 1980. *Black Americans in the Roosevelt Era.* Knoxville: University of Tennessee Press.

Ladd, Everett Carll, Jr., with Charles D. Hadley. 1975. *Transformations of the American Party System.* New York: W. W. Norton.

Page, Benjamin I., and Calvin C. Jones. 1979. "Reciprocal Effects of Policy Preferences, Party Loyalties, and the Vote." *American Political Science Review* 73:1071–90.

Sitkoff, Harvard. 1978. *A New Deal for Blacks.* New York: Oxford University Press.

Sniderman, Paul M., and Thomas Piazza. 1993. *The Scar of Race.* Cambridge, Mass.: Harvard University Press.

Weiss, Nancy J. 1983. *Farewell to the Party of Lincoln.* Princeton, N.J.: Princeton University Press.

Wright, Gerald C., Jr. 1977. "Contextual Models of Electoral Behavior: The Southern Wallace Vote." *American Political Science Review* 71:497–508.

Chapter 6 Understanding Whites' Resistance to Affirmative Action: The Role of Principled Commitments and Racial Prejudice

Laura Stoker

Affirmative action is an increasingly important and divisive issue in American society, so much so that it has been described by one recent commentator as "a time bomb primed to detonate in the middle of the American political marketplace."[1] It has figured prominently in numerous political campaigns, most notably Jesse Helms's 1990 race against Harvey Gantt in North Carolina, and David Duke's unsuccessful bid for the Senate in 1990. Its salience was heightened by legislative battles surrounding the failed 1990 and successful 1991 Civil Rights Acts, by the confirmation controversy surrounding Clarence Thomas's nomination to the Supreme Court, and most recently by the nationally visible campaign surrounding the 1996 California Civil Rights Initiative.

In part because of its political importance, affirmative action has also played a pivotal, and sometimes controversial, role in scholarship on racial attitudes. The fact that whites have continued to resist affirmative action at the same time that they have increasingly come to endorse racial equality in principle and to disavow racially bigoted ideas has helped fuel two major (and related) developments in the literature on racial attitudes in America. The first concerns the so-called princi-ple/policy gap, which has had scholars puzzling over why "white Americans increasingly reject racial injustice in principle but are reluctant to accept the measures necessary to eliminate the injustice" (Pettigrew 1979, p. 119; for re-views, see Carmines and Champagne 1990; Schuman, Steeh, and Bobo 1988). The second is the development of theories emphasizing "modern" or "sym-bolic" racism, which argue that although overt racial bigotry has waned, racial prejudice persists in a new guise, one that serves as the foundation for white opposition to racially egalitarian policies like affirmative action and busing (Dovidio, Mann, and Gaertner 1989; Kinder 1986; Kinder and Sears 1981; McConahay and Hough 1976; McConahay 1986; Sears 1988). Controversially, some of this work has treated opposition to affirmative action as itself indicative of racial prejudice in its modern form.[2]

Despite the political importance of affirmative action and its significance to the development of the literature on racial attitudes, there have been relatively few direct inquiries into the determinants of public opinion on the issue. Several studies have examined the impact of racial prejudice, especially sym-bolic or modern variants, and most have concluded that it plays a substantial role in shaping whites' opinions (Jacobson 1985; Kinder and Sanders 1990; Kluegel and Smith 1986; but see Sniderman and Piazza 1993).[3] Yet as with research on the principle/policy gap more generally, these and other studies have also found evidence of additional influences, especially beliefs about the causes of racial inequality (Kluegel 1985; Kluegel and Smith 1983, 1986), value commitments, particularly individualism and egalitarianism (Kinder and Sanders 1990; Kluegel and Smith 1986; Lipset and Schneider 1978; Lipset 1990), generalized objections to government intervention (Kinder and Sanders 1990; Kuklinski and Parent 1981), and judgments regarding the policy's fairness (Nacoste 1985, 1987; Sniderman and Piazza 1993). As others have noted (e.g., Carmines and Champagne 1990), the basis of whites' opposition to affirmative action remains poorly understood, particularly with regard to the importance of racial beliefs and attitudes on the one hand, and the importance of principled objections to the policy on the other.

The aim of this chapter is to shed new, if not definitive, light on these long-standing questions. The starting point for the analysis is two survey-based experiments, each of which manipulates features of affirmative action that bear on judgments of its fairness. The first experiment varies the circumstances in which racial quotas in hiring are to be implemented. The crucial issue here turns on whether or not they are to be introduced into settings that have been marked by identifiable practices of discrimination, a distinction that is at the heart of the Supreme Court rulings on the fairness, and thus the legality, of affirmative action measures. If they are to be just, says the Court, race-conscious hiring programs must be a remedial response undertaken by a company or governmental unit that had been previously engaging in a wrongful practice of discriminatory hiring, a response that is "narrowly tailored" to counterbalance the nature and extent of the wrong. As we will see, this is a concern about fairness to which the American public also responds.

The second experiment, this time focused on affirmative action in university admissions, varies according to whether the affirmative action program uses race as a selection criteria or instead employs race-targeted measures that operate before the selection stage. Here the crucial issue is the extent to which affirmative action opponents are specifically objecting to procedures that allocate goods on the basis of race, rather than resting allocation decisions solely on the basis of individual qualifications. Put in terms of popular rhetoric, this experiment assesses the importance of objections to "reverse discrimination"— objections that, as we will see, are powerful indeed.

Although the experimental results support the conclusion that whites' attitudes toward affirmative action are partly based on their judgments of the policy's fairness, they do not reveal how whites' racial beliefs and attitudes may also be entering in. White resistance to affirmative action may indeed be principled in part, but, as other analysts have suggested, it may also be grounded in thoughts and feelings that are far less sublime—racially charged feelings of resentment, bigoted and stereotypical beliefs about blacks, and the belief that racial inequality has arisen or persisted because of the failings of blacks themselves. In order to engage this issue, I build upon the earlier aggregate-level analysis of the experimental manipulations by turning to an individual-level analysis of the antecedents of opinions as rendered within each experimental condition. As the results demonstrate, white resistance to affirmative action is neither founded purely on principle nor fueled purely by racial perceptions and prejudice. In important and at times unexpected ways, it finds its roots in both.

EXPERIMENT 1: CONTEXT-SPECIFIC SUPPORT
FOR RACIAL QUOTAS IN HIRING

The typical survey question on affirmative action either generalizes over the contexts in which affirmative action policies are implemented or makes no reference to context whatsoever. The first case is illustrated by the questions below:

> Some large corporations are required to practice what is called affirmative action. This sometimes requires employers to give special preference to minorities or women when hiring. Do you approve or disapprove of affirmative action? (Cambridge Survey Research)
>
> The U.S. Supreme Court has ruled that employers may sometimes favor women and members of minorities over better-qualified men and whites in hiring and promoting, to achieve better balance in their workforces. Do you approve or disapprove of this decision? (Gallup)

The critical words in these questions are "some" and "sometimes." "*Some* corporations are *sometimes* required to implement preferential hiring programs," says the first. "The U.S. Supreme Court has ruled that employers may *sometimes* favor women and members of minorities over better-qualified men and whites in hiring and promoting," says the second. These questions treat the contexts in which affirmative action programs are implemented as irrelevant to the question of what the public thinks of them.

The second case, where the affirmative action opinion question makes no reference to context at all, is illustrated by the formulation used by the National Election Studies (NES):

> Some people say that because of past discrimination against blacks, preference in hiring and promotion should be given to blacks. Others say preferential hiring and promotion of blacks is wrong [Form A: because it discriminates against whites; Form B: because it gives blacks advantages they haven't earned]. What about your opinion—are you for or against preferential hiring and promotion of blacks?

This question abstracts its way away from the contexts in which affirmative action programs are implemented, treating any given affirmative action program as something that one might favor "because of past discrimination against blacks" or oppose "because it discriminates against whites" or "gives blacks advantages they haven't earned."

Such questions miss a key political feature of affirmative action policies in American society: that their legality depends upon the context in which they are implemented. In ruling after ruling over the past two decades, the Supreme Court has stipulated that race-conscious hiring policies are legitimate only when implemented by a business or governmental unit in response to a finding that the unit itself had been engaging in discriminatory hiring practices, and has clearly rejected race-conscious hiring policies whose aim is to compensate blacks for disadvantages rooted in historic or society-wide practices of discrimination in America or to promote racial balance in the workforce.[4] Thus, for example, in *Wygant v. Jackson Board of Education* Justice Lewis Powell wrote: "This Court never has held that societal discrimination alone is sufficient to justify a racial classification. Rather, the Court has insisted upon some showing of prior discrimination by the government unit involved before allowing limited use of racial classifications in order to remedy such discrimination" (1985 476 US 267, 274).

The Court rests its case here on an argument about just compensation: When it has been established that a given company or governmental unit has wrongfully discriminated against blacks, then justice demands that their discriminatory hiring practices be dismantled, and that compensatory or remedial actions be undertaken. Implementing race-conscious hiring policies in such circumstances is just, the Court argues, if it can be shown that they are narrowly tailored to the particular case at hand, and thus yield an appropriate form and level of compensation for the discriminatory practices that were in place. Prior findings as to the existence and nature of the discriminatory hiring practices, as Justice Sandra Day O'Connor put it in a 1988 opinion, are "necessary to define both the scope of the injury and the extent of the remedy necessary to cure its effects" (*Richmond v. J. A. Croson Co.,* 1988 488 US 497). In such cases, affirmative action policies then serve the "focused goal of remedying wrongs worked by specific instances of racial discrimination" rather than "the remedying of the effects of 'societal discrimination,' an amorphous concept of injury that may be ageless in its reach to the past" (ibid., 469).[5] According to the compensatory logic, as one observer put it, it is "black *qua* victim and not black *qua* black person" that is significant (Simon 1977, p. 41).[6]

What makes the typical survey questions problematic is not that they simplify reality, as any survey question must do. Rather, the problem is in the nature of the simplifications that they introduce. If ordinary citizens are moved by the concerns about just compensation that inspire the Court, then we would expect their opinions about affirmative action programs to be sensitive to the context in which those programs are implemented, and specifically to depend upon whether racial preferences are to be introduced in settings marked by a history of discriminatory hiring. Correspondingly, if researchers are interested in knowing what the public thinks about affirmative action programs that the Court has deemed legitimate, then they should be asking affirmative action questions that situate the programs in the circumstances that the Court has identified. At the same time, if they want to know the public's view of affirmative action programs that are or might be found in circumstances that fail to meet the conditions that the Court has identified, then they should ask questions about the use of affirmative action in those circumstances too. Either way, questions that generalize across or ignore the contexts in which affirmative action programs are implemented, may (and, as we will see shortly, often do) yield results that misrepresent the level of public support for affirmative action programs that, as the Court puts it, serve as "narrowly tailored" remedial responses to wrongful practices of discrimination.[7]

The first affirmative action experiment was designed to evaluate the importance of context to opinions on affirmative action. Three different affirmative action questions, each concerning the implementation of a racial quota in hiring, were administered to random thirds of the respondents. The first question was context-free:

Question 1: No Context
Do you think that large companies should be required to give a certain number of jobs to blacks, or should the government stay out of this?

The second and third questions each locate the policy in a particular context. The second defines the policy as one that would be undertaken in companies where "blacks are underrepresented," whereas the third defines the policy as one that would be introduced in companies "with employment policies that discriminate against blacks";

Question 2: Underrepresentation Context
There are some large companies where blacks are underrepresented. . . . Do you think *these* large companies should be required to give a certain number of jobs to blacks, or should the government stay out of this?
Question 3: Discrimination Context
There are some large companies with employment policies that discriminate against blacks. . . . Do you think *these* large companies should be required to give a certain number of jobs to blacks, or should the government stay out of this?

Whereas the first question mimics the abstract framing that affirmative action ordinarily receives, the second locates the policy of race-conscious hiring in companies where the workforce is racially imbalanced, and the third explicitly situates it in the context that the Supreme Court has judged legitimate—in companies whose hiring policies have discriminated against blacks.

Figures 6.1a–c present the distribution of whites' opinions as gauged by each version of the affirmative action opinion question, broken down into responses that range from "strongly favor" to "strongly oppose." Not surprisingly, in light of past research, responses to the context-free question show overwhelmingly opposition to racial hiring quotas (fig. 6.1a). Seventy-six percent of the white

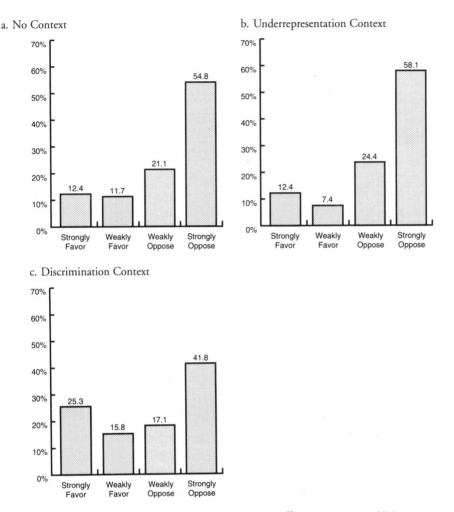

a. No Context

b. Underrepresentation Context

c. Discrimination Context

Figure 6.1 Distribution of Whites' Opinions on Affirmative Action in Hiring

respondents expressed opposition, and over 70 percent of those respondents identified their opposition as strong. In the second condition, when the context is described as one where "blacks are underrepresented," the portrait of opinion remains virtually unchanged (fig. 6.1b). We see a very different distribution of opinion, however, once the policy is situated as a response to identified practices of discrimination. Rather than revealing overwhelming opposition, opinion becomes polarized (fig. 6.1c). Whites opposing racial quotas (59 percent) still outnumber those who express support (41 percent), but the distribution shifts markedly—by roughly 18–20 percent—in the direction of greater support, with those expressing strong opinions outweighing those expressing weak opinions on both sides of the issue.[8]

There are three primary conclusions to draw from these results. First, the fact that racial hiring quotas garner less support when they are implemented by companies identified as having a racially imbalanced workforce (second condition) than when they are implemented by companies identified as having been discriminating against blacks (third condition) tells us that a significant fraction of the public does not consider racial imbalances in the workforce to be indicative of discriminatory hiring practices. Of course, this confirms by inference something about which we also have direct evidence. Research based upon the current survey (see Chapter 8 below), as well as previous surveys (Kluegel 1985; Kluegel and Smith 1986; Kluegel and Bobo 1993; Schuman 1971), has demonstrated that people draw upon a number of different ideas to explain racial differences in economic achievement, including the "lack of effort on the part of blacks, or the lack of skills and preparation, or as the result of a lack of holding the right values" (Kluegel 1985, p. 766) in addition to the forces of prejudice and discrimination.

Second, the enhanced level of support for affirmative action programs that *are*, in fact, situated in contexts where companies had been discriminating against blacks, which is evident for whites and blacks alike, supports the contention that public opinion on affirmative action is partly based on judgments regarding fairness. More specifically, the results suggest that the public is responding to the same concerns about fairness that have inspired the Supreme Court, which has sharply distinguished between race-conscious hiring programs that are introduced to compensate for established practices of discriminatory hiring and those that are implemented simply in order to achieve a racially balanced workforce or to compensate blacks for disadvantages wrought generally by the patterns of racism and prejudice in America.[9]

Finally, the results carry a lesson for how we depict public opinion on affirmative action. When it comes to affirmative action programs that actually meet the requirements set forth by the Supreme Court, programs that are implemented as a "narrowly tailored" remedial response to discriminatory hiring practices, it is not the case that "mass opinion remains invariably opposed to preferential treatment" (Lipset 1991, p. 14), or that "as a civil rights remedy, affirmative action has virtually no mass public support whatsoever" (Carmines and Champagne 1990, p. 197), or that there "is no ambiguity about where the majority stand" (Daniel Yankelovich, quoted in Bunzel 1986, p. 48)—the conventional wisdom about the matter. The portrait of opinion, instead, is of a public that is sharply divided.

EXPERIMENT 2: PREFERENTIAL TREATMENT
VS. COMPENSATORY ACTION POLICIES

Race-conscious hiring or admissions policies—regardless of whether they are introduced to remedy established practices of discrimination, or to achieve racial balance, or to compensate blacks for disadvantages traced to the legacy of racism in America—violate the color-blind ideal of basing decisions solely on the applicants' merit, an ideal that judges race irrelevant to how prospective employees or college applicants should be treated (thus instantiating the principle of equal treatment), and where people of all races compete for jobs or admission slots on the basis of their individual qualifications (thus upholding the principle of equality of opportunity). Although these policies gain legitimacy and, as we have seen, public support when they are implemented to remedy ongoing practices of discrimination, they inevitably remain color-conscious, not blind. In this respect, many affirmative action opponents argue, they are patently unfair.

Yet not all affirmative action policies use race as a criteria for making selection decisions. In fact, the policies that best represent the affirmative action agenda as it was developed in the 1960s and 1970s aim to enhance blacks' educational and employment opportunities without introducing race at the selection stage, as, for example, programs that help blacks learn about available job opportunities or that provide them with educational or job-training assistance. Although such policies fall squarely under the mantle of affirmative action as set forth by the Equal Employment Opportunity Commission and continue to have a widespread presence today, they have become disassociated from the term "affirmative action," as Wilson (1992, p. 177) explains:

> The term "affirmative action" has changed in meaning since it was first introduced. Initially, the term referred primarily to special efforts to ensure that equal opportunities were available for members of groups that had been subject to discrimination. Those special efforts included public advertising for positions to be filled, active recruitment of qualified applicants from the formerly excluded groups, as well as special training programs designed to help them meet the standards for admission or appointment. More recently, the term has come to refer to the necessity of providing some degree of definite preference for members of these groups in determining access to positions from which they were formerly excluded.

Perhaps as a consequence, few studies have investigated the public's view of affirmative action in its preselection-stage guise.

In one of the few studies to do so, which was confined to a review of aggregate polling results on affirmative action, Lipset and Schneider (1978) noticed that the American public is more supportive of affirmative action programs that operate prior to the selection stage ("compensatory action" programs) than of those that introduce race as a selection criterion ("preferential treatment" programs).[10] Whereas American citizens in general, and whites in particular, tend to oppose programs that base selection decisions even partly on the basis of race, white majorities will back other race-conscious measures to enhance blacks' employment and educational opportunities (see also Sniderman and Carmines 1991; for related findings, see Bobo and Kluegel 1993; and Veilleux and Tougas 1989).

The present study introduced an experiment that, by isolating the contrast between preferential treatment and compensatory action, was designed to reveal the extent to which opposition to affirmative action was uniquely tied to the use of racial preferences at the selection stage. Each respondent was asked, at random, one of two questions about affirmative action in university admissions. The first question described the policy as one that would give qualified blacks preference over whites, and the second described the policy as one that would involve making an extra effort to ensure that qualified blacks were considered for admission.

Question 1: Give Blacks Preference

Some people say that because of past discrimination, *qualified blacks should be given preference in university admissions.* Others say that this is wrong because it discriminates against whites. How do you feel—are you in favor of or opposed to *giving qualified blacks preference in admission to colleges and universities?*

Question 2: Make Extra Effort

Some people say that because of past discrimination, *an extra effort should be made to be sure that qualified blacks are considered in university admission.* Others say that this is wrong because it discriminates against whites. How do you feel—are you in favor of or opposed to *making an extra effort to make sure that qualified blacks are considered for admission to colleges and universities?*

Figures 6.2a–b contain the results for the sample of whites. When the question concerns policies that give qualified blacks preference in admission, we see a clear majority in opposition (75 percent), with opposition forces both more numerous and more intense than are the supporting forces (fig. 6.2a). This level of opposition is almost identical to that found when the question concerned racial preferences in hiring, where 76 percent of whites were opposed (fig. 6.1a), although is noticeably less intense (with 38 percent falling in the "strongly oppose" category, compared to 55 percent in fig. 6.1a).[11] The distribution of opinion shifts sharply, however, when the question concerns

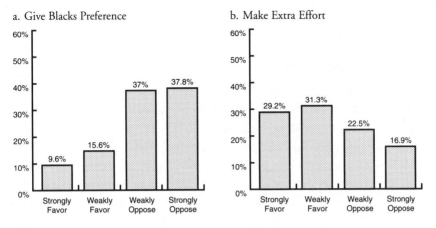

a. Give Blacks Preference

b. Make Extra Effort

Figure 6.2 Distribution of Whites' Opinions on Affirmative Action in Admissions

special efforts to make sure that qualified blacks are considered for admission (fig. 6.2b). The number of opponents drops sharply and the number of supporters more than doubles. In percentage terms, affirmative action support climbs by 35 points to where a clear majority (61 percent) backs the programs, of which half do so "strongly."[12]

As with the first experiment, these results demonstrate that whites' opinions on affirmative action have a principled basis. Whether whites are willing to support race-targeted programs designed to enhance blacks' educational opportunities depends on whether those programs specifically introduce race as a criterion for admissions. Although one sometimes finds political pundits claiming otherwise, it is not the race-targeted aspect of affirmative action programs, per se, that generates majority white opposition. What is crucial is whether they violate the principle of fairness specifying that selection decisions should be based upon applicant qualifications, not race.

INDIVIDUAL-LEVEL ANALYSES

The experimental results support the inference that opinions on affirmative action are partly shaped by judgments about the policy's fairness. Yet as the variation in opinion evident in figures 6.1 and 6.2 reminds us, there is much more that remains to be explained. Understanding the differences of opinion on affirmative action that persist with respect to each of the policy's guises requires a shift in focus—from how different *policy* characteristics provoke different responses to how different *individual* characteristics do so as well. An individual-level analysis will yield a more inclusive sense of the sources of white opposition to affirmative action and, as we will see, a more nuanced understanding of the effects of the experimental manipulations.

My focus in this analysis is on the role played by whites' racial beliefs and attitudes, and on four key variables in particular. The first concerns how whites generally explain the black/white gap in economic status. The importance of these beliefs to whites' opinions on affirmative action has been convincingly demonstrated by James Kluegel and Eliot Smith, in the course of their research into how people think about patterns of gender, racial, and economic inequality (Kluegel 1985; Kluegel and Smith 1983, 1986). In an open-ended question, respondents were asked to provide their own explanations for why blacks were less well-off than whites, followed by a series of closed-ended questions asking them to summarize their views. Whites' responses to the closed-ended question, on which the analysis will rely, ranged from those that placed the blame entirely or mostly on whites (14 percent), through those who placed the blame on whites and blacks equally (68 percent), to those who placed the blame mostly or entirely on blacks (18 percent).

Two variables represent cognitive dimensions of prejudice that have typically been distinguished by contemporary analysts of racial attitudes. The first, which goes under the label of traditional prejudice, Jim Crow racism, or more commonly old-fashioned racism, refers to the belief that blacks are inherently inferior to and different from whites and that they should be treated as such (Bobo and Kluegel 1993; Kinder and Sears 1981; Kluegel and Smith 1983; Jacobson 1985). The "old-fashioned" label captures the fact that although such views used to be widely held by whites, they are less common today. The second dimension, which falls under the rubric of modern or symbolic racism, refers to the belief that blacks violate cherished American values, failing, in particular, to live up to the American work ethic (Kinder and Sears 1981; McConahay and Hough 1976; McConahay 1986; Sears 1988). In this respect, blacks are judged to be contingently, not inherently, inferior to whites, but inferior nonetheless. The "symbolic" or "modern" label reflects the argument that even though prejudice against blacks no longer tends to be expressed through old-fashioned racist beliefs (either because those beliefs have truly eroded or because it is socially unacceptable to admit them), it has not disappeared. Instead, it becomes expressed in a new form—through beliefs that condemn blacks, as a group, for having failed to uphold American values.[13]

To represent these ideas empirically, two indicators were constructed, one assessing old-fashioned racism and one assessing adherence to a stereotype of blacks as having failed to abide by the American work ethic. The indicator of old-fashioned racism combined two component variables: the belief that blacks are unintelligent and opposition to racial integration in housing. When scored to range from 0 (least racist) to 1 (most racist), whites averaged .29 on the scale. This measure reflects the standard conceptualization of traditional prejudice as involving white supremacist and segregationist beliefs, and closely parallels previous indices (Jacobson 1985; Kinder and Sears 1981; Kluegel and Smith 1983; Kluegel and Bobo 1993; McConahay and Hough 1976; McConahay, Hardee, and Batts 1981; McConahay 1982). The indicator of work-ethic stereotyping combined responses to five questions: whether the respondent thinks of blacks as (1) dependable, (2) lazy, (3) determined to succeed, or (4) hard-working, and (5) whether the respondent thinks "most black parents don't teach their children the self-discipline and skills it takes to get ahead in America." Whites averaged .46 on the index, which was scaled to range from 0 (believe blacks are hard-working) to 1 (believe blacks are lazy). The two indices were fairly highly intercorrelated ($r = .54$), and moderately correlated with beliefs about racial inequality ($r = .23$ and .28, respectively).

The fourth variable measures feelings of anger and resentment toward blacks who are making demands for change, which I refer to by the label "racial resentment" in the tables that follow. This variable represents an aspect of modern racial prejudice, as McConahay and others describe it, that is not captured by the stereotyping index—the feeling, in McConahay and Hough's (1976) words, that "blacks are *too* pushy, *too* demanding, *too* angry, things are moving *too* fast, and blacks are getting *more* than they deserve" (p. 38; see also Kinder 1986).[14] It also taps affective reactions to blacks in a more direct fashion than does the work-ethic stereotyping scale. Respondents were asked to indicate, on a scale from 0 to 10, how angry they felt toward "spokesmen for minorities who are always complaining that blacks are being discriminated against." Whites' responses indicated high levels of resentment: less than 6 percent selected the minimum value of 0 (not at all angry), while over one-third gave the maximal value of 10 (extremely angry), and the average was 7.2. Responses to this question were only weakly to moderately correlated with the old-fashioned racism index ($r = .18$), the work-ethic stereotyping index ($r = .21$), and beliefs about the locus of blame for racial inequality ($r = .27$).

The effects of each of these variables were estimated separately within each experimental subsample, where, in the case of affirmative action in hiring, the two samples asked the first (no context) and second versions (underrepresentation context) of the question were combined. Combining the two subsamples in this fashion simplifies things considerably and, as supplementary analysis showed, does not significantly alter the substantive conclusions one would draw. The model is illustrated below for the case of hiring. The only difference in the university admissions case is that the experimental condition variable distinguishes those asked the preferential treatment question (coded 0) from those asked the compensatory action question (coded 1).

Opinion on Racial Quotas in Hiring (coded 0 = strongly favor to 1 = strongly oppose)

$= b_1 + b_2$ Experimental Condition (1 = discrimination context)
$+ b_3$ Blame for Racial Inequality $+ b_4$ (Blame for Racial Inequality)^2
$+ b_5$ Condition * Blame $+ b_6$ Condition * Blame^2
$+ b_7$ Old-Fashioned Racism $+ b_8$ Condition * Old-Fashioned Racism
$+ b_9$ Work-Ethic Stereotype $+ b_{10}$ Condition * Work-Ethic Stereotype
$+ b_{11}$ Racial Resentment $+ b_{12}$ Condition * Racial Resentment
$+ b_j$ Control Variable$_j$ $+ e$

This model yields subsample-specific models as follows:

No Context or Underrepresentation Context

$= b_1$
$+ b_3$ Blame for Racial Inequality
$+ b_4$ (Blame for Racial Inequality)^2
$+ b_7$ Old-Fashioned Racism
$+ b_9$ Work-Ethic Stereotype
$+ b_{11}$ Racial Resentment
$+ b_j$ Control$_j$ $+ e$

Discrimination Context

$= (b_1+b_2)$
$+ (b_3+b_5)$ Blame for Racial Inequality
$+ (b_4+b_6)$ (Blame for Racial Inequality)^2
$+ (b_7+b_8)$ Old-Fashioned Racism
$+ (b_9+b_{10})$ Work-Ethic Stereotype
$+ (b_{11}+b_{12})$ Racial Resentment
$+ b_j$ Control$_j$ $+ e$

The model includes a quadratic version of the blame variable ("blame-squared") in order to represent nonlinearities. Each analysis also controlled for general predispositions that previous research on racial attitudes has identified as important, including objections to government intervention, individualism, general support for social services spending (an indicator of egalitarianism), social tolerance, ideological self-designation, and party identification; as well as a set of socio-demographic variables, including age, sex, education, income, employment status, and region. The effects of the control variables were constrained to be the same across the experimental subsamples.[15] All measures are described further in the Appendix.

The regression results for affirmative action in hiring are found in table 6.1. To facilitate interpretation, the key findings concerning whites' racial beliefs and attitudes are illustrated graphically in figures 6.3–6.6. First, consider how whites' opinions on affirmative action in hiring vary as a function of how they explain the racial gap in economic achievement, which is depicted in figure 6.3. As the figure shows, people who generally attribute blacks' disadvantages to the forces of white racism and discrimination tend to support racial quotas regardless of how the question is posed. These people presumably have the context of discrimination in mind, regardless of whether it is explicitly provided in the question or not. Opposition grows among those whose attributions implicate blacks themselves, and grows especially sharply among those asked the "no context" or "underrepresentation context" versions of the question. There, disagreement about the causes of racial inequality leads to positions on affirmative action that differ by .40 on the 0–1 scale, whereas for the group asked the "discrimination context" version of the question, the comparable figure is less by half (.20).[16] Read another way, the results demonstrate that only whites who view blacks as at least partially responsible for their own economic disadvantages are vulnerable to the experimental manipulation. They take markedly different positions on affirmative action depending upon whether the programs are explicitly situated in a context where discrimination has, in fact, been established.

Thus, when our survey questions treat affirmative action as a general program of assistance to blacks, whites' beliefs about the causes of blacks' poor economic circumstances play an important opinion-shaping role. In other words, the extent to which whites will favor a general effort to remedy racial inequality through affirmative action is powerfully influenced by how they generally explain racial inequality. But when affirmative action is given the narrower reading that the Supreme Court has legitimated, as a remedial re-

Table 6.1. Affirmative Action in Hiring

Independent Variable	No Context or Underrepresentation Context	Discrimination Context	Difference@
Constant	−.27	−.35	−.08
Blame	.88***	.16@@	−.72*
Blame-squared	−.48**	.04	.53#
Old-Fashioned Racism	.03	.42***	.39**
Work Ethic Stereotype	−.05	.01	.06
Racial Resentment	.16***	.13*	−.03
Big Government	.27***	.27***	——
Individualism	.13#	.13#	——
Government Services	.19***	.19***	——
Social Tolerance	.01	.01	——
Liberal/Conservative	.08*	.08*	——
Party Identification	.09**	.09**	——
Age	.16***	.16***	——
Female	−.01	−.01	——
Education	.09*	.09*	——
Political Information	.05	.05	——
Income	.05#	.05#	——
Unemployed	.03	.03	——
South/Border State	.01	.01	——

Note: $N = 1576$ (whites only). $R^2 = .22$. Entries are unstandardized regression coefficients. The dependent and independent variables are each scaled to range from 0 to 1. The direction of coding is as follows: Affirmative Action Opinion 1 = most opposed; Blame 1 = blacks entirely to blame; Old-Fashioned Racism 1 = most racist; Work Ethic Stereotype 1 = believe blacks are lazy; Racial Resentment 1 = most angry; Big Government 1 = most opposed to big government; Individualism 1 = most individualist; Government Services 1 = least supportive; Social Tolerance 1 = least tolerant; Liberal/Conservative 1 = strong conservative; Party Identification 1 = strong Republican; Age 1 = oldest; Female 1 = female (dummy); Education 1 = highest (postgrad); Political Information 1 = highest; Income 1 = highest; Unemployed 1 = unemployed (dummy); South/BorderState 1 = lives in South or border state (dummy).
***$p < .001$; **$p < .01$; *$p < .05$; #$p < .10$
@Blank cells indicate that the variable was constrained to have the same effect in each experimental subsample.
@@The coefficient on blame is significant at $p < .05$ ($b = .20$) when the quadratic term is dropped.

sponse to be implemented specifically when established practices of racial discrimination have left blacks disadvantaged, whites' opinions are at best weakly related to how they explain the general racial gap in economic achievement. Other factors held constant, people with very different ideas about the forces giving rise to the general racial gap in achievement—with some people

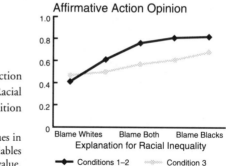

Figure 6.3 Opinion on Affirmative Action
in Hiring, by Explanation for Racial
Inequality and Experimental Condition

Note: In calculating the predicted values in
figs. 6.3–6.10, the other explanatory variables
were set to their mean value.

believing discrimination to be rampant and some believing it rare—come to adopt fairly similar points of view on the programs.

It is interesting, however, that whites' explanations for racial inequality still have some bearing on their opinions even when they are queried about programs specifically situated in the discrimination context. Opposition to racial quotas in cases where discrimination has been established increases reliably, if not strongly, with the extent to which blacks are generally deemed responsible for their own plight. The belief that blacks are to blame for their own poor economic circumstances, and by inference the conclusion that blacks are undeserving of government assistance, continue to bolster opposition to racial quotas even when they are implemented in settings where the presence of discrimination against blacks is not in doubt.

The findings for old-fashioned racism also manifest important differences across the experimental conditions (fig. 6.4). As before, there are two complementary ways to read the results, one focusing on the ability of old-fashioned racism to explain opposition to racial quotas in the two conditions (comparing

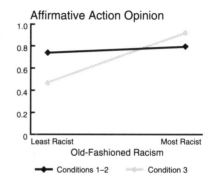

Figure 6.4 Opinion on Affirmative Action
in Hiring, by Old-Fashioned Racism and
Experimental Condition

Affirmative Action Opinion

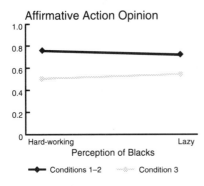

Figure 6.5 Opinion on Affirmative Action in Hiring, by Perception of Blacks' Work Ethic and Experimental Condition

regression coefficients across conditions), and the second focusing on the extent to which racists and nonracists take different positions across the experimental conditions (comparing predicted opinions across conditions at different points along the old-fashioned racism scale).

As seen in both table 6.1 and figure 6.4, there are dramatic differences across conditions in the explanatory power of old-fashioned racism. Among those asked either the first or second version of the question, the effect of old-fashioned racism on opinions is nonexistent ($b = .03$, n.s.), whereas among those asked the third version, the effect is striking in magnitude ($b = . 42, p < .001$). Thus, although in the first two conditions (no context and underrepresentation context) the predicted opinion scores hover around .75 regardless of the respondent's position on the old-fashioned racism scale, in the discrimination condition the predicted opinion scores range from .45 to .87 across the scale. In the equation modeling opinions as gauged in the discrimination condition, the unstandardized regression coefficient for old-fashioned racism exceeds that for any other variable, each of which is scaled to range from 0 to 1,

Affirmative Action Opinion

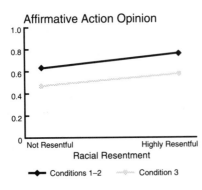

Figure 6.6 Opinion on Affirmative Action in Hiring, by Racial Resentment and Experimental Condition

and its standardized regression coefficient of .18 is also larger than any other variable's as well (not shown).[17]

Taking the second vantage point on the results, we see that those who most vehemently disavow the old-fashioned racist's view take positions on affirmative action that differ markedly across the experimental conditions; on average, they move from firm opponents (.74) to weak supporters (.45) of racial quotas. By contrast, those who adhere to racially bigoted tenets actually became marginally *more* opposed to affirmative action in the third condition, compared to the first or second (.87 versus .76). Old-fashioned racists remain opposed to racial quotas even when they are specifically to be implemented in circumstances where discrimination against blacks has been the norm.

The key to understanding this pattern of findings lies in understanding why the racial bigot remains unmoved by the experimental manipulation that generates a position of greater support in others. I have argued that support for affirmative action grows once it is situated in the discrimination context because it raises concerns about remedial or compensatory justice, epitomized by the judgment that, in all fairness, discrimination against blacks requires a remedial response. This, however, is a judgment that is undermined by the racist's beliefs. The claim that blacks deserve compensation for discrimination rests on the presumption that discrimination against blacks is in fact wrong, which, although a truism for most Americans, is a point at which racial bigots will balk. Indeed, the racist's beliefs undercut the very concept of "discrimination" itself: what others would recognize as discrimination would, to a person who believes that blacks are inherently inferior to whites, be seen as the valid recognition of a racial difference. Hence, those who reject the bigot's white supremacist and segregationist views find a compelling reason to support racial quotas that leaves the traditional bigot unmoved.[18]

Turning to the results concerning the stereotyping of blacks as lazy and undisciplined, we see no sign of the pattern that characterizes old-fashioned racism (fig. 6.5). The extent to which whites think of blacks as failing to live by the standards of the American work ethic is of no consequence to their opinions on racial quotas in either subsample (b's $= -.05$ and .01, respectively), and thus is of no consequence to their response to the experimental manipulation. Those who think of blacks as lazy are no more hostile to racial quotas than are those who believe blacks are hard-working, and both groups offer more support for racial quotas when they are introduced in contexts where discriminatory hiring practices have been established. The irrelevance of whites' stereotypes on the work ethic dimension is striking and, because it goes against expectations derived from symbolic racism theory, quite important. Yet the second aspect of what John McConahay and others have described as prejudice in its "modern" guise, feelings of resentment toward blacks, does have an impact on whites' views of affirmative action. Unlike that found for old-fashioned racism, however, it has a comparable effect in each of the experimental subsamples (fig. 6.6), with estimated coefficients of .16 and .13, respectively.

The broader set of findings in table 6.1 carries little in the way of surprises. As gauged by the regression analysis, whites' opinions on affirmative action also reflect other considerations that, on their face, are race-neutral. Especially potent are generalized objections to a powerful federal government ($b = .27$, $p < .001$) and opposition to government services for the disadvantaged ($b = .19$, $p < .001$). Whites' commitments to individualism also play a role ($b = .13$, $p < .10$), as does their party identification ($b = .09$, $p < .01$) and ideological orientation ($b = .08$, $p < .05$). Higher levels of opposition are also found among older whites ($b = .16$, $p < .001$) and, to a lesser extent, wealthier whites ($b = .05$, $p < .10$). Perhaps the only surprise lies in a final significant predictor, education, whose estimated effect is such that higher levels of education correspond to greater resistance to affirmative action ($b = .09$, $p < .05$). Although it would be going too far to read this result as indicating that education leads only to a "superficial commitment" to racial egalitarianism (Jackman and Muha 1984)—support for the principle, but not the requisite policies—it is clear that better-educated respondents manifest greater, not less, opposition to affirmative action once other variables are controlled.

The results for affirmative action in university admissions show both similarities to and differences from those for affirmative action in hiring (table 6.2, figs. 6.7–6.10). Again we find that beliefs about the causes of racial inequality play a powerful role in shaping whites' opinions on affirmative action (fig. 6.7). But, one caveat aside, their effect is equivalent in each experimental subsample—among those asked the question about preferential treatment, on the one hand, and those asked the question about compensatory action, on the other. Other factors held constant, whites who hold diametrically opposed views about the locus of blame for racial inequality take positions on affirmative action that differ by .26 in the preferential treatment condition (ranging from .41 to .67), and that differ by .30 in the compensatory action condition (ranging from .25 to .55).

The caveat concerns the fact that the functional form relating beliefs about inequality and opinions on affirmative action varies dramatically in the two conditions, which is due to the positions that are taken by those with mixed

Table 6.2. Affirmative Action in University Admissions

Independent Variable	Give Preference	Make Special Effort	Difference@
Constant	−.16	−.29	−.13
Blame	.90***	.28@@	−.63**
Blame-squared	−.63**	.03	.66*
Old-Fashioned Racism	.00	.22**	.22*
Work Ethic Stereotype	.18*	−.12#	−.30**
Racial Resentment	.17***	.23***	.06
Big Government	.01	.01	———
Individualism	.19**	.19***	———
Government Services	.25***	.25***	———
Social Tolerance	.04	.04	———
Liberal/Conservative	.10**	.10**	———
Party Identification	−.01	−.01	———
Age	−.08*	−.08*	———
Female	.01	.01	———
Education	.08*	.08*	———
Political Information	.05	.05	———
Income	.01	.01	———
Unemployed	.01	.01	———
South/Border State	−.03*	−.03*	———

Notes: N = 1578 (whites only). R^2 = .27. Entries are unstandardized regression coefficients. See the note to table 1 for variable coding.
***p < .001; **p < .01; *p < .05; #p < .10
@Blank cells indicate that the variable was constrained to have the same effect in each experimental subsample.
@The coefficient on blame is signficant at p < .001 (b = .30) when the quadratic term is dropped.

views on what gives rise to the racial disparity in economic achievement. When it comes to preferential treatment, those who "blame whites and blacks equally" stand in firm opposition, much closer to the position taken by those who blame blacks for their own economic problems than to the position taken by those who blame whites. The curvilinearity evident here is fully parallel to that found for preferential treatment in hiring (fig. 6.3).[19] Yet in the compensatory action condition, their opposition drops significantly, falling twice as far as those with more extreme views on the subject, and thus the curvilinearity fully disappears. In what I read as a sign of ambivalence, whites with mixed views concerning the causes of racial inequality—which, recall, is the vast majority (68 percent)— show the most marked difference of opinion across the experimental conditions, going from clear opposition to preferential treatment programs (.70) to clear support for compensatory action measures (.39).

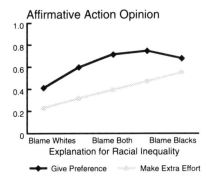

Figure 6.7 Opinion on Affirmative Action in Admissions, by Explanation for Racial Inequality and Experimental Condition

The old-fashioned racism results manifest a similar, though less stark, pattern to that found for the hiring case (fig. 6.8). The extent to which whites adhere to racist beliefs is completely unrelated to their opinions on programs of preferential admissions for blacks ($b = .004$) but is engaged when it comes to opinions on programs designed to ensure that qualified blacks are considered for admission ($b = .22, p < .01$). Comparing opinions across the two programs, we see that although racial bigots demonstrate somewhat more support for compensatory action than for preferential treatment programs (with scores of .56 versus .69), this difference is less than half of that found for whites who reject the bigot's views (.34 versus .69). Thus, whites who repudiate the racist's derogatory views about blacks again take positions on affirmative action that demonstrate a sensitivity to the policy's specific features, here exhibiting more support for affirmative action in the compensatory action case. In this, they leave the racist standing alone, continuing to resist affirmative action no matter the guise.

Whereas traditionally racist beliefs function similarly in the hiring and

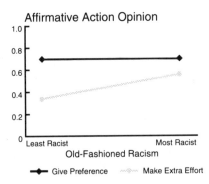

Figure 6.8 Opinion on Affirmative Action in Admissions, by Old-Fashioned Racism and Experimental Condition

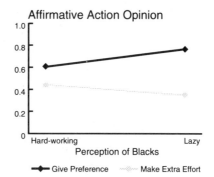

Figure 6.9 Opinion on Affirmative Action in Admissions, by Perception of Blacks' Work Ethic and Experimental Condition

admissions cases, that is not true of whites' beliefs about whether blacks are lazy or otherwise unwilling to do what it takes to succeed. First of all, notice from table 6.2 that stereotypes on this dimension bear a reasonably strong relationship to opinions in the preferential treatment condition ($b = .18, p < .05$), which was not true of the hiring results, a difference that to my mind is inexplicable. More interesting, notice that this relationship entirely disappears—even reverses—in the compensatory action condition ($b = -.12, p < .10$ one-tailed, $< .20$ two-tailed). The upshot of this is that, other things held constant, whites who have adopted the stereotype of the lazy black show a striking difference of opinion across the two conditions, as figure 6.9 illustrates. They are more opposed to preferential treatment in university admissions than are those who reject the stereotype, but both groups are willing to support race-targeted efforts to assist qualified blacks in their educational endeavors.

Although it would not be prudent to read too much into this lone result, there are two reasons to give it at least some attention. First, the pattern is plausible. As Kluegel (1985) and Bobo and Kluegel (1993) have argued, the

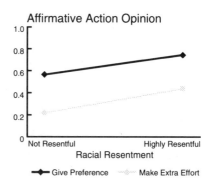

Figure 6.10 Opinion on Affirmative Action in Admissions, by Racial Resentment and Experimental Condition

public's regard of compensatory action programs is enhanced because they, in effect, "help blacks help themselves" and reward only the motivated, hard-working, diligent—deserving—black. As a consequence, they are more likely to draw the support of whites who are skeptical of blacks' qualifications than are programs which implement a racial preference.[20] The second reason the result is worthy of notice is that it works in precisely the opposite direction of the result for old-fashioned racism. Persistent resistance to affirmative action is characteristic of whites whose beliefs take the traditionally prejudiced form (that racial differences are innate and racial segregation is desirable), but not of whites whose beliefs take the "modern" prejudiced form (that blacks have failed when judged by the standards of the American work ethic). Given these results and those for the hiring case as well, it is evident that the two aspects of prejudice deserve to remain clearly delineated in our thinking.[21]

The final aspect of prejudice under investigation here, whites' feelings of racial resentment, is clearly important to opinions on affirmative action in university admissions (fig. 6.10). Regardless of whether one is talking about programs that implement a racial quota or about programs that simply ensure that qualified blacks are considered for admission, white resistance is fueled by feelings of anger and resentment toward blacks ($b = .17$, $p < .001$, and $b = .23$, $p < .001$, respectively). Recall that these feelings were similarly influential in shaping opinions on affirmative action in hiring. Indeed, no other aspect of whites' racial beliefs and attitudes bears such a consistent pattern of effects, as we have seen. Given their importance in this context, racially charged emotions deserve to receive more careful attention in future investigations of racial attitudes and racial conflict in America.

The remaining findings in table 6.2 show that, as in the case of hiring, opinions on affirmative action in university are linked to whites' general level of support for social services programs ($b = .25$, $p < .001$), commitments to individualism ($b = .19$, $p < .01$), and ideology ($b = .10$, $p < .01$). In addition, higher levels of education are once again associated with greater opposition to affirmative action ($b = .08$, $p < .05$). Closer investigation demonstrates, however, that this education effect is limited to the preferential treatment condition alone. In a model that allows all of the "control" variables to interact with the experimental condition, the education effect is sizable in the preferential treatment condition ($b = .18$, $p < .01$), and negligible in the compensatory action condition ($b = -.01$, n.s.; not shown). Therefore, the greater opposition to affirmative action among the highly educated is limited to affirmative action in its preferential treatment form, and disappears when it comes to compensatory action measures.

Several other findings differ from the hiring case. First, older whites and those residing in a southern or border state are marginally more supportive of affirmative action after controlling for other variables ($b = -.08$, $p < .05$ and $b = -.03$, $p < .05$, respectively).[22] The much more striking difference between the results, however, concerns whites' objections to big government. Whereas the extent to which whites generally object to a powerful federal government was one of the most potent predictors of their views on affirmative action in hiring ($b = .27$, $p < .001$; table 6.1), it appears to have nothing to do with their views on affirmative action in university admissions ($b = .01$, n.s.; table 6.2). One might read this result as suggesting that the specter of federal intervention looms only in the employment, but not the educational, context. However, this difference probably has less to do with the hiring/admissions contrast itself than with the particular question wording that was used in the two instances here. Only the question about affirmative action in hiring explicitly invoked the governmental role: "Should companies be required to give a certain number of jobs to blacks, or should the government stay out of this?" The question-wording caution raised by Kuklinski and Parent (1981) remains fully relevant here.

CONCLUSION

There is a noticeable discrepancy between how the typical survey question has framed affirmative action in employment and how it has been framed by the law that has emerged under the guidance of Supreme Court rulings. Survey questions usually pose the issue abstractly; they treat racial preferences in employment as a general measure designed to enhance the employment status of blacks, in light of discrimination generally experienced by blacks in the past. The Court, by contrast, has treated racial preferences in employment as a limited remedial measure designed to "eliminate those discriminatory practices and devices which have fostered racially stratified job environments to the disadvantage of minority citizens,"[23] appropriate only when implemented in occupational contexts marked by a history of racial discrimination. Their purpose is circumscribed—to remedy the effects of identifiable practices of discrimination; as are the circumstances in which they may legally be imple-mented—in companies where established practices of discrimination have left blacks disadvantaged.

The practice of studying public opinion on affirmative action through the use of abstract and general survey questions has several consequences, as demonstrated here. First, it fails to reveal that the American public, white and black alike, is sensitive to an issue of fairness that has preoccupied the courts: whether or not the programs are specifically tailored to respond to wrongful practices of discrimination and to compensate blacks for disadvantages suffered as a result. On the whole, Americans are significantly more supportive of programs that meet the "narrowly tailored" remedial purpose that the Supreme Court has established than of programs simply designed to eradicate racial stratification in the workforce, whatever its cause. Although it is standard practice to describe the American public as overwhelmingly and invariably opposed to racial quotas, that conventional wisdom should be revised.

Second, analyses based on responses to abstract affirmative action questions lead to an exaggerated sense of the opinion-shaping role played by whites' explanations for racial inequality—though exaggerated in one sense alone. These beliefs are indeed important to how whites evaluate affirmative action, but they are especially so when the program is framed as a general policy tool through which to enhance blacks' status. They become much less important, though not completely irrelevant, when the policy is treated as a limited measure only to be utilized in circumstances where discrimination against blacks has been operating. Whites who disagree about the forces giving rise to the general racial gap in economic status (with some tending to blame whites and some tending to blame blacks themselves) take widely differing positions on affirmative action in its general guise, yet converge in their level of support for programs specifically located in occupational contexts where the existence of discrimination against blacks has been established.

Finally, the typical question-wording strategy has the consequence of masking the important effects of traditional racist beliefs in sustaining white opposition to affirmative action. When it comes to the use of affirmative action as a general remedial measure, the opinions of whites who adhere to racist tenets are indistinguishable from the opinions of those who reject the racist's views. Racist beliefs, it appears, are not a source of white opposition to racial quotas. Yet that is decidedly not the perspective that emerges once we consider opinions that are rendered with respect to affirmative action in its narrowly tailored guise. There, stark differences of opinion between racists and nonracists appear. The key to understanding these results, I have suggested, is to read them in conjunction. It is true that old-fashioned racism fails to account for differences of opinion in the first instance, as whites who repudiate the traditional bigot's views come to express opposition on other grounds. Yet it is also true that when those same whites find a compelling reason to support affirmative action in its narrower guise, they leave the racist behind. Old-fashioned racism may not explain variation in opinion in each case, but, as the contrast across the cases reveals, the force of racist beliefs is there just the same.

Despite the importance of the remedial context to how racial quotas are received, they continue to meet with resistance specifically because they introduce race as a criterion by which selection decisions will be made. Thus, whereas whites are divided over the use of racial preferences as a remedy for discrimination, they stand firmly behind race-targeted affirmative action measures that operate before the selection stage. In this result we again see signs that whites' reactions to affirmative action are partly structured by principled commitments. The implementation of a racial preference violates the color-blind ideal of merit-based selection, which evidently leads some whites to judge racial quotas unfair.

At the same time, racial prejudice is very much a part of the story of white opposition to affirmative action, though not always in ways that, on the basis of previous research, one would have predicted in advance. A large fraction of the white public subscribes to the negative stereotype of blacks as lazy, undisciplined, and generally failing to do what it takes to succeed in America. Although these beliefs are at the heart of the thesis of symbolic racism, and thus one would expect to find them sustaining white opposition to affirmative action, they in fact play a surprisingly limited role. Adherence to the stereotype of the "lazy black" is, of course, one of the reasons that some whites come to blame blacks for their own economic disadvantages, and those judgments of responsibility are themselves very consequential to whites' opinions on affirmative action. That given, however, the influence of these stereotypical beliefs is remarkably weak.

Of greater consequence are whites' feelings of resentment toward blacks, feelings generated by blacks' insistence that American citizens and policies recognize the forces of discrimination to which they have been, and continue to be, subject—feelings palpably present in the vast majority of whites. Whites' resistance to affirmative action may not be directly grounded in the derogatory beliefs about blacks that have received emphasis in scholarly accounts of modern prejudice, but it has been directly fueled by racially charged emotions also emphasized by the modern-prejudice school. Indeed, these emotions sustain white opposition to affirmative action no matter how the policy is framed or defined.

And then there are plain old-fashioned racist beliefs, a source of opposition that is all too often overlooked by contemporary analysts working under the assumption that "since the explicitly segregationist, white supremacist view has all but disappeared, it no longer can be a major political force" (Kinder and Sears 1981, p. 416). These beliefs play an important and underappreciated role in explaining white opposition to affirmative action. Not only does the racist's animus toward blacks undergird his opposition to racial quotas even when they are implemented in response to discrimination, as noted above, but it also sustains his opposition to affirmative action programs regardless of whether they take a preferential treatment or compensatory action form. The lesson these results carry for analysts of racial attitudes is clear: the presence and force of old-fashioned racist beliefs have, unfortunately, not disappeared.

In light of the full set of arguments and findings presented here, it is apparent that this study adds to the growing weight of evidence suggesting the importance of issue framing, an argument that has been developed by a number of analysts studying public opinion on affirmative action (Fine 1992; Fletcher and Chalmers 1991; Gamson 1992; Gamson and Modigliani 1987; Kinder and Nelson 1990; Kinder and Sanders 1990; Sniderman et al. 1993). The framing argument holds that the opinions citizens take on an issue are affected by the way the issue is "packaged" by elites or the mass media, and accordingly by our survey questions as well. In the survey context, however, this idea has usually been developed by thinking about the different ways in which a given policy stance—support or opposition—might be justified. Kinder and Sanders (1990), for example, experimentally manipulated the reason given for opposing a general policy of racial preferences, in one condition using the phrase "because it discriminates against whites," and in a second condition using the phrase "because it gives blacks advantages they haven't earned." What this investigation has emphasized, instead, is not how support or opposition to a given affirmative action policy is justified in our questions, but rather how our questions—and ultimately political elites—come to describe affirmative action policies themselves.

Affirmative action promises to remain a contested subject on the broader political agenda. As of this writing, the Republican majority in Congress is taking aim at affirmative action, hoping to use it as a "wedge issue" to elicit the conversion or defection of conservative white Democrats. New court cases challenging the legitimacy of race-conscious hiring and admissions programs continue to make their way through the legal system. Thinking about the broader political ramifications of the affirmative action debate provides a final way to put in perspective the findings and arguments presented here. In the electoral arena, the debate over affirmative action is typically waged in terms of symbols and slogans. It's about "quotas," "a color-blind society," "racism," "reverse discrimination," and the like. As Jesse Helms's infamous 1990 advertisement reminds us even more forcefully, it is often not about the parameters of actual policies at all.[24] There is every reason to believe that the controversies over affirmative action will continue to operate rhetorically in ways that fully ignore the policy distinctions I have focused upon here. As Theodore M. Shaw, associate director-counsel for the NAACP Legal Defense Fund, put it recently: "These issues are very complex and sensitive. The courts have struck a balance that allows affirmative action in limited circumstances. But the political process and the nature of political discourse these days do not insure these issues will be dealt with in a thoughtful and sensitive way."[25] To the extent that this is so, what will be of consequence to the electoral arena is not the fact that Americans will support this or that affirmative action policy, or support a given policy in one circumstance more than in another. Simplistic appeals and emotionally charged rhetoric may come to rule the day.

NOTES

1. Steven V. Roberts. "Affirmative Action on the Edge," *U.S. News and World Report,* February 13, 1995.
2. Kinder and Sears's (1981) index of "expressive racism," for example, included responses to two questions tapping opinions on racial quotas in university admissions. Less blatant is the logic embodied in the implicit syllogism with which McConahay, Hardee, and Batts (1981) begin their article "Has Racism Declined in America?": "In recent years as public opinion polls have shown a decline in racist responses, white Americans have strongly resisted school desegregation and affirmative action programs. Hence, there has been a debate over the extent to which racism has really declined." See Sniderman and Tetlock (1986) for a critique of the thesis of symbolic racism in general, and the reading of opposition to affirmative action as equivalent to prejudice in particular.
3. The only study I am aware of that explicitly compares the effects of old-fashioned and modern versions of prejudice, Jacobson (1985), found smaller effects for the former than for the latter. This is consistent with what has been found for other race-policy opinions (Kinder 1986). Kinder and Sanders (1990) found that racial prejudice bore a moderately strong relationship to opinions on affirmative action, more so when the policy was framed as "giving blacks advantages they haven't earned" than when it was framed as "discriminating against whites." Although they do not describe their measure, it was presumably based on the symbolic racism items carried by the National Election Studies, as described

in Kinder (1986). Kluegel and Smith's (1986) measure of racial prejudice, which combined "the perception of blacks' demands for change as legitimate or illegitimate, and evaluations of civil rights groups" (p. 160), proved to be one of the best predictors of opinions on affirmative action. Sniderman and Piazza (1993) examined the effects of a variety of racial stereotypes, finding effects for stereotypes that concern blacks' work ethic (e.g., the belief that blacks are lazy or undisciplined), but these effects were noticeably weaker with respect to affirmative action opinions than with respect to opinions concerning general social assistance programs for blacks. They conclude that "although it has become fashionable to assert that opposition to affirmative action is driven by racism, as though the reason so many whites object to racial quotas and preferential treatment is prejudice pure and simple, it turns out that the politics of affirmative action has remarkably little to do with whites' feelings toward blacks" (p. 109). Other studies of public opinion on affirmative action have not examined whites' racial beliefs and attitudes at all, because they focus either on aggregate polling results (e.g., Bunzel 1986; Fine 1992; Lipset and Schneider 1978; Lipset 1990) or on the results of controlled experiments (e.g., Nacoste 1985, 1987).

4. The Court has reached similar conclusions with respect to other areas in which affirmative action is practiced, although the legal details vary considerably. Discrimination throughout the construction industry, for example, has been judged relevant to the use of affirmative action in the awarding of government contracts (a point under contention in the 1995 case *Adarand Constructors v. Pena,* which otherwise affirmed the "narrowly tailored" rationale), and the value of diversity has been recognized in cases concerning university admissions. It is also worth noting that any business that voluntarily implements an affirmative action program must be able to provide evidence of prior discrimination if the legality of the program is challenged. Rosenfeld (1991) contains a useful review of affirmative action rulings from the 1970s and 1980s. Dansicker (1991) discusses more recent cases and legislation.

5. Here, Justice O'Connor is partially quoting from Justice Powell's opinion in *University of California Regents v. Baake* (1978 438 US 265). Court rulings also repeatedly warn about "the myriad of innocent causes that may lead to statistical imbalances in the composition of their work forces" (*Watson v. Fort Worth Bank and Trust,* 1988 487 US 977, 992; quoted in *Wards Cove Packing Co. v. Atonia,* 1989 490 US 642, 657).

6. Compensatory justice requires reparation or restitution to victims. One problematic issue that remains revolves around the question of whether preferential treatment policies are only acceptable if they compensate "actual victims" or whether they may apply to the entire "class of victims" (e.g., blacks) affected by the discriminatory practice (see, e.g., Groarke 1990). This continues to be debated by the Court (for example, see Justice Scalia's separate opinion in *Richmond v. J. A. Croson Co.* 1988 488 US 469), but in *Local 25, Sheet Metal Workers' Intern. Ass'n v. EEOC* the Court explicitly rejected the argument that Title VII, section 706(g) of the 1964 Civil Rights Act "authorizes a district court to award preferential relief only to the actual victims of unlawful discrimination" and concluded that it "does not prohibit a court from ordering, in appropriate circumstances, affirmative race-conscious relief as a remedy for past discrimination. Specifically, we hold that such relief may be appropriate where an employer or a labor union has engaged in persistent or egregious discrimination, or where necessary to dissipate the

lingering effects of pervasive discrimination" (1985 478 US 421, 444–445, opinion delivered by Justice Brennan).

7. Ironically, it is quite clear that affirmative action opinion questions have been formulated with Supreme Court decisions in mind. The first two questions listed above refer explicitly or implicitly to Court pronouncements. And, like the NES question, many others include such phrases as "because of past discrimination" or "to make up for past discrimination," language prominent in Supreme Court decisions on affirmative action. Yet, whereas the Court's use of the phrase "past discrimination" refers to past discrimination in the hiring unit in which the affirmative action policy serves as the remedial response, when it finds its way into abstract survey questions like that used by the NES, it instead evokes images of discrimination as a generalized social phenomenon, perhaps found only in the distant past.

8. It is important to note that although blacks exhibit much more support for racial quotas than do whites, they show a pattern of differences across the experimental conditions that is very similar to (and statistically indistinguishable from) that for whites. The percentage of blacks who express opposition to racial quotas drops from 33% and 37% in the first two conditions, respectively, to 19% in the third condition. For the sample as a whole, the comparable figures are 72%, 76%, and 54%.

9. Only two studies that I am aware of provide further evidence of this point, and do so only obliquely. The first was an experimental study undertaken by Rupert Nacoste (1985), where undergraduate subjects played the role of a female professor awarded a university grant through affirmative action, and which manipulated whether or not there was a history of discrimination against women in the awards committee. Subjects in the prior discrimination condition felt significantly more deserving of their grant, and Nacoste concluded that "overall, it appears that history of discrimination is an important contextual variable to consider within the domain of responses to affirmative action" (p. 240). The second study, undertaken by Francine Tougas, Ann Beaton, and France Veilleux (1991), examined the attitudes of female workers in Canada. It found that perceptions regarding the extent to which women were disadvantaged by the organization's existing hiring and promotional practices strongly affected the level of support given to affirmative action programs.

10. The findings reported by Lipset and Schneider have also been noted by other analysts of public opinion on affirmative action, including Bunzel (1986), Kluegel and Smith (1983), and Lynch and Beer (1990).

11. Data from NES reported by Fine (1992) and from GSS reported by Kluegel and Smith (1986) have also shown that the American public responds similarly to quotas in hiring and in university admissions.

12. By way of comparison, the shift in blacks' opinions across the two conditions is not nearly as stark. Twenty-three percent of the black respondents expressed opposition in the preferential treatment condition, dropping to 9% in the compensatory action case. The smaller experimental shift among blacks (14%) than among whites (35%), however, is apparently due to floor effects. Because the rate of black opposition to preferential treatment in university admissions is so low to begin with, there is not much further it could fall.

13. The term "symbolic racism" is usually associated with the work of David Sears and Donald Kinder and the early work of John McConahay, but McConahay has come to adopt the term "modern racism." McConahay's conception of modern racism bears a close connection to that of symbolic racism, as Kinder (1986) points out, and as is evident from the definition of modern racism that McConahay offered in 1976 and reiterated in 1986: "the expression in terms of abstract ideological symbols and symbolic behaviors of the feeling that blacks are violating cherished values and making illegitimate demands for change in the racial *status quo*" (1986, p. 95). But McConahay's recent conceptual arguments and operational measures have emphasized the second component (feeling blacks are making illegitimate demands for change) rather than the former (feeling blacks are violating cherished values), suggesting that there may be two different ideas here (McConahay 1986). I represent feelings concerning blacks' demands for change with a separate indicator. See below.

14. Although the expression of feelings of racial resentment and the stereotyping of blacks as failing to abide by the American work ethic both fall under the rubric of modern or symbolic racism (see n. 13), I treat them separately here. This is advisable in light of research showing emotional and cognitive processes to be partially independent, with each contributing to attitude formation (e.g., Ottati and Wyer 1993). The two measures perform differently as well.

15. With two exceptions, there are no statistically significant differences in the effects of these variables across the experimental conditions. The two exceptions are age and education, and only for experiment 2 (preferential treatment versus compensatory action), about which I will say more below. If the effects of all of the variables are estimated separately within each experimental subsample, one find results for whites' racial beliefs and attitudes that are nearly identical to those presented here.

16. Multiplying the "blame" and "blame-squared" coefficients for each subsample by the overall sample mean for these variables provides another way to indicate relative importance ("level importance," following Achen 1982). The figures are .32 (no context or underrepresentation context) versus .10 (discrimination context), for a difference of .22. Thus the greater power of beliefs about racial inequality in the first subsample has the effect of shifting the mean .22 units in the direction of greater opposition.

17. The variable measuring objections to big government carries the next largest unstandardized coefficient (.27), as table 6.1 shows, and has the next largest standardized coefficient as well (.16). If importance is judged using Achen's (1982) "level-importance" measure— by the product of the variable's coefficient and mean—then old-fashioned racism falls to second (score .12) behind objections to big government (score .17).

18. So understood, the analysis underscores the importance of concerns about fairness at the same time, ironically, that it uncovers a larger role for racist sentiments than one would otherwise see. In this, it provides evidence in support of an argument that others have advanced more speculatively, to wit, that although racism leads some whites to oppose affirmative action, whites who reject racist ideas may come to oppose affirmative action either because they object on grounds of fairness (e.g., Sniderman et al. 1993; Sniderman and Piazza 1993) or because of their beliefs about the causes of racial stratification (e.g., Kluegel 1985; Kluegel and Smith 1986). As Kluegel (1985) put it, when discussing why the

over-time decline in racist beliefs has not given rise to an enhanced level of support for affirmative action: "Although we may expect that persons who express traditional racial prejudice also oppose affirmative action, based on prevailing beliefs about the scope and causes of the black-white gap in socio-economic status there is no reason to expect that, *ceteris paribus,* rejecting traditional racial prejudice of any necessity leads to support of affirmative action" (p. 778). Only through an analysis that experimentally removes what some nonracist whites judge to be an objectionable feature of affirmative action is the importance of racist beliefs in undergirding white opposition revealed.

19. Indeed, when the two curvilinear figures are carefully juxtaposed, they are almost identical. The only difference is a slightly higher level of opposition in the hiring case among those who place the blame for racial inequality upon blacks themselves.

20. As Kluegel (1985) put it, "If the lack of necessary motivation, skills and values is believed to be the only problem, and if one believes that white America owes black America a debt for perceived past injustice, then it logically follows that one should support programs to train blacks to have the 'proper' skills and attitudes to compete equally with whites" (p. 776). Kluegel distinguishes between "structuralist" and "individualist" programs, where individualist programs correspond to those described here under the compensatory action label. Bobo and Kluegel (1993) do not directly analyze opinions on affirmative action but examine differences between how whites evaluate "results enhancing" and "opportunity enhancing" programs, a distinction that corresponds to the preferential treatment/compensatory action distinction.

21. Although this is fairly standard practice, some come close to treating them as manifestations of a single dimension of racial hostility, one overtly racist and old-fashioned, and the other covertly racist and modern. McConahay and Hough (1976), for example, devote several pages to the question, "If both red-neck and symbolic racism are expressions of the same anti-black feeling, why does the first appear to be on the decline . . . while the second is possibly on the rise?" (p. 39).

22. The only other significant interaction in the full analysis-of-covariance model that allows the effects of each variable to vary across the experimental subsamples concerns age. There is no age effect in the preferential treatment subsample ($b = .001$, n.s.) but a marginally significant negative relationship in the compensatory action subsample ($b = -.14$, $p < .05$ one-tailed, $p < .10$ two-tailed).

23. From Justice Brennan's opinion in *Local 25, Sheet Metal Workers' Intern. Ass'n v. EEOC* (1985 478 US 421, 450).

24. The advertisement showed "white hands holding a rejection slip, while a narrator intoned, 'You needed that job, and you were the best qualified. But it had to go to a minority because of a racial quota.'" Priscilla Painton. "Quota Quagmire," *Time,* May 27, 1991.

25. *New York Times,* February 7, 1995.

REFERENCES

Achen, Christopher H. 1982. *Interpreting and Using Regression.* Beverly Hills, Calif.: Sage.

Bobo, Lawrence. 1988. "Group Conflict, Prejudice, and the Paradox of Contemporary Racial

Attitudes." In *Eliminating Racism: Profiles in Controversy,* ed. Phyllis A. Katz and Dalmas A. Taylor. New York: Plenum.

Bobo, Lawrence, and James R. Kluegel. 1993. "Opposition to Race-targeting: Self-interest, Stratification Ideology, or Racial Attitudes?" *American Sociological Review* 58:443–64.

Bunzel, John H. 1986. "Affirmative Re-actions." *Public Opinion* February/March:45–49.

Carmines, Edward G., and Richard A. Champagne, Jr. 1990. "The Changing Content of American Racial Attitudes: A Fifty-Year Portrait." *Journal of Micropolitics* 3:187–208.

Dansicker, Andrew M. 1991. "A Sheep in Wolf's Clothing: Affirmative Action, Disparate Impact, Quotas, and the Civil Rights Act." *Columbia Journal of Law and Social Problems* 25:1–50.

Dovidio, John F., Jeffrey Mann, and Samuel L. Gaertner. 1989. "Resistance to Affirmative Action: The Implications of Aversive Racism." In *Affirmative Action in Perspective,* ed. Fletcher A. Blanchard and Faye J. Crosby. New York: Springer.

Fine, Terri Susan. 1992. "The Impact of Issue Framing on Public Opinion Toward Affirmative Action Programs." *Social Science Journal* 29:323–34.

Gamson, William A. 1992. *Talking Politics.* New York: Cambridge University Press.

Gamson, William A., and Andre Modigliani. 1987. "The Changing Culture of Affirmative Action." *Research in Political Sociology* 3:137–77.

Groarke, Leo. 1990. "Affirmative Action as a Form of Restitution." *Journal of Business Ethics* 9:207–13.

Jackman, Mary R., and Michael J. Muha. 1984. "Education and Intergroup Attitudes: Moral Enlightenment, Superficial Democratic Commitment, or Ideological Refinement?" *American Sociological Review* 49:751–69.

Jacobson, Cardell. 1985. "Resistance to Affirmative Action: Self-interest or Racism?" *Journal of Conflict Resolution* 29:306–29.

Kinder, Donald R. 1986. "The Continuing American Dilemma: White Resistance to Racial Change 40 Years After Myrdal." *Journal of Social Issues* 42:151–71.

Kinder, Donald R., and Lynn M. Sanders. 1990. "Mimicking Political Debate with Survey Questions: The Case of White Opinion on Affirmative Action." *Social Cognition* 8:71–103.

Kinder, Donald R., and David O. Sears. 1981. "Symbolic Racism Versus Racial Threats to the Good Life." *Journal of Personality and Social Psychology* 40:414–31.

Kluegel, James R. 1985. "If There: Isn't a Problem, You Don't Need a Solution: The Bases of Contemporary Affirmative Action Attitudes." *American Behavioral Scientist* 28:761–64.

Kluegel, James R., and Lawrence Bobo. 1993. "Dimensions of Whites' Beliefs About the Black-White Socioeconomic Gap." In *Prejudice, Politics, and the American Dilemma,* ed. Paul M. Sniderman, Philip E. Tetlock, and Edward G. Carmines. Stanford, Calif.: Stanford University Press.

Kluegel, James R., and Eliot R. Smith. 1983. "Affirmative Action Attitudes: Effects of Self-interest, Racial Affect, and Stratification Beliefs on Whites' Views." *Social Forces* 61:797–824.

———. 1986. *Beliefs About Inequality.* New York: Aldine de Gruyter.

Kuklinski, James H., and Wayne Parent. 1981. "Race and Big Government: Contamination in Measuring Racial Attitudes." *Political Methodology* 8:131–59.

Lipset, Seymour Martin. 1991. "Two Americas, Two Value Systems: Blacks and Whites." Hoover Institution Working Paper P-91–1.

Lipset, Seymour Martin, and William Schneider. 1978. "The Bakke Case: How Would It Be Decided in the Bar of Public Opinion?" *Public Opinion* 1:38–44.

Lynch, Frederick R., and William R. Beer. 1990. "You Ain't the Right Color, Pal." *Policy Review* Winter:64–67.

McConahay, John B. 1982. "Self-Interest Versus Racial Attitudes as Correlates of Anti-busing Attitudes in Louisville: Is It the Buses or the Blacks?" *Journal of Politics* 44:692–720.

———. 1986. "Modern Racism, Ambivalence, and the Modern Racism Scale." In *Prejudice, Discrimination, and Racism,* ed. John F. Dovidio and Samuel L. Gaertner. New York: Academic.

McConahay, John B., Betty B. Hardee, and Valerie Batts. 1981. "Has Racism Declined in America?" *Journal of Conflict Resolution* 25:563–79.

McConahay, John B., and J. C. Hough, Jr. 1976. "Symbolic Racism." *Journal of Social Issues* 32:23–45.

Nacoste, Rupert W. 1985. "Selection Procedure and Responses to Affirmative Action: The Case of Favorable Treatment." *Law and Human Behavior* 9:225–42.

Nacoste, Rupert W. 1987. "But Do They Care About Fairness? The Dynamics of Preferential Treatment and Minority Interest." *Basic and Applied Social Psychology* 8:177–91.

Ottati, Victor C. and Robert S. Wyer, Jr. 1993. "Affect and Political Judgment." In *Explorations in Political Psychology,* ed. Shanto Iyengar and William J. McGuire. Durham, N.C.: Duke University Press.

Pettigrew, Thomas F. 1979. "Racial Change and Social Policy," *Annals of the American Academy of Political and Social Science* 44:114–31.

Rosenfeld, Michael. 1991. *Affirmative Action and Justice.* New Haven: Yale University Press.

Schuman, Howard. 1971. "Free Will and Determinism in Public Beliefs about Race." In *Majority and Minority: The Dynamics of Racial and Ethnic Relations,* ed. Norman R. Yetman and C. Hoy Steele. Boston: Allyn and Bacon.

Schuman, Howard, Charlotte Steeh, and Lawrence Bobo. 1985. *Racial Attitudes in America.* Cambridge, Mass.: Harvard University Press.

Sears, David O. 1988. "Symbolic Racism." In *Eliminating Racism: Profiles in Controversy,* ed. Phyllis A. Katz and Dalmas A. Taylor. New York: Plenum.

Simon, Robert 1977. "Preferential Hiring: A Reply to Judith Jarvis Thomson." In *Equality and Preferential Treatment,* ed. Marshall Cohen, Thomas Nagel, and Thomas Scanlon. Princeton, N.J.: Princeton University Press.

Sniderman, Paul M., and Thomas Piazza. 1993. *The Scar of Race.* Cambridge, Mass.: Harvard University Press.

Sniderman, Paul M., and Philip E. Tetlock. 1986a. "Symbolic Racism: Problems of Motive Attribution in Political Analysis" *Journal of Social Issues* 42:129–50.

———. 1986b. "Reflections on American Racism." *Journal of Social Issues* 42:173–87.

Sniderman, Paul M., Philip E. Tetlock, Edward G. Carmines, and Randall S. Peterson. 1993. "The Politics of the American Dilemma: Issue Pluralism." In *Prejudice, Politics, and the American Dilemma,* ed. Paul M. Sniderman, Philip E. Tetlock, and Edward G. Carmines. Stanford, Calif.: Stanford University Press.

Tougas, Francine, Ann M. Beaton, and France Veilleux. 1991. "Why Women Approve of Affirmative Action: The Study of a Predictive Model." *International Journal of Psychology* 26:761–76.

Veilleux, France, and Francine Tougas. 1989. "Male Acceptance of Affirmative Action Programs for Women: The Results of Altruistic or Egotistical Motives?" *International Journal of Psychology* 24:485–96.

Chapter 7 Racial Attitudes and Race-Neutral Social Policies: White Opposition to Welfare and the Politics of Racial Inequality

Martin Gilens

In almost every aspect of social and economic well-being, black Americans remain worse off than whites. African-Americans' median income today is 74 percent that of whites, a feeble improvement of only five percentage points in the past twenty-five years. Racial differences in high school completion rates and achievement scores on standardized tests have narrowed dramatically in the past two decades. But the racial gap in college education remains large, with 26 percent of whites and only 15 percent of blacks completing four years of college. In other areas, racial differences have not narrowed at all. The racial gap in unemployment has not changed over the past twenty-five years and remains over twice as high for blacks as it is for whites (currently 11.5 percent compared to 5.3 percent). And racial differences in home-ownership rates have actually increased slightly since 1970.[1]

Although racial inequality remains a pressing problem in the United States, remedies that are both economically effective and politically popular have proved elusive. In particular, racially targeted policies such as affirmative action often elicit strong opposition from whites (Citrin 1996; Gilens, Sniderman, and Kuklinski, 1998; Kinder and Sanders 1996; Steeh and Krysan 1996). Responding to the lack of political support for race-targeted remedies, some observers have called for a "surreptitious" social policy of combating racial inequality through race-neutral programs that will address the needs of poor people of all ethnic and racial groups. William Julius Wilson, for example, approvingly quotes from Vivian Henderson: "The economic future of blacks in the United States is bound up with that of the rest of the nation. Policies, programs, and politics designed in the future to cope with the problems of the poor and victimized will also yield benefits to blacks. In contrast, any efforts to treat blacks separately from the rest of the nation are likely to lead to frustration, heightened racial animosities, and a waste of the country's resources and the precious resources of black people" (Wilson 1991, p. 477).

The problem, Wilson writes, is that "many white Americans have turned, not against blacks, but against a strategy that emphasizes programs perceived to benefit only racial minorities" (Wilson 1990, p. 74). Consequently, in *The Truly Disadvantaged,* Wilson (1987) urged liberals to adopt a "hidden agenda" of using race-neutral policies to address racial inequality. "The real challenge," he later wrote, "is to develop programs that not only meaningfully address the problems of the underclass but that draw broad support. . . . I now believe that this is best achieved not simply through a combination of targeted and universal initiatives, but through targeted and universal initiatives that are clearly race neutral" (Wilson 1991, p. 478).

The strategy of using race-neutral programs to combat racial inequality has a number of potential shortcomings. Because blacks are disproportionately poor, antipoverty programs should benefit blacks disproportionately. But race-neutral programs are by their nature unable to address the *race-specific* causes of racial inequality. Poor blacks suffer not only from the problems common to all poor people but also from the burden of racial discrimination and stereotyping.[2] Although income-targeted programs can help poor blacks, just as they can help the nonblack poor, such programs cannot address the racially specific sources of African-Americans' economic problems.

In this chapter, however, I am concerned not with the practical limitations of race-neutral programs to redress racial inequality, but rather with the nature and extent of public support for such programs. The political argument for race-neutral social programs rests on the belief that public attitudes toward such programs are, to some substantial degree at least, insulated from racial politics. But how plausible is this belief? Do white Americans react to race-neutral antipoverty policies in nonracial terms, or do their racial attitudes also permeate their thinking about programs that target the poor of all races?

The notion that whites' racial views are a stronger influence on race-targeted than on race-neutral antipoverty policies receives some support from previous analyses of public opinion. For example, Bobo and Kluegel (1993) examined the impact of whites' racial attitudes on similar race-targeted and income-targeted social policies. (These policies included government spending to assist blacks and the poor, government responsibility for improving the standard of living of blacks and of the poor, and support for enterprise zones and educational spending targeted at blacks and at the poor.) Bobo and Kluegel found strong and consistent effects of racial attitudes on race-targeted policies, but weaker and inconsistent effects on support for income-targeted policies. (See also Bobo and Smith 1994 for similar comparisons across a different set of social policies.)

The claim that income-targeted antipoverty policies are somewhat insulated from the impact of whites' racial attitudes can also draw support from much of the research on public attitudes toward welfare. Past studies of welfare attitudes have tended either to ignore racial attitudes (Alston and Dean 1972; AuClaire 1984; Cook and Barrett 1992; Curtin and Cowan 1975; Feagin 1975; Hasenfeld and Rafferty 1989; Williamson 1974) or to assign them a secondary role among the determinants of the public's welfare views (Kluegel and Smith 1986). Rather than racial attitudes, this research has focused on Americans' individualism, their perceived economic self-interest, or their explanations for poverty and perceptions of the poor as the primary influences on attitudes toward welfare.

But other studies have placed more emphasis on racial attitudes in understanding public opposition to welfare. Gilens (1995), Sears and Citrin (1985), and Smith (1987) all found racial views to be important predictors of Americans' attitudes toward welfare. I shall take another look at the importance of racial attitudes in understanding opposition to welfare among white Americans, paying particular attention to the problem of distinguishing between attitudes toward blacks and attitudes toward poor people in general. Blacks compose a disproportionate share of poor people in the United States—currently about 27 percent (U.S. Bureau of the Census 1996). But more to the point, the public *thinks* that blacks make up an even larger share of the poor. In one survey, respondents were asked, "Of all the people who are poor in this country, are more of them black or are more of them white?"[3] Fifty-one percent of respondents chose black, and only 17 percent white (the remainder said about equal, or had no opinion). In the 1991 Race and Politics Study (RPS), respondents were simply asked, "What percent of all the poor people in this country would you say are black?" The median guess in response to this question was 50 percent.

Because African-Americans constitute a disproportionate share of America's poor, apparently nonracial survey questions tapping respondents' attitudes toward the poor may reflect their racial attitudes as well. Similarly, survey measures of racial attitudes may reflect not only specific evaluations of and beliefs about blacks but also beliefs about the poor in general. Because these two sets of attitudes are confounded, the apparent power of each to predict whites' welfare views may be misleading: a strong connection between racial attitudes and welfare views is not in itself compelling evidence that whites think about welfare in racial terms. The belief, for example, that blacks' economic problems are their own fault may simply reflect a broader judgment that the economically disadvantaged of all races have only themselves to blame. Conversely, a strong connection between respondents' welfare views and their attitudes toward the poor may in fact arise from racial considerations, even if entirely nonracial questions are used to measure attitudes toward the poor.

In this chapter, I address the overlap between attitudes toward blacks and toward the poor with a randomized experiment from the RPS. In this experiment, one randomly selected half of the survey respondents were asked questions about a poor black person, while the other half were asked otherwise identical questions about a poor white person. Because respondents were randomly assigned to the different versions of the questions, the two subsamples should be nearly identical, differing only because of chance variations (and with the large number of respondents to the RPS, such chance variations between two subsamples are likely to be quite small). With proper consideration for sampling error, we can estimate the difference in respondents' attitudes toward poor blacks and poor whites by comparing responses to the two different versions of these questions.

PUBLIC ATTITUDES TOWARD WELFARE

Race-neutral antipoverty programs include an array of policies, from public housing to Medicaid to the Earned Income Tax Credit. The most prominent among these programs—although not the most costly—consists of what has come to be known simply as "welfare." As it is usually understood, welfare includes means-tested cash-transfer programs for the able-bodied, working-age poor—that is, programs that provide a cash benefit for recipients who must meet a "means test" by showing that they are poor enough to qualify. Understood in this way, welfare includes Aid to Families with Dependent Children (AFDC) and the state-run General Assistance (GA) programs. The Food Stamp program also serves the able-bodied working-age poor, but provides a cashlike scrip that can be used to purchase approved foodstuffs.

These means-tested transfer programs represent only a small fraction of social welfare spending, and such programs raise fewer people out of poverty than social insurance programs like Social Security and Unemployment Insurance (Marmor, Mashaw, and Harvey 1990). Nevertheless, both public thinking and elite policy debates over government antipoverty policy focus disproportionately on these means-tested programs. Perhaps because of the controversy that surrounds them, welfare programs such as AFDC, GA, and Food Stamps have become the center of debate over public efforts to help the poor.

Previous efforts to explain Americans' opposition to welfare have often pointed to the economic self-interest of middle-class taxpayers. From this perspective, support for welfare is most likely to be found among lower-income Americans who are welfare recipients themselves, who have friends or family who receive welfare, or who envision the possibility of needing welfare in the future. At the same time, middle- and upper-class taxpayers are expected to oppose welfare out of a desire to reduce their tax burden.

The economic self-interest explanation is widely assumed to be true, and debates over public policy often rest on the assumption that middle-class taxpayers resent paying for programs that benefit only the poor (Jencks 1992; Skocpol 1990; Skocpol 1991). For example, discussing the politics of welfare in the 1970s and 1980s, Skocpol (1990, p. 63) writes: "This political situation was rooted in a split between people who benefited most from policy changes and people who saw themselves as burdened with higher taxes. Surely many working- and middle-class families have elderly parents or grandparents who gained from Medicare and increases in Social Security, but higher 'welfare' transfers to the poor produced no gain for them." This explanation for opposition to welfare is intuitively plausible, and is bolstered by survey analyses showing that support for welfare is greatest among the least well off, whereas opposition increases among those with higher incomes (AuClaire 1984; Cook and Barrett 1992; Curtin and Cowan 1975; Hasenfeld and Rafferty 1989; Williamson 1974). But although this association of economic status and welfare attitudes is found consistently by survey analysts, it is often quite modest; many poor Americans nevertheless oppose welfare, while many well-off taxpayers support it, despite their apparent self-interest in cutting welfare spending.

A second widespread explanation for opposition to welfare focuses on individualism. A belief in individual effort and responsibility, and a suspicion of government, have long been viewed as essential elements of American political culture (de Tocqueville [1835] 1969; Hartz 1955; Lipset 1979; McClosky and Zaller 1984; Williams 1956). Along with self-interest, this "culture of individualism" account of antiwelfare sentiment figures prominently in policy debates (Marmor, Mashaw, and Harvey 1990; Mead 1986). For example, Marmor, Mashaw, and Harvey (1990, p. 240) write: "Commitments to individual and family autonomy, market allocation of most goods and services, and limited and decentralized governance . . . tell us much about why we have the welfare state arrangements we do and about the probable direction of future developments. These commitments bound the feasible set of policy initiatives." Once again, this popular belief has received support from survey studies of public attitudes. In a nuanced study of individualism and the welfare state, Feldman and Zaller (1992) argue that individualist values constitute the most common among a variety of ideological orientations that Americans draw upon in thinking about social welfare. Feldman and Zaller's analysis is consistent with that of other researchers who have found that respondents with a greater commitment to individualist beliefs express greater opposition to welfare (Feagin 1975; Hasenfeld and Rafferty 1989; Kluegel and Smith 1986; Williamson 1974).

Explanations for poverty and perceptions of the poor constitute a third influence on public attitudes toward welfare. The key distinction among the many possible explanations for poverty is between accounts that place the blame on the poor themselves and those that attribute poverty to circumstances beyond the control of the poor. Closely related to these judgments of causal attribution for poverty are perceptions of the poor as either trying hard to overcome their situational disadvantages or lacking in thrift or effort. When past research has included measures of causal attribution, they have invariably shown strong associations with attitudes toward welfare. For example, Kluegel and Smith (1986) found explanations for poverty to be the single most important attitudinal predictors of welfare views, while Hasenfeld and Rafferty (1989) found an index of attitudes toward the work ethic of the poor to be an important influence on respondents' support for welfare.

In contrast to the attention devoted to economic self-interest, individualism, and beliefs about the poor, racial attitudes have been largely neglected in prior studies of welfare views. Most studies, including some of the most recent and ambitious analyses, have completely omitted racial attitudes from their models of welfare support (Alston and Dean 1972; AuClaire 1984; Cook and Barrett

1992; Curtin and Cowan 1975; Feagin 1975; Hasenfeld and Rafferty 1989; Williamson 1974). When racial attitudes have been examined, researchers have found that negative attitudes toward blacks are associated with greater opposition to welfare (Gilens 1995; Kluegel and Smith 1986; Sears and Citrin 1985; Smith 1987). But, as noted above, this research has failed to deal with the central difficulty that measures of racial attitudes are confounded with respondents' broader nonracial attitudes toward the poor.

The major hypothesized influences on welfare views, then, consist of economic self-interest, individualism, perceptions of the poor, and racial attitudes. But two additional factors might be thought to shape welfare attitudes, and we will need to take them into account in our analyses. First, partisan identification has long been recognized as an important influence on political policy preferences, and previous research has shown that Republicans express greater opposition to welfare than Democrats (Cook and Barrett 1992). Similarly, conservatives are more likely to oppose welfare than are liberals (Cook and Barrett 1992), so ideological self-identification is also taken into account in examining welfare views.

DATA AND MEASURES

All of the analyses reported here are based on the 1991 RPS telephone survey and its mail-back follow-up. African-American respondents are excluded from all of the analyses presented below. This is because racial attitudes clearly play different roles in shaping policy preferences among blacks and nonblacks. Consequently, separate analyses would be necessary to understand the welfare attitudes of African-Americans. (For analyses of blacks' welfare attitudes see Sigelman and Welch 1991 and Gilliam and Whitby 1989.) This chapter, then, will be based on the 2,022 nonblack respondents to the RPS.

As in previous research, economic self-interest will be measured by family income. Those with higher incomes are expected to express greater opposition to welfare, both because they are less likely to see it as a potential benefit and because they bear a disproportionate share of its costs in the form of taxes. Although commonly used as an indicator of self-interest, income is clearly not an ideal measure. First, income represents only a "snapshot" of a respondent's economic status; recent changes in income or future expectations might be more directly tied to perceptions about potential benefits from welfare or burdens from taxes. Second, income represents an objective measure of a respondent's social condition, but does not directly tap respondents' *perceptions* of the potential personal economic costs and benefits of welfare, or the likelihood that those costs or benefits will be realized. Despite these limitations, family income has been shown to be far and away the best objective measure of economic condition for the purpose of assessing welfare views (Gilens 1995) and is virtually the only such measure used in previous studies of this topic (Cook and Barrett 1992 provide the lone exception).

Individualism concerns the proper balance of individual and government responsibility, and is measured quite straightforwardly by asking whether "the government in Washington tries to do too many things that should be left up to individuals and private businesses," with responses expressed on a four-point agree/disagree scale.

To measure perceptions of the poor, respondents' scores on two questions regarding the work ethic of the poor are summed. The first question asks whether "most people who don't succeed in life are just plain lazy," with responses on a four-point agree/disagree scale. The second asks whether most poor people are poor because "they don't try hard enough to get ahead" or because "they don't get the training and education they need." Respondents who indicate that both explanations for poverty are wrong are given an intermediate score. The resulting index is rescaled to run from 0 (for those who reject the belief that poor people are lazy) to 1 (for respondents who are most blaming of the poor).[4]

Perceptions of blacks as lazy are assessed by the difference in respondents' scores on two items from a series of personal characteristics applied to African-Americans. The series is introduced as follows:

> Now I'll read a few words that people sometimes use to describe blacks. Of course, no word fits absolutely everybody, but, as I read each one, please tell me using a number from 0 to 10 how well you think it describes blacks as a group. If you think it's a very good description of most blacks, give it a 10. If you feel a word is a very inaccurate description of most blacks, give it a 0.

The measure of blacks as lazy is constructed by subtracting a respondent's score for "hard-working" from their score for "lazy" and rescaling to a 0–1 interval.[5]

Partisanship and ideological self-identification are measured with the standard seven-point scales ranging from strong Democrat to strong Republican, and from strong liberal to strong conservative. Educational attainment is measured on a six-point scale ranging from "eighth grade or lower" to "some graduate work or graduate degree"; age is measured in years; marital status is coded 1 for currently married and 0 for not currently married; and region of residence is coded 1 for the South and 0 for the non-South.[6] Like the other predictor variables, these measures are all scaled to a range of 0 to 1.

Respondents' welfare views are measured by (1) a single variable asking whether federal spending for welfare should be increased, decreased, or kept the same, and (2) a summated index of four agree/disagree questions measuring respondents' attitudes toward welfare (see table 7.1 for full text). Both of these measures are scored from −1 for the most negative views toward welfare to +1 for the most positive.

Table 7.1. Whites' Welfare Attitudes and Welfare Spending Preferences

Welfare Attitudes	Agree Strongly	Agree Somewhat	Disagree Somewhat	Disagree Strongly
When people can't support themselves, the government should help by giving them enough money to meet their basic needs.	29%	51%	16%	5%
Most people on welfare could get by without it if they really tried.	17	42	33	8
Most people on welfare would rather be working than taking money from the government.	13	41	33	13
The high cost of welfare puts too big a burden on the average taxpayer.	43	41	13	2

	Positive Attitudes	Neutral Attitudes	Negative Attitudes
Welfare Attitudes Index	35%	15%	50%

	Spend More	Keep Same	Spend Less
Welfare Spending Preference			
Suppose you had to say in making up the federal budget, would you prefer to see more spent, less spent, or the same amount of money spent on welfare as in the past?	19%	31%	49%

FINDINGS

Whites' Welfare Views

Whites' ambivalence toward welfare can be seen clearly in table 7.1, which shows both strong support for the *principle* of welfare (that is, for direct government payments to poor individuals or families) and high levels of cynicism toward current welfare recipients, as well as a clear belief that too much money is being spent on welfare. The first question in the table shows whites' overwhelming support for welfare in principle. Fully 80 percent of white respondents agree that "when people can't support themselves, the government should help by giving them enough money to meet their basic needs." But these same respondents believe that many, or even most, current welfare recipients could manage without government help. Fifty-nine percent agree that "most people on welfare could get by without it if they really tried."

This cynical view of welfare recipients is balanced somewhat by the more positive belief (subscribed to by 54 percent of whites) that "most people on welfare would rather be working than taking money from the government."[7] Finally, 84 percent of white respondents express concern over welfare's financial costs, agreeing that "the high cost of welfare puts too big a burden on the average taxpayer." When the four welfare attitude questions are combined into a welfare attitudes index,[8] we find that 15 percent of the white respondents express "neutral" attitudes, by agreeing (or disagreeing) equally with the negative and positive questions about welfare. Thirty-five percent of whites express positive welfare attitudes on balance, while 50 percent hold negative attitudes.

A similar distribution of attitudes is found with regard to welfare spending preferences. In this case, 49 percent of whites express negative attitudes, preferring to cut welfare spending. In contrast, only 19 percent think welfare spending should be increased, with the remainder (31 percent) preferring to keep spending at its current level.

In sum, we see a pattern of responses consistent with the notion that white Americans view the poor as being composed of two distinct groups: the "deserving poor" and the "undeserving poor" (Katz 1989). This perspective suggests that help should be provided for the truly needy, but that most current welfare beneficiaries are not, in fact, truly needy. Instead, most welfare recipients could get along without welfare if they really tried and should therefore be counted among the undeserving poor. Consequently, the welfare roles are filled with freeloaders who should be cut off from aid, thereby lifting the undue financial burden from taxpayers.

To what extent does this cynicism toward welfare recipients and desire to trim the welfare roles stem from whites' perception that blacks in particular (who compose a disproportionate share of welfare recipients) fall primarily into the category of the undeserving poor? Or are these attitudes rooted in middle-class whites' concern with their own economic self-interest, in their genuine commitment to individual effort and responsibility, or in broader nonracial perceptions of the poor in general?

Sources of Welfare Opposition

To understand the sources of white opposition to welfare, we need to assess the separate and independent effects of each influence on welfare views. In statistical terms, we need to estimate the impact of each variable while "controlling for" the other predictors of whites' welfare attitudes. This is accomplished with OLS regression. Table 7.2 displays the regression results for both welfare spending preferences and the welfare attitudes index. The unstandardized regression coefficients (the b's in table 7.2) indicate the predicted change in respondents' welfare spending preferences or welfare attitudes associated with a one-unit change in the predictor variable. For example, −.73 in the top left of the table indicates that a one-unit change in perceptions of blacks as lazy (the difference between respondents who most strongly reject this stereotype and those who most strongly accept it) is associated with a .73-unit decrease in support for welfare spending (on the −1–+1 scale). Also reported are the associated standardized regression coefficients (or betas) that provide similar information but measure the association between welfare views and each of the predictor variables in standard deviations.[9]

As table 7.2 shows, the perception of blacks as lazy is the strongest predictor of both whites' welfare spending preferences and their scores on the welfare attitudes index. Whites who fully accept the stereotype of blacks as lazy have predicted scores on welfare spending that are .73 units lower than whites who fully reject this stereotype. This same difference in racial attitudes is associated with a .54-unit change in score on the welfare attitudes index. Since both measures of welfare views are scored on a two-point scale (from −1 to +1), these coefficients indicate quite a substantial impact.

After perceptions of blacks as lazy, the strongest association with welfare views is the perception that poor people are lazy. White respondents who most strongly subscribe to this explanation for poverty express more negative views of welfare, scoring .44 units lower on welfare spending preferences, and .33 units lower on the welfare attitudes index.

Table 7.2. Regression Analysis of Whites' Welfare Spending Preferences and Welfare Attitudes

	Welfare Spending			Welfare Attitudes Index		
	b	s.e. of b	Beta	b	s.e. of b	Beta
Blacks Are Lazy	-.73	.13	-.17***	-.54	.06	.27***
Poor People Are Lazy	-.44	.10	-.14***	-.33	.04	-.22***
Individualism	-.27	.08	-.10**	-.22	.04	-.17***
Family Income	-.25	.09	-.10**	.00	.04	.00
Age	-.28	.11	-.08*	.09	.05	.05
Party Identification (high = Democrat)	.18	.05	.11***	.04	.02	.06
Married (1 = yes, 0 = no)	-.13	.05	-.08*	-.06	.02	-.08**
Ideology (high = liberal)	.07	.06	.04	.07	.03	.07*
Education	.05	.11	.01	.10	.05	.06*
Region (1 = South, 0 = non-South)	-.01	.06	.00	.04	.03	.04
R^2	.13			.24		
N	988			983		

*$p < .05$; **$p < .01$; ***$p < .001$

Note: b is the unstandardized regression coefficient; s.e. of b is the standard error of the regression coefficient; beta is the standardized regression coefficient. All independent variables are recorded to a 0–1 range. Welfare spending indicates respondents' preferences for increasing, maintaining, or decreasing spending on welfare, scored +1, 0, and -1, respectively. The welfare attitudes index is comprised of four variables measuring respondents' attitudes toward welfare (see table 7.1 for question wording), with the index scored from -1 for the most negative to +1 for the most positive attitudes.

The third hypothesized influence on welfare views—individualism—is also related to both welfare spending preferences and the welfare attitudes index, although less strongly than are perceptions of blacks and of the poor. White respondents who strongly agree that the government "tries to do too many things that should be left up to individuals and private business" score .27 units lower on welfare spending preferences and .22 units lower on the welfare attitudes index.

Table 7.2 also shows that family income, our indicator of economic self-interest, is related to welfare spending preferences (with a coefficient of -.25) but not to the welfare attitudes index (b = .00). This difference supports the validity of income as an indicator of economic self-interest, as it appears that whites with higher incomes (and therefore higher taxes) do not hold more negative views of welfare or welfare recipients, but are nevertheless less likely to favor welfare spending. Even with regard to welfare spending, however, the impact of family income is rather modest: a difference of $60,000 in income (between the lowest and the highest categories) is associated with a .25-unit difference on the two-point welfare spending scale (scored from −1 to +1).

In addition to these four influences on welfare views, table 7.2 shows that opposition to welfare spending is higher among older white respondents, but that age is unrelated to the welfare attitudes index. Repeating the pattern found for family income, this difference suggests that age influences welfare policy preferences not because older white respondents hold different attitudes toward those on welfare, but because they see their self-interest as better served by cutting welfare spending. Perhaps this should not be surprising, since welfare programs are most closely associated with young families and the most prominent welfare program, AFDC, is restricted to families with dependent children. In contrast, programs that direct more of their resources to the elderly, including means-tested programs such as Medicaid or Supplemental Security Income (SSI), are not often thought of as "welfare."

The remaining predictor variables in table 7.2 show weak-to-moderate relationships with the welfare measures. White Democrats are more likely than Republicans to support welfare spending, while married respondents express greater opposition than those not married. Opposition to welfare as measured by the welfare attitudes index is also higher among married whites, while liberals and those with higher education are more supportive than their conservative or less-educated counterparts.

Most of the predictors in table 7.2 show some relationship to white Americans' welfare views, but only beliefs about the character of blacks and of poor people and respondents' general preferences for individual versus government responsibility have strong and consistent influences on both measures of welfare. Of these, perceptions of blacks as lazy emerge as the single most powerful predictor of white Americans' welfare views. These results suggest that the popular belief that welfare is a "race-coded" issue is warranted; whatever other reasons whites may have for opposing welfare, their negative views of blacks appear to constitute an important factor in generating that opposition.

It is, perhaps, no great shock to find that the belief that blacks are lazy can generate opposition to welfare among whites. But two things must be kept in mind to fully appreciate the importance of this finding. First, it is not just poor blacks, or blacks on welfare, who were asked about; instead respondents were instructed to indicate how well "lazy" and "hard-working" describe *most blacks*. This suggests that not only are whites' evaluations of welfare steeped in racial considerations, but that these considerations appear to involve little distinction between the minority of blacks who receive welfare and the majority who do not.

The second thing we must keep in mind is that the impact of racial views on welfare support is even stronger than the impact of views about the poor in general. Remarkably, whites' perceptions of blacks as lazy are more important in shaping opposition to welfare than their perceptions of poor people as lazy. Once again, this suggests that the welfare debate has become so thoroughly racialized that what matters most to the white public is perceptions of a single subgroup of welfare recipients—blacks. Although only 36 percent percent of current welfare recipients are black (U.S. House of Representatives 1996, p. 474), beliefs about blacks appear to dominate whites' thinking when it comes to evaluating welfare.

Measuring Racial Attitudes
with a Survey-Based Experiment

One difficulty in analyzing the influences on Americans' welfare views is that attitudes toward blacks are confounded with attitudes toward the poor. In the analyses presented above, I attempted to deal with this problem by using OLS regression to statistically "hold constant" attitudes toward the poor (along with all the other variables in the model) in order to estimate the independent impact of respondents' racial attitudes. (Similarly, of course, racial attitudes, along with the other predictor variables, were held constant when estimating the impact of attitudes toward the poor.) This is the standard technique for dealing with correlated predictors, and is clearly an important improvement over models of welfare views that include only racial attitudes or attitudes toward the poor but not both. Nevertheless, OLS regression and related statistical models are necessarily imperfect solutions to this problem.

In the analyses in table 7.2, perceptions of the work ethic of blacks and of the poor are not assessed with identical questions. Perceptions of blacks were ascertained by asking respondents to rate the applicability of "lazy" and "hardworking" to "most blacks," while perceptions of the poor were measured by questions asking whether "most people who don't succeed in life are just plain lazy," and whether most poor people are poor because "they don't try hard enough to get ahead" or because "they don't get the training and education they need."

Although these questions appear to be valid measures of perceptions of blacks and of the poor, we would prefer to have strictly identical measures to assess their importance in shaping welfare attitudes. Without parallel questions, we cannot be sure that our survey measures are serving as adequate statistical controls for each other. For example, if the measure of racial perceptions is a more reliable measure than the index of perceptions of the poor, or if it better taps the particular attitudinal dimension relevant to welfare views, than racial attitudes may appear to have more explanatory power than perceptions of the poor. Without parallel questions, we cannot be sure that we have successfully "purged" the measure of racial attitudes of its nonracial components, nor can we be sure that the estimated impact of attitudes toward the poor does not still reflect respondents' racial perceptions, despite our inclusion of the racial attitudes measure in the regression model.

Unfortunately, we cannot simply ask respondents to evaluate both blacks and poor people using the same questions, due to the social desirability and consistency pressures that operate within the interview setting (Schuman and Presser 1981). Because social norms of equality apply to racial issues, respondents may feel pressured to provide the same responses to questions about blacks and about whites. Thus if white respondents acknowledge their belief that black welfare recipients are lazy, they face pressure to say that white welfare recipients are lazy as well, if asked on a subsequent question. Alternatively, if they first indicate that whites on welfare would prefer to be working, they might feel pressured to respond that African-American welfare recipients would rather be working too.

In order to gauge white respondents' true views of poor blacks and poor whites with identical questions, I use an experimental manipulation in which half the respondents are asked only about blacks and the other half are asked

otherwise identical questions which refer instead to whites. Because each respondent is asked only about one racial group, consistency pressures are absent.
Thus, rather than compare two questions (or sets of questions) asked of the
same respondent, I compare the answers given by two different groups of
respondents. But because respondents are randomly assigned to the "black" or
"white" versions of these questions, the two groups can be assumed to be
identical in every way, within the limits of sampling error.

This technique combines the advantages of the randomized experiment with
those of the sample survey (see Piazza, Sniderman, and Tetlock 1989). By
randomly assigning respondents to different question "treatments" we ensure
that differences in responses result from differences in the questions asked, and
since the random assignment is uncorrelated with respondents' characteristics
we need not worry that differences in responses to poor blacks and poor whites
are confounded with other factors such as education, region, or political attitudes. By embedding this experiment within a large-scale national survey, we
also retain the ability to generalize to the American population at large, an
ability that is severely limited in the typical small-scale experiment.

By means of a "survey experiment" we can reveal something of the thought
process or judgmental heuristic (Sniderman, Brody, and Tetlock 1991) that
respondents use in evaluating welfare. When white Americans assess welfare in
general, or identify their preferences with regard to welfare spending, are they
thinking more about black welfare recipients, white welfare recipients, or both
equally?

In the "welfare mother" experiment respondents are asked their impressions
of a welfare recipient described as either a black or white woman in her early
thirties, who has a ten-year-old child and has been on welfare for the past
year.[10] Respondents are asked first how likely it is that the woman described
will try hard to find a job, and second, how likely it is that she will have more
children in order to get a bigger welfare check. Half of the respondents are
randomly assigned to the "black version" of the question and the other half to
the "white version." For this analysis, the responses to the questions about jobs
and children are combined into an index of welfare mother stereotypes,[11] with
those saying it is very unlikely that the welfare mother will look for a job and
very likely that she will have more children receiving the highest scores.

If respondents are thinking more about black welfare mothers when they
offer their overall views of welfare, then we would expect the black version of
the welfare mother experiment to be more strongly related to welfare views than
the white version. Most important, because the two versions of these questions

are identical except for the race of the hypothetical welfare mother, and because respondents were randomly assigned to one version of the questions or the other, we can feel certain that if the two versions differ in their ability to predict whites' welfare views, this difference reflects the influence of respondents' racial attitudes.

To assess the relative importance of black and white welfare mother stereotypes I repeat the regression analyses of table 7.2, using responses to the black and white versions of the welfare mother experiment in place of the measures of attitudes toward blacks and toward the poor. Because different groups of respondents were asked the black and white versions of the welfare mother questions, separate analyses are conducted for each of the two experimental groups.[12] Tables 7.3a–c show the results of these analyses in predicting whites' welfare spending preferences, their scores on the welfare attitudes index, and their perceptions of the poor as lazy (using the same index that was used as a predictor variable in table 7.2).

The results of each of these analyses, based on the three different aspects of attitudes toward welfare and poverty, are the same: whites' perceptions of black welfare recipients are clearly more important predictors than their perceptions of white welfare recipients. Table 7.3a shows that the black version of the welfare mother experiment predicts whites' welfare spending preferences at −.55, while the white version produces an analogous coefficient of −.32. With regard to the welfare attitudes index, the black version of these questions again proves to be the better predictor, with a coefficient of −.49 compared with −.28 for the white version. Finally, if we use these same questions to predict respondents' perceptions of the poor as lazy, we find that once again whites' attitudes toward the poor are dominated by their views of poor blacks, not poor whites. In this case the black version of the welfare mother experiment produces a coefficient of .36, compared to only .14 for the white version. This last finding confirms the suspicion that the ostensibly race-neutral question about the work ethic of the poor, which was used as a predictor in table 7.2, is not race-neutral at all, but is in fact *primarily* reflective of respondents' perceptions of poor blacks.

The results of the welfare mother experiment are unambiguous. Whites' perceptions of black welfare mothers are consistently better predictors of their overall views on welfare and poverty than their perceptions of white welfare mothers. For the three attitudinal measures used in tables 7.3a–c, the black version of the welfare mother questions outperforms the white version by factors of 1.7, 1.8, and 2.6 (each of the black/white comparisons is statistically significant at the .05 level).[13]

Table 7.3A. Whites' Welfare Spending Preferences as Predicted by Perceptions of Black and White Welfare Mothers

	Using Black Welfare Mother Questions			Using White Welfare Mother Questions		
	b	s.e. of b	Beta	b	s.e. of b	Beta
Negative Perceptions of Black or White Welfare Mother	−.55	.10	−.18***	−.32	.10	−.11**
Individualism	−.21	.09	−.07*	−.22	.09	−.08*
Family Income	−.24	.09	−.09**	−.24	.09	−.09**
Age	−.24	.12	−.07*	−.24	.12	−.07*
Party Identification (high = Democrat)	.19	.05	.12***	.17	.05	.11**
Married (1 = yes, 0 = no)	−.10	.05	−.06	−.11	.05	−.07*
Ideology (high = liberal)	.11	.06	.06	.13	.06	.07*
Education	.16	.11	.05	.16	.11	.05
Region (1 = South, 0 = non-South)	−.02	.06	−.01	−.05	.06	−.03
R^2	.09			.07		
N	944			942		

*$p < .05$; **$p < .01$; ***$p < .001$

Note: b is the unstandardized regression coefficient; s.e. of b is the standard error of the regression coefficient; beta is the standardized regression coefficient. All independent variables are recoded to a 0–1 range. Welfare spending indicates respondents' preferences for increasing, maintaining, or decreasing spending on welfare, scored +1, 0, and −1, respectively. See n. 12 for metholodological details.

Table 7.3B. Whites' Welfare Attitudes as Predicted by Perceptions of Black and White Welfare Mothers

	Using Black Welfare Mother Questions			Using White Welfare Mother Questions		
	b	s.e. of b	Beta	b	s.e. of b	Beta
Negative Perceptions of Black or White Welfare Mother	−.49	.06	−.34***	−.28	.06	−.20**
Individualism	−.21	.05	−.17***	−.22	.05	−.18***
Family Income	−.03	.05	−.02	−.04	.06	−.03
Age	.07	.07	.04	.08	.07	.05
Party Identification (high = Democrat)	.09	.03	.12**	.06	.03	.08*
Married (1 = yes, 0 = no)	−.06	.03	−.08	−.06	.03	−.08
Ideology (high = liberal)	.08	.04	.09*	.10	.04	.11*
Education	.15	.07	.09*	.15	.07	.09*
Region (1 = South, 0 = non-South)	−.02	.04	−.02	−.06	.04	−.06
R^2	.22			.14		
N	529			539		

*$p < .05$; **$p < .01$; ***$p < .001$

Note: b is the unstandardized regression coefficient; s.e. of b is the standard error of the regression coefficient; beta is the standardized regression coefficient. All independent variables are recoded to a 0–1 range. The welfare attitudes index is comprised of four variables measuring respondents' attitudes toward welfare (see table 7.1 for question wording), with the index scored from −1 for the most negative to +1 for the most positive attitudes. See n. 12 for methodological details.

Table 7.3C. Whites' Perceptions of the Poor as Lazy as Predicted by Perceptions of Black and White Welfare Mothers

	Using Black Welfare Mother Questions			Using White Welfare Mother Questions		
	b	s.e. of b	Beta	b	s.e. of b	Beta
Negative Perceptions of Black or White Welfare Mother	.36	.08	.19***	.14	.08	.07
Individualism	.19	.07	.11**	.21	.08	.12**
Family Income	.14	.08	.08	.14	.08	.09
Age	-.09	.10	-.05	-.10	.10	-.04
Party Identification (high = Democrat)	-.08	.04	-.08	-.07	.04	-.06
Married (1 = yes, 0 = no)	-.01	.05	-.01	-.01	.05	-.01
Ideology (high = liberal)	-.08	.05	-.07	-.10	.05	-.08
Education	-.14	.09	-.07	-.16	.10	-.08
Region (1 = South, 0 = non-South)	-.06	.05	-.05	-.04	.05	-.03
R^2	.08			.05		
N	538			545		

*$p < .05$; **$p < .01$; ***$p < .001$

Note: b is the unstandardized regression coefficient; s.e. of b is the standard error of the regression coefficient; beta is the standardized regression coefficient. All independent variables are recoded to a 0–1 range. Perceptions of the poor as lazy are measured by an additive index of two variables and scored to −1 (for the strongest disagreement that the poor are lazy) to +1 (for strongest agreement). See text for index construction and n. 12 for methodological details.

Clearly, perceptions of black welfare recipients play a different, and more important, role in shaping white Americans' thinking about poverty and welfare than do perceptions of white welfare recipients. Do white Americans also hold more negative views of black welfare recipients? The welfare mother experiment is of only limited value in answering this question, because the black and white welfare mothers are described identically and in considerable detail. Both the black and white welfare recipients are described as being in their early thirties, with one child, and as having been on welfare for the past year. In contrast, respondents may hold rather different impressions of the "average" black and white welfare recipients, thinking, for example, that black welfare recipients are younger, have more children, or have been on welfare for longer. Thus the degree of positive or negative response to these hypothetical welfare mothers can tell us only how white respondents view *similarly described* black and white welfare mothers, not how they view what they regard as "typical" black and white welfare recipients.

With this limitation in mind, table 7.4 shows that white respondents do not seem to apply a racial double standard; black and white welfare mothers—when similarly described—elicit similar levels of positive and negative imagery from the white public. As the bottom panel of table 7.4 indicates, 39 percent of white respondents offered negative reactions to both questions about the hypothetical white welfare mother, while a nearly identical 38 percent offered negative reactions to both questions about the black welfare mother.[14] Similarly, 22 percent of whites had positive reactions to both questions when the hypothetical welfare mother was black, while 25 percent offered positive reactions to both questions in response to a white welfare mother.

The Salience of Negative Racial Stereotypes

Both the traditional regression model shown in table 7.2 and the results of the survey experiment reported in table 7.3 show that white Americans' welfare views are clearly not "race-neutral" expressions of their economic self-interest, their commitment to individualism, or their evaluations of poor people. Instead, whites' views are, to a remarkable degree, rooted in their perceptions of blacks in general and of black welfare recipients in particular.

The racial character of whites' response to ostensibly race-neutral welfare programs is significant in itself. But the most pressing question is whether the racialized nature of whites' thinking about welfare results in decreased levels of support. It might appear from the similar responses to the black and white welfare mothers shown in table 7.4 that this is not the case. After all, if whites'

Table 7.4. Whites' Perceptions of Black and White Welfare Mothers

	Black Welfare Mother	White Welfare Mother
How likely do you think it is that she [the black or white wefare mother] will really try hard to find a job?		
Very likely	13%	14%
Somewhat likely	40	40
Somewhat unlikely	30	30
Very unlikely	17	17
How likley is it that she will have more children in order to get a bigger welfare check?		
Very likely	28	23
Somewhat likely	42	43
Somewhat unlikely	21	23
Very likely	8	11
Negative perceptions on both questions	39	38
Mixed perceptions	40	36
Positive perceptions on both questions	22	25

Notes: For the job question, $N = 960$ cases each for the black and white welfare mother versions; for the children question, $N = 951$ cases for the black welfare mother version and 950 cases for the white welfare mother version. "Negative perceptions on both questions" includes respondents who said the welfare mother was very or somewhat unlikely to look for a job and very or somewhat likely to have more children. "Positive perceptions on both questions" includes respondents who said the welfare mother was very or somewhat likely to look for a job and very or somewhat unlikely to have more children.

views of white welfare mothers are no more positive than their views of black welfare mothers, it might appear not to matter that whites' welfare views are dominated by their perceptions of blacks.

But the similarity of whites' evaluations of black and white welfare mothers does not mean that racial considerations do not impact support for welfare, because the *consequences* of holding negative beliefs about black and white welfare mothers are not the same. Figure 7.1 shows that, as expected, respondents with positive perceptions of welfare mothers express greater support for welfare than those with negative views. But there is a racial asymmetry apparent in this figure. The welfare attitudes of white respondents with positive perceptions of white welfare mothers are the same as those with positive perceptions of black welfare mothers (.10 versus .09, a statistically nonsignificant difference), and the welfare attitudes of those with neutral views of white and black welfare

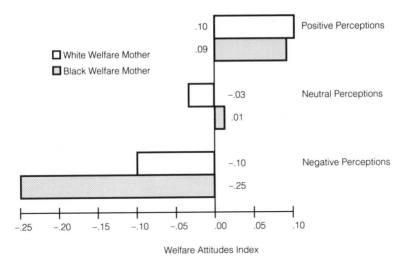

Note: The welfare attitudes index is scored from −1 for the most negative to +1 for
the most positive attitudes toward welfare. See text and table 7.1 for question wording,
and table 7.4 for the coding of perceptions of welfare mothers.

Figure 7.1 Whites' Welfare Attitudes, by Perceptions of Black and White Welfare
Mothers

mothers are the same (−.03 versus .01, also statistically nonsignificant). However, the consequence of holding negative perceptions depends on whether the
perceptions are of white welfare recipients or of black white welfare recipients.
Negative perceptions of black welfare mothers are associated with significantly
more negative views of welfare in general than are negative perceptions of white
welfare mothers (−.25 versus −.10, statistically significant at $p < .0002$).

We saw in tables 7.2 and 7.3 that racial attitudes figure prominently in
whites' evaluations of welfare and that perceptions of black welfare mothers are
stronger influences on whites' welfare views than perceptions of white welfare
mothers. Figure 7.1 reveals just why this is so. The greater power of perceptions
of black welfare mothers to shape white respondents' welfare views comes from
the particular salience of *negative* images of blacks. Positive images of black or
white welfare mothers are associated with mildly positive scores on the welfare
attitudes index, while neutral perceptions of black or white welfare mothers are
associated with neutral scores. Negative perceptions of *white* welfare mothers
also show a modest impact on welfare attitudes, but negative perceptions of
black welfare mothers have a dramatically stronger impact on whites' welfare
views. For many whites, the image of a black welfare mother has become a

"condensation symbol" (Edelman 1985) of what is wrong with America's welfare system, and, indeed, of what is wrong with American blacks.

CONCLUSIONS

In this chapter I have explored one aspect of the claim that race-neutral anti-poverty policies can be expected to garner greater political support because they are less vulnerable to racial politics. Focusing on welfare—a prominent component of current antipoverty programs—I examined the role of racial attitudes in shaping policy preferences and overall support among white Americans. Both conventional modeling techniques and a survey-based randomized experiment showed that whites' responses to welfare, and their thinking about the poor in general, strongly reflect their views of blacks. First, using a traditional regression model, I compared the predictive power of economic self-interest, attitudes toward individualism, beliefs about the poor in general, and perceptions of blacks as lazy, and found the last of these to be the most important influence on whites' welfare spending preferences and their attitudes toward welfare. Then, using a randomized experiment to disentangle respondents' attitudes toward poor blacks and poor whites, I confirmed the importance of the specifically racial elements of white Americans' thinking about welfare and poverty, showing that whites' perceptions of black welfare recipients are considerably more important than their perceptions of white welfare recipients in shaping their views on welfare and their perceptions of the work ethic of the poor. Finally, I showed that negative images of black welfare mothers have a particularly strong impact on whites' attitudes toward welfare, far exceeding the influence of negative images of white welfare mothers, as well as the influence of positive images of either black or white welfare recipients.

Although blacks constitute barely one out of three welfare families,[15] perceptions of black welfare mothers—especially negative perceptions—appear to dominate whites' evaluations of welfare recipients and their preferences with regard to welfare spending. This negative "racialization" of welfare calls into question the "hidden agenda" strategy for fighting racial inequality. It is clear that simply making benefits available to all poor Americans is not enough to divorce antipoverty programs from racial politics; as this chapter has shown, even race-neutral antipoverty policies can fall prey to racial stereotyping.

To the extent that antipoverty programs become associated with African-Americans, and in particular to the extent to that such programs evoke the public's negative stereotypes of blacks, support among whites will remain limited. Welfare seems especially susceptible to just this kind of negative racial politics. First, welfare has become strongly associated with blacks, so much so that many now consider welfare to be a "code word" for race (Edsall and Edsall 1991; Jamieson 1992). Just as important, welfare evokes precisely the kinds of negative stereotypes that still afflict African-Americans.

Over the past few decades, whites' racial attitudes have become markedly more sympathetic along many dimensions (Carmines and Champagne 1990; Schuman, Steeh, and Bobo 1985). Nevertheless, negative stereotypes of blacks remain widespread, and the belief that blacks lack commitment to the work ethic appears to be an especially widespread perception among white Americans. When the General Social Survey asked respondents to rate blacks and whites with regard to six different social characteristics, blacks were viewed more negatively on each one (Davis and Smith 1994). White respondents perceived blacks to be more violent, less patriotic, less intelligent, poorer, lazier, and more likely to prefer living off welfare rather than to be self-supporting. Of the six characteristics, however, the preference for welfare over self-support elicited by far the largest difference between the qualities attributed to blacks and those attributed to whites. Using a seven-point scale in which one side indicates that the group being evaluated prefers to live off welfare and the other side indicates the group prefers to be self-supporting, 74 percent of white respondents placed whites as a group on the "self-supporting" side of the scale, but only 13 percent placed blacks on this side of the scale.

As long as African-Americans make up a disproportionate share of the poor it is unlikely that antipoverty policy can be fully divorced from racial politics (and this separation is made all the more unlikely by the public's exaggerated perception that blacks constitute the majority of the poor). However, whites' race-based opposition to antipoverty programs is not rooted in a general antipathy toward blacks, but rather in the more specific belief that many African-Americans lack commitment to the work ethic. In the analysis in this chapter, the perception of blacks as lazy proved to be the strongest predictor of whites' welfare views, and in previous research comparing many dimensions of racial attitudes, the perception that blacks lack commitment to the work ethic emerged as the most powerful influence on whites' thinking about welfare (Gilens 1995).

If white opposition to antipoverty programs reflected a general antipathy toward blacks, than any program perceived to benefit primarily African-Americans would be unlikely to gain wide public support. But if the most relevant racial attitudes involved are more narrowly focused, as appears to be the case, then the vulnerability of antipoverty programs should vary, depending on the degree to which they evoke the relevant negative stereotypes of blacks. Those antipoverty programs (like welfare) that are thought to undermine the work ethic, or reward those who are too lazy or undisciplined to support themselves, should be most vulnerable to racial politics, while those that are viewed as enhancing self-sufficiency—even if strongly identified with minorities— should sustain more support among the white public.

Of existing government antipoverty programs, welfare and Food Stamps are clearly associated with blacks and consistently receive the lowest levels of public support. But other programs that are just as strongly associated with racial minorities receive much greater support from the public. For example, in one survey 67 percent of white respondents indicated that they believed the majority of food stamp recipients are racial minorities, while 80 percent of white respondents believed this to be true for public housing (Sanders 1996). Yet public housing programs are far more popular than food stamps: while only 36 percent of Americans object to cutting food stamps in order to balance the federal budget, 59 percent oppose cuts in public housing for this purpose (Times Mirror 1995). Furthermore, survey data show that some of the most popular antipoverty programs are among those most strongly associated with minorities. Both Head Start and job training programs receive overwhelming support from the public, with majorities saying that spending should be increased in both areas.[16] Yet 59 percent of whites believe that most children enrolled in Head Start classes are minorities, and 68 percent think that minorities account for most of those in job training programs (Sanders 1996).

Although antipoverty programs cannot be divorced from racial politics simply by adopting a race-neutral benefit structure, it is equally clear that a program's strong association with racial minorities does not preclude high levels of public support. Whites' racial attitudes can and do produce opposition to some antipoverty programs, despite these programs' race-neutral structure; the "hidden agenda," it appears, is not very well hidden at all. But all antipoverty programs are not equally vulnerable to the antiblack attitudes that so strongly impact whites' thinking about welfare. Programs that are seen as enhancing the ability of poor people to support themselves, rather than rewarding the lazy with government "handouts," do not evoke the same negative racial imagery. Unlike welfare, public housing can be viewed as a supplement to, not a substitute for, self-support; after all, public housing tenants pay rent for their apartments. And Head Start and job training programs can be seen as an investment in individuals which, it is hoped, will pay off by allowing them to support themselves. These programs are seen as helping people help themselves, not undermining their motive to work, and as a result are less vulnerable to the politics of racial stereotyping.

The impulse behind the "hidden agenda" is not wrong. Programs that limit their benefits to racial minorities clearly face perceptions of unfairness that income-targeted programs do not. But public perceptions of poverty are now so steeped in racial thinking that even race-neutral antipoverty programs are strongly associated with African-Americans. An effective strategy, from the standpoint of attracting popular support, is not to promote programs that will surreptitiously help blacks without the public noticing, but rather to support programs that the public will gladly endorse, knowing full well that a disproportionate share of the benefits will accrue to African-Americans. The popularity of Head Start, job training, and public housing attests to the feasibility of this agenda. The challenge now is to enlist the public, and the country's political elites, in the effort to improve and expand such programs.

NOTES

1. For statistics on the racial differences cited see, for income: U.S. Census Bureau web page (http://www.census.gov), Table P-2a, "Median Income in Current Dollars for 1970 and 1994"; for education: U.S. Census Bureau web page (http://www.census.gov), "March Current Population Survey for 1970 and 1995"; for unemployment: U.S. Bureau of the Census 1995, p. 400; for homeownership: U.S. Bureau of the Census 1995, p. 733.
2. For evidence of racial discrimination in housing see Massey and Denton 1993; for evidence of employment discrimination see Kirschenman and Neckerman 1991.
3. CBS/*New York Times* National Survey, March 1982.
4. Cronbach's alpha for the scale measuring perceptions of the work ethic of the poor is .38.
5. Cronbach's alpha for the scale measuring perceptions of blacks as lazy is .35.
6. The South is defined as Alabama, Arkansas, Florida, Georgia, Louisiana, Mississippi, North Carolina, South Carolina, Texas, and Virginia.
7. The willingness to agree to both of these apparently contradictory statements could result from the perception among some white respondents that most welfare recipients could get along without welfare, but at an even lower standard of living, and that although they would prefer to be working, they are not willing to make the financial sacrifice that leaving welfare would entail. Alternatively, acquiescence bias, or the tendency among some respondents to agree to any statement (or at least any statement about which they have mixed feelings or are unsure), could result in majority support for each of these beliefs about welfare recipients.
8. Cronbach's alpha for the four-item welfare attitudes index is .61.
9. The standard deviation is a measure of the "average" or "typical" amount of spread or variation in the distribution of a variable. Thus the standardized coefficients reflect the

amount of change in welfare attitudes associated with a typical or average amount of change in each of the predictor variables.

10. In addition, the hypothetical welfare mother is described to one random subsample as a high school graduate and to the other random subsample as a high school dropout. This experimental manipulation is orthogonal to the race of the hypothetical welfare mother, so that one-quarter of the respondents receive the "black dropout" version, one-quarter the "black graduate" version, one-quarter the "white dropout" version, and one-quarter the "white graduate" version. For the analyses in this chapter, the two educational variations are combined.

11. Cronbach's alpha for the welfare mother index is .61.

12. Randomized assignment to experimental treatment groups (in this case the black and white versions of the welfare mother experiment) is used to ensure that respondents assigned to each group are as similar as possible in every way except for the version of the welfare mother questions they are asked. But in any finite-size sample some differences between randomly constructed groups are likely to emerge. To decrease the likelihood that such randomly occurring differences between the experimental groups are responsible for the observed effects of the black and white welfare mother questions, the variance/covariance matrices of the other variables included in the analyses in tables 7.3a–c are constrained to be equal for the two experimental groups.

13. Significance levels for the differences between the regression coefficients produced by the black and white versions of the welfare mother experiment, using one-tailed tests, are .05, .007, and .03 for welfare spending preferences, welfare attitudes, and perceptions of the poor as lazy, respectively.

14. The positive views of welfare recipients expressed by many white respondents may reflect the description of the welfare mother in our experiment. She is described as being in her early thirties, having only one child who is ten years old, and having been on welfare only one year. In addition, for a random half of the respondents, the welfare mother is described as being a high school graduate (see n. 10). Therefore she does not appear to be a "chronic" welfare recipient and may have been perceived more sympathetically by respondents than would be the case for other (more typical) welfare recipients.

15. Currently 36% of families receiving AFDC are headed by African-Americans (U.S. House of Representatives 1996).

16. For example, 61% of respondents to the 1990 General Social Survey said spending for Head Start should be increased, while only 5% wanted spending for Head Start cut (Davis and Smith 1994). In another recent poll, 60% of respondents said they would be willing to pay higher taxes in order to increase spending on job training programs, compared to 37% who were not willing to pay higher taxes for this purpose (NBC News 1994).

REFERENCES

Alston, Jon P., and K. Imogene Dean. 1972. "Socioeconomic Factors Associated with Attitudes Toward Welfare Participants and the Causes of Poverty." *Social Service Review* 46:13–23.

AuClaire, Philip Arthur. 1984. "Public Attitudes Toward Social Welfare Expenditures." *Social Work* 29:139–44.

Bobo, Lawrence, and James R. Kluegel. 1993. "Opposition to Race-targeting: Self-interest, Stratification Ideology, or Racial Attitudes?" *American Sociological Review* 58:443–64.

Bobo, Lawrence and Ryan A. Smith. 1994. "Antipoverty Policy, Affirmative Action, and Racial Attitudes." In *Confronting Poverty: Prescriptions for Change*, ed. Sheldon H. Danziger, Gary D. Sandefur, and Daniel H. Weinberg. Cambridge, Mass.: Harvard University Press.

Carmines, Edward G., and Richard A. Champagne Jr. 1990. "The Changing Content of American Racial Attitudes." In *Research in Micropolitics*, vol. 3, ed. Samuel Long. Greenwich, Conn.: JAI Press.

Citrin, Jack. 1996. "Affirmative Action in the People's Court." *Public Interest* 122:39–48.

Cook, Fay Lomax, and Edith J. Barrett. 1992. *Support for the American Welfare State*. New York: Columbia University Press.

Curtin, Richard T., and Charles D. Cowan. 1975. "Public Attitudes Toward Fiscal Programs." In *1972–1973 Surveys of Consumers*, ed. Burkhard Strumpel. Ann Arbor: University of Michigan Institute for Social Research.

Davis, James Allan, and Tom W. Smith. 1994. *General Social Surveys, 1972–1994* [machine-readable data file]. Chicago: National Opinion Research Center.

Edelman, Murray. 1985. *The Symbolic Uses of Politics*. Urbana: University of Illinois Press.

Feagin, Joe R. 1975. *Subordinating the Poor: Welfare and American Beliefs*. Englewood Cliffs, N.J.: Prentice-Hall.

Feldman, Stanley, and John Zaller. 1992. "The Political Culture of Ambivalence: Ideological Responses to the Welfare State." *American Journal of Political Science* 36:268–307.

Gilens, Martin. 1995. "Racial Attitudes and Opposition to Welfare." *Journal of Politics* 57:994–1014.

Gilens, Martin, Paul M. Sniderman, and James H. Kuklinski. 1998. "Affirmative Action and the Politics of Realignment." *British Journal of Political Science* (forthcoming).

Gilliam, Franklin D., Jr. and Kenny J. Whitby. 1989. "Race, Class and Attitudes Toward Social Welfare Spending: An Ethclass Interpretation." *Social Science Quarterly* 70:88–100.

Hartz, Louis. 1955. *The Liberal Tradition in America*. San Diego, Calif.: Harcourt Brace Jovanovich.

Hasenfeld, Yeheskel, and Jane A. Rafferty. 1989. "The Determinants of Public Attitudes Toward the Welfare State." *Social Forces* 67:1027–48.

Jencks, Christopher. 1992. *Rethinking Social Policy*. Cambridge, Mass.: Harvard University Press.

Katz, Michael B. 1989. *The Undeserving Poor*. New York: Pantheon.

Kinder, Donald R., and Lynn M. Sanders. 1996. *Divided by Color: Racial Politics and Democratic Ideals in the American Republic*. Chicago: University of Chicago Press.

Kirschenman, Joleen and Kathryn M. Neckerman. 1991. "'We'd Love to Hire Them, But. .': The Meaning of Race for Employers." In *The Urban Underclass*, ed. Christopher Jencks and Paul E. Peterson. Washington, D.C.: Brookings Institution.

Kluegel, James R., and Eliot R. Smith. 1986. *Beliefs About Inequality: Americans' Views of What Is and What Ought to Be*. New York: Aldine de Gruyter.

Lipset, Seymour Martin. 1979. *The First New Nation.* New York: W. W. Norton.

Marmor, Theodore R., Jerry L. Mashaw, and Philip L. Harvey. 1990. *America's Misunderstood Welfare State.* New York: Basic Books.

Massey, Douglas S. and Nancy A. Denton. 1993. *American Apartheid: Segregation and the Making of the Underclass.* Cambridge, Mass.: Harvard University Press.

McClosky, Herbert, and John Zaller. 1984. *The American Ethos.* Cambridge, Mass.: Harvard University Press.

Mead, Lawrence M. 1986. *Beyond Entitlement.* New York: Free Press.

NBC News. 1994. NBC News/ *Wall Street Journal* Survey, conducted June 10–14.

Piazza, Thomas, Paul M. Sniderman, and Philip E. Tetlock. 1989. "Analysis of the Dynamics of Political Reasoning: A General-Purpose Computer-Assisted Methodology." In *Political Analysis,* ed. James A. Stimson. Ann Arbor: University of Michigan Press.

Sanders, Lynn M. 1996. "Racialized Interpretations of Economic Reality." Paper presented at the annual meeting of the American Political Science Association, San Francisco.

Schuman, Howard, and Stanley Presser. 1981. *Questions and Answers in Attitude Surveys.* San Diego, Calif.: Academic.

Schuman, Howard, Charlotte Steeh, and Lawrence Bobo. 1985. *Racial Attitudes in America: Trends and Interpretations.* Cambridge, Mass.: Harvard University Press.

Sears, David O. and Jack Citrin. 1985. *Tax Revolt.* Cambridge, Mass.: Harvard University Press.

Sigelman, Lee, and Susan Welch. 1991. *Black Americans' Views of Racial Inequality.* Cambridge: Cambridge University Press.

Skocpol, Theda. 1990. "Sustainable Social Policy: Fighting Poverty Without Poverty Programs." *American Prospect* 2:58–70.

———. 1991. "Targeting Within Universalism." In *The Urban Underclass,* ed. Christopher Jencks and Paul E. Peterson. Washington, D.C.: Brookings Institution.

Smith, Tom W. 1987. "That Which We Call Welfare by Any Other Name Would Smell Sweeter: An Analysis of the Impact of Question Wording on Response Patterns." *Public Opinion Quarterly* 51:75–83.

Sniderman, Paul M., Richard A. Brody, and Philip E. Tetlock. 1991. *Reasoning and Choice: Explorations in Political Psychology.* Cambridge: Cambridge University Press.

Steeh, Charlotte, and Maria Krysan. 1996. "Trends: Affirmative Action and the Public, 1970–1995." *Public Opinion Quarterly* 60:128–58.

Times Mirror. 1995. Times Mirror Company Survey, conducted Aug. 17.

Tocqueville, Alexis de. 1969 [1835]. *Democracy in America.* Trans. George Lawrence. Garden City, N.Y.: Anchor.

U.S. Bureau of the Census. 1995. *Statistical Abstract of the United States: 1992.* Washington, D.C.: U.S. Government Printing Office.

U.S. Bureau of the Census. 1996. "Historical Poverty Tables—Table 14." Available online at http://www.census.gov/hhes/poverty/histpov/hstpov14.html.

U.S. House of Representatives. 1996. *Background Material and Data on Programs Within the Jurisdiction of the Committee on Ways and Means.* Washington, D.C.: U.S. Government Printing Office.

Williams, Robin M. 1956. *American Society.* New York: Alfred A. Knopf.

Williamson, John B. 1974. "Beliefs About the Motivation of the Poor and Attitudes Toward Poverty Policy." *Social Problems* 21:634–48.

Wilson, William Julius. 1987. *The Truly Disadvantaged.* Chicago: University of Chicago Press.

———. 1990. "Race-neutral Programs and the Democratic Coalition." *American Prospect* 1:74–81.

———. 1991. "Public Policy Research and *The Truly Disadvantaged.*" In *The Urban Underclass,* ed. Christopher Jencks and Paul E. Peterson. Washington, D.C.: Brookings Institution.

Chapter 8 In Their Own Words: Citizens' Explanations of Inequality Between the Races

Kathleen Knight

Racial inequality is generally acknowledged to be a central issue in modern American political life. Although progress in removing barriers to equality between blacks and whites cannot be denied, there are still great areas of inequality. Policy proposals, as prospective solutions to problems about which the government should concern itself, carry implicit assumptions about how the problem came about. Assumptions about the cause of a problem define the range of response options considered (Snyder and Paige 1958; Tversky and Kahneman 1974), and, indeed, the suitability of any government intervention (Schattschneider 1960). Thus, as Sniderman, Piazza, and Harvey argue in Chapter 2, asking respondents *why* "the average black American is worse off than the average white" provides an opportunity to explore public perceptions of causality in a way which can shed further light on opinion about a whole range of racial issues.

The Race and Politics Study (RPS) provided respondents with the opportunity to explain the reasons for racial inequality *in their own words*. In the following pages these unstructured, open-ended responses are explored in depth. The goal here is twofold: first, to provide a sense of the variety and flavor of citizens' explanations for racial inequality, and second, to examine the role of causal attributions for racial inequality in predicting policy and other racial attitudes.[1]

ATTRIBUTIONS AND INEQUALITY

Causal attribution is widely regarded as the building block of cognitive organization—the means by which individuals "make sense" out of the stimuli that are continually bombarding them from gross reality. To ask respondents to make an attribution is to ask them to summarize their understanding of how this particular part of reality functions (Heider 1958; Kahneman, Slovic, and Tversky 1982; Nisbett and Ross 1980). A considerable tradition in the study of racial attitudes is also based upon the central notion of causal attribution (Allport 1954; Pettigrew 1979; Sniderman with Hagen 1984; Sigelman and Welch 1991; Gilens 1995).

The "fundamental attribution error" is the underestimation of the contextual, or situational, factors in explaining one's own behavior, and the overestimation of individual dispositional factors in explaining the behavior of others (Heider 1944). In the American culture, this general human tendency is reinforced by the high value placed on individualism and self-reliance (Sniderman and Brody 1977; Hochschild 1981; Kluegel and Smith 1986; Feldman 1982). According to Allport, the tendency "to regard causation as something people are responsible for . . . predisposes us to prejudice. While in reality our frustrations and ills are due to impersonal causes" (Allport 1954, p. 170).

In applying this perspective to racial inequality in an earlier study, Sniderman and Hagen (1985) pointed to an ethic of self-reliance coupled with a moralistic style of thought. It is this intersection, characterized most particularly by the moralistic "propensity to convert wrongs into wrongdoing" (Sniderman 1985, p. 21), which most closely approximates Allport's (1954) definition of prejudice. If inequality is the outcome of failures in effort or will, then it is hardly up to "the taxpayer" to redress the imbalance. The internal, or dispositional, attribution relieves society of responsibility, while reaffirming the basic justice of the system (Schlozman and Verba 1979; Kluegel 1990). Further, in Allport's (1954) theory, rather than denying the value of equality, people project a norm violation onto the outgroup. Thus, punitive moralism is warranted. Subsequently, Sniderman, Brody, and Tetlock (1991) illustrated that the "desert heuristic" played a central and reciprocal role in attitude toward policies intended to promote racial equality. "Attributions for racial inequality provide people with a simple easy-to-execute heuristic for evaluating appeals for assistance" (Sniderman, et al. 1991, p. 87). A "test" is applied and, if the answer is unambiguous, the inference is compelling. Adopting the terms of *Reasoning and Choice,* the desert heuristic is a "quasi-ideology," a "scripted," or "prepackaged" attribution "drawing on stereotypes about the group in question and expressing widely shared beliefs about the causes of success or failure." (Sniderman et al. 1991, p. 87).

This theme has also been pursued at length by Sigelman and Welch (1991) in their examination of blacks' attitudes about inequality. They found, for example, black/white differences about the impact of discrimination (an external, or situational, attribution) to be most pronounced and consistent over time. Black/white attitudes about the impact of internal, or dispositional, factors like "willpower" were more similar to each other. Majorities of both races were found willing to agree that although "discrimination has unfairly held down blacks, many of the problems which blacks in this country have today are brought on by blacks themselves" (Sigelman and Welch 1991, p. 91). Kluegel and Smith (1986) pointed to a similar mix of "structuralist" and "individualist" explanations.

Recently, Gilens (1995b) identified blaming blacks for racial inequality as a major component in white racial attitudes. His more detailed analysis suggested that whites' racial attitudes play an overriding role in determining attitudes about welfare policy generally. Further, "even with a wide range of demographic and attitudinal controls, support for these [direct assistance] programs is strongly related to respondents' attribution of blame for racial inequality" (Gilens 1995, pp. 108–09). Gilens stressed, as did Wright (1976), that the significance of this relationship lies in the fact that attitudes about blacks' deservingness drive preferences for a policy that is *not* targeted toward blacks explicitly, and which, as a matter of fact, benefits more white native-born Americans than it does blacks.[2]

The most sophisticated research on causal explanations of racial inequality has been content controlled either by using multi-item scales (Sniderman and Hagen 1985; Sniderman et al. 1991; Sigelman and Welch 1991) or by experimental manipulation (Sniderman et al. 1991, 1996; Sniderman and Piazza 1993). These various efforts have yielded a good deal of insight about inequality, but they have also left some issues unresolved. Sigelman and Welch (1991) point out that Heider's theoretical assumption of unidimensionality has not been borne out by the empirical evidence. They found that dispositional and situational explanations form separate dimensions that are not highly negatively correlated. Sniderman, Brody, and Tetlock (1991) were satisfied that principal-components analysis of six items yielded a single strong dimension, although Sniderman (with Hagen 1984) has expressed objections to unidimensionality at a theoretical level.

The American National Election Studies (see Kinder and Sanders 1996), the General Social Survey (see Schuman, Steeh, and Bobo 1985), opinion polls sponsored by the media, and the Bay Area Study employed by Sniderman and Hagen (1984) carry sets of agree/disagree items designed to capture separate components of these explanations for inequality. Citizens can, and do, agree with several of the explanations in ways which may appear confused or inconsistent. On the other hand, recognizing that a problem can have multiple causes can be seen as a sign of realistic sophistication, or cognitive complexity (Tetlock 1984). Sigelman and Welch's (1991) finding that a majority of both blacks and whites agreed with an ABC News/ *Washington Post* item which mentions both discrimination and lack of effort points to a different kind of complexity.

The difficulty is that all of the explanations for racial inequality provided to survey respondents in public opinion polls are plausible, or they would not have been included in the survey to begin with. Most of the resultant patterns of responses are, likewise, plausible. Ultimately, we know a good deal about "what goes with what" in the minds of the survey analysts, but we do not know what kinds of reasons respondents might put together on their own. The modern theory of the survey opinion (Zaller and Feldman 1992) suggests that citizens will construct their explanations from a distribution of considerations (Feldman 1995). The range of the distribution of considerations will be constrained both by factors affecting the individual and by factors affecting the circumstances under which the explanations are produced (Sniderman et al. 1993; Lodge 1995).

Providing respondents with sets of agree/disagree items exerts maximum control over the circumstantial factors affecting the response. As Ginsberg (1986) points out, respondents may "strongly agree" with plausibly phrased statements that they might not think of by themselves. Objections to the question wording, reservations, and amendments offered by respondents are generally noted by interviewers but ignored by researchers. An unstructured format provides respondents greater opportunity to express more individualized (idiosyncratic) views. The strategy employed in this exercise is deliberately "in-between." It takes advantage of word processing technology to store and review citizens' verbal responses to an open-ended question. In so doing it seeks to improve upon traditional depth interviews of small nonprobability samples (Lane 1963; Hochschild 1981, 1995) by yielding data that are generalizable and compatible with quantitative analysis but still preserve the richness of natural language with all its attendant ambiguities.[3]

Posing the Question

The stimulus question read as follows: "Statistics show that the average black person in America is worse off than the average white person. What do you suppose caused this difference? (Just tell me in your own words.)"[4] The question occurred about a third of the way through a long telephone interview about race relations, which should insure that respondents were well "warmed up" by the time the open-ended question was posed, and that any racial schema they possessed should have been fully accessed (see Fiske and Taylor 1982; Lau and Sears 1986; Lodge and McGraw 1995).[5]

The range of explanations for racial inequality generally mirrors the complexity of issues concerning race in America. The complex reality of racial issues today necessarily leads to confusion and ambivalence, even exasperation, on the part of the public (Hochschild 1981, 1995). Value conflict is also evident, since sympathy toward African-Americans may coexist with conflicting preferences about the appropriate means of distributing economic value in society (Sniderman and Piazza 1993; Hochschild 1981).

The responses also provide examples of what Sniderman, Brody, and Tetlock (1991) refer to as "scripted attributions." These "pre-packaged" explanations frequently mimic political rhetoric at the elite level. Citizens may absorb these scripts[6] and reproduce them faithfully, or reorder them, or mix and match to arrive at their own unique construction, or misunderstand them entirely. However, when asked to explain apparent racial inequality in American society, respondents clearly do not "start from scratch." Nor do they uniformly parrot the last consideration they were asked about in the survey. Some respondents clearly borrowed from the framing of earlier questions, but they do not seem to do so systematically. And they go well beyond this in their efforts to explain the causes of racial inequality to some stranger on the phone.

Coding Attributions

When citizens are asked to explain the reasons for inequality between whites and African-Americans, most of them are quite willing to construct an answer. For the most part, they accept that the statement "the average black person in America is worse off that the average white person" is a realistic depiction of racial inequality. Seventy-four white respondents (4 percent of all whites) did reject the premise of the question, along with three black respondents. Another 5 percent of whites and nearly 10 percent of African-Americans responded "don't know." But by and large the survey respondents made a real effort to come to grips with this complex and enduring problem. More than 90 percent of white respondents provided some verbal explanation. This is a high level of opinionation even compared to standard fixed-format questions (see for example Sniderman and Hagen 1984), and substantially higher than open-ended evaluations of the candidates and parties in the American National Election Studies.

Verbatim responses were separated from the other RPS data and coded in isolation to prevent knowledge of demographic or other attitudinal characteristics of the respondent from contaminating the judgment. All open-ended responses were classified into one of four categories. Two of these were for attributions which could be unambiguously assigned. Unqualified *external* responses are those which made reference to situational, structural, circumstantial, or environmental reasons for inequality. Unqualified *internal* responses are those which place the blame for inequality on volitional or dispositional factors internal to individuals, or to the culture of black Americans.

Two mixed categories were provided for responses that expressed some degree of ambivalence. Ambivalent responses are by their nature ambiguous, but in order to avoid a catchall middle category the coder was required to judge whether the internal or external attribution predominated. In External/ internal (E/i) responses, references to situational factors predominated, but some kind of internal attribution was also mentioned. Internal/external (I/e) responses are those in which the dispositional elements predominated, but reference was also made to systemic elements like prejudice or discrimination. If no other means was available to decide which attribution predominated, the response was coded according to first mention.[7]

Table 8.1 provides a breakdown of the content of the attribution coding of explanations for racial inequality for both white and black respondents. Although the rest of the analysis is restricted to whites, taking a look at the way African-Americans explain inequality between the races provides one kind of baseline from which we can interpret the explanations offered by whites.[8] The lack of a black oversample means that the range of error around estimates for blacks is much larger than that for whites (roughly ±8 percent for blacks versus ±3 percent for whites).

Although just a little less than a majority of whites offered unqualified external attributions, a solid majority of blacks located the reasons for racial

Table 8.1. Open-ended Explanations for Racial Inequality, by Race

	White	Black
External/Situational, Unqualified	892	128
	(48.45%)	(63.68%)
External Predominant, Internal	254	18
Mention	(13.80%)	(8.96%)
Internal Predominant, External	156	8
Mention	(8.47%)	(3.98%)
Internal/Dispositional,	365	24
Unqualified	(19.83%)	(11.94%)
Rejects Premise of Question	74	3
	(4.02%)	(1.49%)
Don't Know/Refused	100	20
	(5.43%)	(9.95%)
Total	1,841	201
	(100.00%)	(100.00%)

inequality in societal prejudice and historic discrimination. African-American respondents were by no means unwilling to identify dispositional elements that contributed to racial inequality. Roughly 25 percent of black respondents made some mention of individual failings in effort or character that contributed to the disadvantaged position of African-Americans in modern society, including 12 percent who offered internal attributions only.

By comparison, white respondents were much more likely to attribute inequality between the races to the individual failings of black people. Thirty-two percent of whites made at least some internal attribution, and nearly 20 percent offered exclusively dispositional explanations for the continuing inequality between the races. Differences between blacks' and whites' propensities to make unqualified external attributions for the causes of racial inequality are large enough to be considered statistically significant by any reasonable criteria. Racial differences in propensity toward unqualified internal attributions are not statistically significant according to normal conservative criteria (for example, the confidence intervals around the estimates for blacks and whites overlap).

THE CONTENT OF ATTRIBUTIONS
FOR RACIAL INEQUALITY

The purpose of this exercise was not to find a more complicated, and admittedly less reliable, way of producing a measure of citizens' attributions for the causes of racial inequality. Causal attributions for racial inequality are theoretically important predictors of prejudice,[9] and have been found to exert a good deal of explanatory influence on other racial attitudes. The primary purpose of this part of the RPS enterprise was to explore citizens' explanations for racial inequality *in their own words.* The causal attribution coding scheme used here can be thought of as a device for organizing the verbatim data that follows logically from the question wordings. It also reflects an important dimension of content, but not the only one that might be considered relevant by other researchers.

The remainder of this chapter illustrates the open-ended comments in depth and then looks briefly at the consequences of causal attributions for attitudes about other policy issues. An important philosophical issue about the nature of open-ended data in survey research underlies the decision to follow a broad general coding strategy and to quote verbatim responses at length. It is simply that the richness of what randomly interviewed members of the public tell us in their own words has, for the most part, been lost in the abstraction process involved in rendering the data in numeric form. A decent respect for our respondents' efforts to explain their views requires that researchers be willing to read what the respondents actually tell us. The process of reading what the respondents say may also provide some insights about what their fixed-format responses mean, and may serve as a useful corrective to the reification of concepts in question wording.

Another "Dog that Didn't Bark"

One particular element among the explanations for racial inequality commonly offered in fixed-format items simply doesn't occur when respondents are asked to explain the reasons for racial inequality in their own words. This is the "biological inferiority" thesis. As a number of researchers who have examined trends in racial attitudes have pointed out (Schuman, Steeh, and Bobo 1985; Sniderman and Piazza 1993; Kinder and Sanders 1996), explanations for blacks' inequality that are based on notions of the inherent inferiority of the black race seem to have died out. Some respondents may still be cued by question wording to agree with statements ascribing racial inequality to innate or biological origins, but they don't seem to provide such explanations on their own.

The overall lack of biological explanations for racial inequality is important to note for two reasons. First, it is indicative of progress in white Americans' attitudes about African-Americans. Second, it is an important indication that when ideas are not "scripted" by intellectual and political elites, they do not emerge from the mass public. It is, of course, possible that the biological inferiority explanation was avoided by respondents in the RPS because it is deemed socially undesirable, but even this is progress. Some responses did indicate that blacks were judged inferior to whites, but the reasons were not rooted in biology.[10]

Unqualified Internal Attributions

Internal attributions are those which locate the causes of racial inequality in the individual dispositions of black people. Although unqualified internal attributions were offered by only a fifth of white respondents in the RPS, they deserve more than a cursory examination. This is because internal attributions constitute rationales for opposing public policy initiatives aimed at redressing inequality on the grounds that the potential recipients are undeserving. Undeservingness is a logical "stopper." In this sense it is more powerful than other arguments because once it is made, or agreed with, the implication—opposition to a policy designed to "help"—is unavoidable. To argue someone out of opposition to policies designed to help blacks, when such opposition is based on the perception of undeservingness, it is not enough to offer other reasons for supporting the policy. Instead, it is necessary to go back and change the perception of undeservingness (see Sniderman and Piazza 1993).

In addition to the logical strength of the desert heuristic, it is useful to examine unqualified internal attributions in depth because of Allport's (1954) thesis that the fundamental attribution error "predisposes us to prejudice." Racism may not be as much of a problem now as it has been in the past, but it is still an important problem. Not everyone who makes an internal attribution for the causes of racial inequality can be considered a racist. But the hypothesis that racial hostility and animosity are more likely to be found among individuals who blame blacks for racial inequality is straightforward, and worthy of examination.

The following response, from an older white man living in the mid-Atlantic region who actually called himself a liberal Democrat, is a classic example of the tendency to attribute responsibility for economic disadvantage to lack of individual effort, or lack of disposition toward self-reliance and initiative.

Ah, too lazy to get out and get a job.

(Anything else?)

Well, they're just lazy and they think more of dope and drinking than earning a living. They are all on welfare all the way, in other words.

(Anything else?)

Well, in my neighborhood, in my state, all of the state that is, the only issues I can find are that they are too lazy, and welfare takes care of them.

Economic inequality among blacks *as a group* is attributed to failings of individual character and values. The respondent's hostility is further magnified by the injustice of state support for indolence and criminality. Blacks are seen as a group to be violating the rules of the game, and taking unfair advantage of the system.

In the following explanation, offered by a seventy-one-year-old white man who identified himself as a conservative Republican, the dispositional emphasis is also clear. The negative behavior is willful, a matter of preference rather than misfortune or disability.

Lack of wanting to do something. They prefer to get by without working. I think anybody can get a job if they try hard enough.

(Anything else?)

Well, I myself work and I feel like anybody can get a job if they want to.

A sixty-two-year-old white male college graduate responded in a similar fashion:

Lack of ambition to go out and work.

(Anything else?)

No, I think that's what I think. I just feel that a lot of 'em could get a job if they wanted to go do it, rather than requesting a handout.

In each of the preceding cases, the respondent's complete answers have been presented, and these examples are quite typical of the bulk of internal-attribution responses. The explanation is unicausal. The stereotype of laziness, a personal attribute, is used to explain the economic disadvantage of blacks in general. Blacks prefer not to work. "Anybody" can get a job.

The tendency to attribute the disadvantage of a group to the personal failings of its members can also be seen in the following response, but the tone is not as punitive:

I think, uh, bad managing, managing your business wrong.

(Can you tell me a little more about that?)

When a black and white man are working on the same job, the white man will manage his money better than the black man.

(Anything else?)

Well, uh, I don't know, it's hard, yes hard, your ideas from a long way back. They never really had it.

(Repeat question.)

> Now they can't afford it but can get it, can afford a Volkswagen, but will go buy a Cadillac.
>
> (Anything else?)
>
> That's about the size of it, spending money.

Here, the personal failing is not one of ambition but of a lack of understanding, or rejection, of the value of thrift. The moralism is muted but still apparent. Blacks as individuals do not measure up; they have failed to grasp the fundamentals of the work ethic and the dynamic of capitalism. The respondent, in this case a middle-aged black man from the South who expressed no partisan or ideological identification, offered a vignette of behavior, or a "moral tale," which includes the presumption that the world is racially unbiased "when a black and white man are working on the same job."

The following, more contextualized explanation features the same themes (poverty, too many children, lack of education), but the implications are much more negative:

> Ah, they are worse off than the average one, is that what you're saying?
>
> (Yes.)
>
> I think they have a lack of incentive due to their environment. I think where they are coming from and where they are heading to looks the same to the average black.
>
> (Anything else?)
>
> I don't feel that any of it is discrimination any more, not in this area.
>
> (Anything else?)
>
> Well, I think it's the old saying, the sins of the parents fall on the children.
>
> (Sins?)
>
> I would say it would involve probably use of the welfare system.
>
> (Anything else?)
>
> I don't know, I don't think so. I know some very affluent blacks who send their children to better schools than I send mine to.

A superficial reading of this response from a younger white male high school graduate might suggest an external, or environmental, attribution. There is a sense of historical dysfunction somehow linked to the "welfare system" which deprives blacks of incentives for economic advancement. They have no initiative—"where they are coming from and where they are heading to looks the same." Still, it is the individual's failure to take advantage of opportunities that causes the aggregate inequality. Discrimination against African-Americans is *explicitly dismissed* as a cause of the current imbalance of economic outcome. Indeed, there is a mild challenge of the premise of the question—that blacks are "worse off" than whites—obtained by differentiating within the categories of black and white. The fact that there are some "very affluent blacks," certainly better off than the respondent, argues that economic rewards are not biased by race. The exception is used to further confirm the fairness of the system.

The preceding response, and the one cited directly below, highlight a sense of historic and intergenerational dysfunction. The "sins of the parents" *are* visited on the children. Not only are children not taken care of, they are produced to take advantage of the welfare system. The "scripts" reproduced by the respondents contain the themes favored by right-wing television commentators and talk show hosts. Differentiation within the category of blacks—"I don't think all of them are like that"—not only reaffirms the ultimate justice of the distribution, it also serves as a kind of disclaimer of personal prejudice.

> Gosh, I don't know, um, I really don't. I don't know just to put it in a few words. (Just give me some ideas about how you think about it now.)
>
> I think too many want something for nothing, and don't get out and try to get work. (Anything else?)
>
> Gosh, not getting enough education. I guess, I honestly think some of the parents some of the lower blacks don't take care of their children at home and don't care about where they are half the time, and it just gets out of control. I think a lot of them get babies just to get on welfare. That's how it was at one time. I don't think all of them are like that, I think a lot of them are.

Here laziness is reinforced by the perception of irresponsibility in caring for the young. The notion that women have children to obtain or increase welfare payments is a prominent part of the explanation for blacks being *worse off.*

Even if a punitive attitude toward the violation of economic norms is not regarded as racist, since it can be applied to whites as well as African-Americans, it is not comforting to realize that such attitudes are held by a *minimum* of one out of every five white Americans. And this 20 percent only counts respondents whose dispositional attributions were unqualified. An additional 22 percent of white respondents made some internal attribution as part of an ambivalent response. Even the estimate of 42 percent may be low, however, if a social desirability bias depresses respondents' willingness to blame blacks for the economic disadvantages they suffer.

Unqualified External Attributions

Respondents who make unqualified external attributions explain racial inequality in a fashion that absolves African-Americans of responsibility for their disadvantaged status. Blacks as a group are seen as victims of discrimination and prejudice. These are circumstances over which blacks have no control. The reasons for blacks' disadvantage may also be attributed to inequity in the economic system, and to a lack of opportunity to obtain education and jobs. Just a little under half of all white respondents in the Race and Politics Survey provided unqualified external attributions.

It is possible that blaming inequality between the races on prejudice, an unjust social economic system, or other factors beyond the control of individual black people might require extra cognitive effort. First, it is necessary to overcome the fundamental attribution error by seeing inequality as a result of a situation in which blacks find themselves, and which they would change if they could.[11] Making a situational attribution also requires overcoming the prevailing cultural bias in favor of individual initiative and responsibility. It might additionally be said to require a more sophisticated understanding of the quirks of chance, or an ability to put oneself in the other's place. In essence, external attributions might be said to require a "second thought" that considers the situational factors, or the broader course of history.

The following response, offered by a middle-aged southern white male with some experience in graduate school who identified himself as a moderate Democrat, provides a classic example of external attribution.

Why minorities are worse off? How it came about?

(Yes.)

Oh, me, it came about, it's an odd thing in the sense that, mm, it is because of the superior feeling of the Caucasian groups from taking over the country from minority groups and slavery. PBS has been carrying a four or five night historical series, Shelby Foote on that. [I'm] reading up on the books themselves, it's very interesting.

(Can you tell me more?)

Feeling of superiority of race and blacks were imported from other nations and felt to be inferior, and felt to be limited. How to say this, limited I don't know in capacities of life. I don't know how to say that, just in general they're an inferior race to be produced for the Caucasian people who were taking over the country. That's not my personal feeling, but you asked why that happened.

(Anything else?)

That summed it up pretty well, from the feeling of superiority, the socioeconomical barriers, no recognition of the individual or the individual mind, the capability or equality of humans.

In this response, blame for racial inequality is clearly attributed to the attitudes and behavior of white people. The respondent specifically disavows such attitudes on his own part. Further, he is able to cite public educational television programming and the name of a specific historian as his sources. Although generally not evident in such detail, this response offers another example of what Sniderman et al. (1991) call a "scripted attribution."

Attribution to the environment, or to a situation beyond the control of individual African-Americans, need not sound sophisticated or go into great detail, as the following complete response illustrates.

> I have no idea, discrimination.
>
> (Can you tell me more about that?)
>
> The Civil War, slavery, the sinful heart of man.
>
> (Anything else?)
>
> No.

This explanation by a white male college graduate clearly locates the cause of disadvantages faced by African-Americans beyond their control. It is long-standing and seems to have a certain air of inevitability.

The following respondent offers a more contextualized version of the attribution to historical, and apparently inevitable, discrimination.

> Hmm, slavery. I think it's just history at this point.
>
> (Could you go into that please?)
>
> Well, I just think we're paying for slavery now. All of us, whites and blacks. I don't know what else to say, I just know that, especially in Chicago, it's a very bigoted town, but I just think it's what we're paying for.
>
> (Anything else?)
>
> I really think that's the basis of it, if you want to go into present day things, it's so hard to start. It's the families, not that they're not important, I don't know how to tell you. I can only speak for this area, but blacks are thrown into these high-rise ghettos, with an invisible wall around them. The family isn't available for the children, it isn't supportive, and the sad part is that a lot of it isn't intentional. The mothers are doing the best that they can do, but they have to work, it's hard.
>
> (Anything else?)
>
> I think that's enough.

This respondent, a thirty-six-year-old white woman who refused to identify herself ideologically, and who called herself an independent when asked about party identification, makes her sympathy clear. She not only provides an attribution which relieves the "average black American" of responsibility for racial inequality, but specifically argues against the stereotype of laziness.

In the following response, it also seems quite clear that systemic discrimination is to blame for the economic disadvantage of blacks.

I think prejudice, prejudism.

(Anything else?)

No I just feel that, um, I don't know how to explain that the blacks are put down a lot, they're not given the same opportunity as the whites. The inner-city schools don't give them the opportunity that the white kids have. I believe that if you're born in poverty you don't have the same chance, and a lot of the black kids are.

(Can you say anything more about that?)

I just feel that, I think that birth control had a lot to do with it. I think that they just keep having kids, and more kids, and the blacks don't have a chance to break out of their environment.

(Repeat question.)

I just believe it's their poverty. I don't know of any other reason.

(Can you say anything more about poverty specifically?)

I told you they just keep having children, and the younger children keep having children, and I think there should be some kind of birth control.

(Anything else?)

No.

This explanation from a middle-aged white Republican woman who also refused ideological identification is clearly sympathetic, even seemingly anguished over the frustrating inevitability of discrimination and poverty. The respondent does not condemn blacks for their own poverty, but sees a connection between having children and poverty. The repeated reference to "birth control" might carry the implication that African-Americans do not exercise proper self-discipline with respect to sexual matters. In this sense, even if sympathetic, the explanation feeds into racial stereotypes. Nonetheless, to be true to the logic of the coding scheme, this must be regarded as an external or environmental explanation because there is no explicit statement or insinuation that the lack of "birth control" is intentional.

The fact that 48 percent of white Americans attribute the lack of material equality between the races exclusively to causes over which neither the black community nor individual African-Americans have control may be cause for some optimism that the social value of racial equality has penetrated fairly deeply into the public at large. Fully 70 percent of white respondents in the Race and Politics Study attributed at least part of the reason for racial inequality to circumstances that could not be held to be the fault of blacks. This figure is very likely a maximum, and may well be inflated by social desirability bias.

Attributions and Ambivalence

Of course, not all respondents in the Race and Politics Survey offered clear-cut dispositional or environmental attributions. In some cases, respondents were willing to talk out contending considerations. The following response is typical of the ambivalence expressed in attempting to explain the reasons for the disparate circumstances of black and white Americans.

> Well, I think, ah, they could be just about the same as the other people if they buckle down and try to get a job.
> (Anything else?)
> Well, it's, ah, let's see, their environment, and, you know, the education.
> (How did this come about in the first place?)
> I don't think they were, it's not that they didn't want to go. It's just that they were so doggone discriminated against. They didn't go to school just so that they wouldn't get in conflict, a fight, you know.
> (Anything else?)
> No.

Several strands of explanation are apparent even in this relatively compact response. Initially the respondent, a middle-aged Hispanic man who identified himself as a Republican, attributes the inequality to individual differences in efforts, implying a certain degree of trust in the fairness of the economic outcome. On probing, lack of education is identified as an additional cause of racial inequality. But this is followed by an acknowledgment of systemic prejudice, perhaps evoking images of school integration confrontations of the 1950s, where blacks who attempted to get an equal education faced the organized hostility of whites.

The implications of these alternative attributions for public policy solutions are quite different. According to the dominant ideology of individualism, if the disparity results from lack of individual effort, it is to be expected and tolerated (Kluegel and Smith 1986). It can be regarded as a just outcome—consistent with the work ethic. Even more, it is possible to regard the disadvantaged group "itself" as responsible for the outcome through willful violations of the accepted norms.

If, on the other had, the inequality results from forces that are outside the control of individual black people, or because of injustice visited on African-Americans as a group, then some degree of government intervention to redress the imbalance might be acceptable. In fact, many respondents acknowledged historic discrimination and inequality, but some also took pains to indicate that the situation has been subsequently rectified.[12] This kind of response makes up the bulk of the mixed attributions category.

The following respondent, a twenty-eight-year-old white female college graduate from the South with no partisan or ideological identification, also compares the situation today to that of the past. But she is less forgiving in her ambivalence:

> I think if they had more education they could get better jobs and that would help.
>
> (Why can't they get more education?)
>
> Um, well, the parental support, they don't get it because the parents don't have the educational background to help the children. So if they could upgrade themselves, the parents that is, then the parents could help the children further themselves.
>
> (Anything else?)
>
> Some are not as ambitious as others, some find it easier to go through the system and have it handed to them.
>
> (How do you mean they aren't ambitious?)
>
> Um, they are satisfied with the government giving them a check and they could spend it on drugs, alcohol and the children then have to do without.
>
> (Anything else?)
>
> Maybe substance abuse.
>
> (Can you tell me more about that?)
>
> Well, it's just that they feel put down, so their self-esteem is low and that will make them feel better, and that just doesn't work.
>
> (Anything else?)
>
> I think that's about it nowadays.
>
> (Were things different in the past?)
>
> In the past it would have been discrimination, but now it's not much of an issue, and it's been blown up to more than what it should be.

Several familiar themes reappear in this response. There is the linking of dependence on government "handouts" with dependence on drugs and alcohol abuse. There is the notion of intergenerational dysfunction; parents may have been deprived of education due to past discrimination, but they exacerbate the problem for their children by irresponsible behavior. Even this weakness is, to some extent, understandable because of past damage to self-esteem, but it is nonetheless a failing. Thus, although this respondent is not without sympathy, ultimately greater self-worth on the part of individual blacks will solve the inequality problem. Systemic discrimination is acknowledged but again explicitly dismissed as a problem in the current era.

A thirty-seven-year-old white woman from the South offered a similar explanation:

Educational difference.

(Anything else?)

Poverty, well, birth control, welfare—all of that adds to it. They haven't the education [or] knowledge to exercise birth control. Too many children, some in poverty, and then on welfare, and we've paid for this. I don't believe their living styles are as structured. Their morals aren't as strong.

(Anything else?)

That's probably it.

In this case, there is some evidence that the dysfunctional behavior of blacks is not regarded as necessarily willful: "They haven't the education . . . to practice birth control" and it is "too many children" that ultimately keep them in poverty. Still, "their morals aren't as strong," and the cost of the unconstrained behavior of blacks is borne by society as a whole.

The following two responses exhibit the "helplessness, anger, [and] inconsistency" that Hochschild (1981, pp. 240–41) regards as emblematic of ambivalence. The first, by a thirty-year-old white male Republican high school graduate, considers several explanations for continuing racial inequality. Discrimination is acknowledged but ultimately dismissed. African-Americans are compared to other minorities and found wanting in ambition and effort. The second example by a white woman of about the same age, but much greater educational attainments, expresses an even greater sense of intractability.

Ah, without profanity? Boy what caused that? I suppose the beginning of it started with discrimination, but a lot of it today is laziness. Well, ah, I'm trying to figure [it] out, I feel that they have same opportunities I have, went to same schools I did, but it's a matter of going out and getting it. I think they are too used to having system work for them, all the social programs, the Mexican people are as hard hit, but they are trying to work themselves out of it, also lack of education.

(How did this come about in the first place?)

Well, as to what caused it in the first place I can't speak for that. Back in '50s or '60s I went to school where I was mostly minority. I had the same teachers they had. My parents weren't rich. I really can't say why. (Pause.) Ah, I think it's environmental. Ah, how do I say this, a lot of it is opportunity, a lot is environmental. Not having desire, or ambition, or hope that they can make it on their own.

(Repeat question.)

Ah, no it all had to do with that. Probably there is income, but which came first, chicken or egg? If you don't have income to go to school, one breeds the other, and they have oppressed group behavior, horizontal violence.

This response can be read as a direct contradiction, and signaled enough confusion that the interviewer repeated the question. The respondent, however, confirmed her ambivalence and employed something that sounds like social science concepts to attribute at least part of the disadvantages faced by blacks to their own doing.

The explanations for racial inequality in the mixed categories provide particularly nice illustrations of the process hypothesized by Zaller and Feldman (1992) to underlie the survey response. Asking citizens open-ended questions gives them an opportunity to review and share the considerations that play a role in their opinions. Only 22 percent of white people in the RPS expressed ambivalence. This is less than might be expected on the basis of Hochschild's (1981) or Feldman and Zaller's (1992) studies of open-ended answers about welfare not explicitly targeted toward blacks. It is also substantially less than the majority Sigelman and Welch (1991) found to agree with a fixed-format item containing both situational and dispositional attributions for the disadvantaged position of blacks. But it is a typical theme in the open-ended responses.

EXPLAINING INEQUALITY

The question posed to the RPS interviewees is generally not considered an easy one to answer. It is in some respects surprising to find that 90 percent of the public offered an explanation. It must, however, be granted that respondents had been thoroughly stimulated to think about racial issues by the time they were offered a chance to reply in their own words. Only about a fifth of white Americans responded to the question with ambivalence, and reading these responses in detail makes clear that apparently contradictory considerations are not signs of confusion or inattention. Another fifth of the sample attributed the inequality between the races to lack of effort, or will, on the part of black people.

Nearly half of the RPS sample attributed the inequality between blacks and whites to factors which African-Americans could not be expected to overcome as individuals. Given the fundamental attribution error, the individualistic biases in the culture, and even the weight of ideological rhetoric in the recent past (see Feldman and Zaller 1992), this figure is both surprising and encouraging. Even more, 70 percent of white respondents attributed racial inequality at least partially to factors outside the control of African-Americans. Even if a good deal of social desirability bias affects these responses, one can be consoled by the knowledge that the vast majority of white Americans have at least learned that it is "politically correct" to explain inequality between the races with some reference to factors beyond the control of individual black Americans.

Demographic Correlates
of Causal Attributions

With the sample restricted to white respondents, those who blamed racial inequality exclusively on the individual failings of black people were significantly older than those who attributed inequality entirely to external, environmental, or systemic causes (forty-six years, on average, versus forty-two). White respondents living in the South were also significantly more likely than those living elsewhere to blame continuing racial inequality on blacks. In fact, with a control for region, the relationship between age and internal attribution is nonsignificant in the South but remains significant elsewhere. In other words, young white southerners are just as likely to blame blacks' disadvantaged status on the individual dispositions of black people as are older white southerners.

White respondents who made exclusively internal attributions were also significantly less educated than those who made exclusively external attributions. Sixteen percent of white respondents who made internal attributions had no more than a high school diploma, compared to only 6 percent of whites who attributed racial inequality exclusively to the environment. Only 20 percent of whites who attributed economic inequality between the races exclusively to the failings of individual blacks had graduated from college. Nearly twice as many whites (37 percent) who made external attributions held a college degree.[13] As might be expected, liberal identifiers were significantly more likely than conservatives to make external attributions, but Democrats were no more likely to make external attributions than Republicans.

Consequences of Causal Attributions

A wealth of items available in the survey allow the relationship between causal attributions and other racial and political attitudes to be examined. As Gilens (1995) proposed, attribution of the causes of racial inequality should affect respondents' positions on policy issues such as welfare spending. This might be particularly likely, since "welfare dependency" is an available scripted attribution for racial inequality.

Table 8.2 Impact of Attribution for the Causes of Racial Inequality
on Attitude Toward Welfare Spending (Whites Only)

	External (%)	E/i (%)	I/e (%)	Internal (%)	Total
Spend More	25.06	15.38	15.03	8.82	19.10
Spend the Same	34.54	33.60	30.07	20.94	30.99
Spend Less	40.41	51.01	54.90	70.25	49.91
Total	100.00	100.00	100.00	100.00	100.00
	(886)	(247)	(153)	(363)	(1,649)

Pearson chi^2 (6) = 102.3611
Pr = 0.000
Rearson's r = .201

Table 8.2 provides a breakdown of attitudes toward welfare spending by attributional category. Seventy percent of white respondents who made exclusively internal attributions for racial inequality preferred to see less spent on welfare, as opposed to 40 percent of white respondents who made exclusively external attributions. Blacks were not an explicit target in the welfare spending question, so it appears that thinking of blacks as the authors of their own disadvantaged position spills over into welfare attitudes more generally, as Gilens (1995b) suggests.

One of the many experiments in the survey asked respondents whether they agreed with the statement "Most [randomly varied group] these days would rather take assistance from the government than make it on their own through hard work," where the group was randomly varied as "poor people," "blacks," and "poor blacks." Table 8.3 reveals an interesting pattern of differences between external and internal attributers. The percentages agreeing somewhat and agreeing strongly with the statement in each condition have been combined to simplify the presentation.

Table 8.3. Percentage Agreeing (Strongly or Somewhat, Combined)
that "Most [Randomly Varied Group] These Days Would Rather
Take Assistance from the Government than Make It on Their
Own Through Hard Work."

Attribution	"poor"	"blacks"	"poor blacks"	N
Unqualified External	47	30	44	881
Unqualified Internal	69	81	82	357

When the target group was described simply as "poor people," 47 percent of respondents who made exclusively external attributions agreed with the statement, as did 69 percent of respondents who made exclusively internal attributions. Only 30 percent of white respondents who made external attributions agreed that the group would rather take assistance than work when it was identified as "blacks." By contrast, 81 percent of internal attributers agreed with the statement when the group was described as "blacks."

When both descriptors were used simultaneously—"poor blacks"—internal and external attributers appear to respond differently to the combined description. Forty-four percent of respondents who made exclusively external attributions for the causes of racial inequality agreed that poor blacks would rather take assistance than work. Among internal attributers, however, 82 percent agreed that poor blacks would rather take assistance than work. In essence, white respondents who made exclusively situational attributions for racial inequality seemed to think that taking government assistance is more likely to be explained by poverty than by race. The same cannot be said for the internal identifiers.[14]

Overt Expressions of Anger

The survey also asked respondents to rate how angry various conditions made them. Among the conditions, situations, and behaviors described were several particularly relevant to perceptions of blacks; they are detailed in Table 8.4. Everyone reported feeling quite angry "when people are treated unfairly because of their race," as indicated by the grand mean of nearly 9 on a scale that ranged from 0 to 10, and a fairly narrow variance. Nonetheless, whites making unqualified external or unqualified internal attributions differed significantly[15] in the level of anger they expressed in reaction to the statements.

Those who made unqualified internal attributions for the causes of racial inequality were significantly[16] more angry about "giving blacks and other minorities special advantages" than individuals who considered situational explanations (that is, made external attributions) at all. The greater anger toward "special advantages" for blacks and other minorities would seem appropriate among respondents who believe that blacks are to blame for their own disadvantage. Individuals who made unqualified external attributions were significantly less angry about "spokesmen for minorities complaining that blacks are being discriminated against" than those whose responses included *any* reference to dispositional factors. Likewise, those who made unqualified internal attributions were significantly more angry at the spokesmen for minor-

Table 8.4. Level of Anger at Various Racial Situations
by Attributions of the Causes of Racial Inequaity

"How much does this anger you?" (0 = doesn't bother you at all, 10 = extremely angry).

A. "When people are treated unfairly because of their race."

Cause	Mean	S.D.	Freq.
External	9.01	1.68	887
E/i	8.79	2.03	253
I/e	8.72	2.09	156
Internal	8.51	2.36	359
Total	8.84	1.95	1,655

B. "Giving blacks and other minorities special advantages in jobs and school."

Cause	Mean	S.D.	Freq.
External	5.67	3.06	885
E/i	6.37	2.86	252
I/e	6.23	3.22	156
Internal	7.23	3.05	359
Total	6.17	3.10	1,652

C. "Spokesmen for minorities who are always complaining that blacks are being discriminated against."

Cause	Mean	S.D.	Freq.
External	6.51	2.88	885
E/i	7.56	2.45	252
I/e	7.61	2.95	156
Internal	8.34	2.70	358
Total	7.17	2.88	1,651

ities than individuals who were classified as making predominantly or entirely external attributions.

Open Housing

The two experiments described above were both aimed at trying to disentangle the effect of attitudes toward welfare and individual effort from the effect of attitudes toward blacks. The results are suggestive at the bivariate level, but not conclusive. As a final effort in this direction, the following analysis considers an attitude which should be theoretically unrelated to welfare. Respondents were asked, "How do you feel about blacks buying houses in white suburbs?" Responses were collected using a four-point scale ranging from "strongly favor" to "strongly oppose."

Among white respondents, the Pearson's correlation coefficient between the four-value internal/external attribution coding and feelings about blacks buying houses in white suburbs is .20. In the South, the correlation is .24, and in the North it is .16. As illustrated in Table 8.5, fewer than 3 percent of whites reported that they were strongly opposed to blacks buying houses in white suburbs in the nation as a whole. Individuals who made exclusively internal attributions for the causes of inequality between blacks and whites were, however, more than twice as likely to oppose blacks buying houses in white suburbs.

The idea of blacks buying houses in white suburbs has no explicit welfare component, so the "desert heuristic" should not be triggered by this question. What is at issue here is willingness to see African-Americans moving into neighborhoods where whites live. Individuals who are willing to say they strongly oppose this notion are few enough that their attributions for racial inequality can be considered in more detail.

Of the forty-four respondents in the entire survey who said they strongly opposed blacks buying houses in white suburbs, thirty-two made some kind of internal attribution and twenty-three made exclusively internal attributions. The bulk of these responses manifested a particularly punitive quality. The reasons for inequality between blacks and whites are given as: "It's their own fault. Anyone who wants to work can." Another respondent said, "Because they're too damn lazy to work." Still another said, "They don't work as much as white people." Among all of the respondents who strongly opposed housing

Table 8.5. Opinion About Blacks Buying Houses in White Suburbs, by Causal Attribution (Percentages)

	External	E/i	I/e	Internal
Strongly Favor	54	48	43	32
Somewhat Favor	38	40	46	49
Somewhat Oppose	7	9	9	13
Strongly Oppose	1	3	1	6
Total	100	100	100	100
	(881)	(247)	(153)	(355)

integration, a dozen explicitly mentioned something to do with an unwillingness to work. Eight respondents mentioned something about welfare and "government handouts."

The following full responses provide some sense of the flavor of these explanations, and particularly the tendency to project norm violations onto the "out group."

> Well, the only thing that I would say is that they don't work hard enough. They just take it off other people. That's the way people are here, they think it should be given to them.
>
> (Anything else?)
>
> Not that I know of. (Pause.) Well, I think a lot of them are really lazy and I've been raised about them, you know.
>
> (What do you know?)
>
> Having babies one right after the other, there's such a thing as birth control you know, I had that done when I was 24, I was ahead of this, I had three boys, I had my tubes [tied]. I've never had any problems since. (Pause.) Well, the way everything is handled.
>
> (What do you mean?)
>
> I'm not against the colored people but the colored people are getting advantage of everything. If you are colored you can go to the grocery store and get everything, if you are white you don't see that kind of thing.

Although these respondents were generally among the less educated, about a third of them reported at least some college experience. They were also older and more likely to come from the South. Several college graduates provided answers too long to quote in their entirety. The following is atypical in its length, but not in its sentiment:

> One word: education.
>
> (Can you tell me more?)
>
> . . . The Negro as a race are their own worse enemy, and even their own exalted leaders are coming around to the fact . . . . It's not the whites' fault but the Nigger race themself. It's their own fault, every time you turn the TV on you get these pictures of murder, rapes, drugs, um, disrupted families . . . and they are black, and 98 percent of it is black.
>
> (Can you tell me how it came about in the first place?)
>
> Well, OK, segregation, and that was a big issue, but when Eisenhower called the troops in Arkansas that was the beginning of forced integration of the schooling. That was the beginning of the downfall of education for the Negro, yeah, and that

alone is one of the reasons the Negroes keep killing the Negroes, and the Negroes keep selling the dope to the Negroes. . . . But if the Negro race would wake up and quit blaming everyone else for their own fortunes and plight and make a real honest to God effort to improve on their own lot then there is no question that they would be better off but . . . they've done really nothing but murder and steal from each other. . . . They are a very violent people.

Clearly, a person who provides this kind of explanation of why "the average black person in America is worse off than the average white" would hardly want African-Americans to buy houses in white suburbs. Citing television as the source of this information provides another example of where stereotypes come from (see Gilens 1995a and n. 2 above). Whether they say it in brief or at length, individuals who make internal attributions and who strongly oppose integration of suburban housing are accusatory in their attribution of blame for inequality to the willful failings of black people.[17]

Again, it is important to stress that unqualified dispositional attributions for the causes of racial inequality were provided by only a fifth of white respondents in the survey. Negative stereotypes, hostility, and punitive moralism seem to be heavily concentrated in one segment of the public. Although blaming blacks for racial inequality is not by itself an indicator of racism, it may be enough reason for a closer look.

CONCLUSION

The intent of this exercise was to try to get some sense of explanations for racial inequality based on what respondents are willing to say in their own words. Until quite recently, open-ended responses have received relatively little attention in mass survey research. Part of the reason for their absence can be traced to the difficulty of rendering them into the numerical form required for most analytic purposes. Current word processing capabilities do not fully solve these difficulties, but they do make it possible to preserve the data in a form accessible to other researchers. Refinements in theory and/or methodology require replication. Another advance in the RPS is that responses to the open-ended questions were typed into the CATI record by the interviewer. These responses (edited only to expand abbreviated and truncated words, and to correct spelling) are available in electronic form to interested researchers for replication and further analysis.[18]

In many respects, it is more disturbing to quote the kinds of unenlightened and prejudiced things respondents tell us in their own words than it is to report that a certain percentage of citizens agree with some negative stereotype or prejudiced statement. Fixed-format survey items have a certain sanitized quality that encourages detachment and "value-free" analysis. At the very least, it can be argued that responses which cast the public in a negative light are the contrivances of the researcher and would not occur in "real life" without prompting (Ginsberg 1986).

Because negative information generally has a greater impact than positive, it is important to stress, once again, that this analysis suggests that only a fifth of the public blames blacks in an unqualified fashion for their disadvantaged position in society. Another fifth of the public expresses some degree of ambivalence about the causes of racial inequality. On the positive side, roughly half of the American public looks to the situation in which African-Americans find themselves today to explain continued inequality.

That even half of the public in the early 1990s can construct verbal explanations for racial inequality that locate responsibility for the current state of affairs beyond the control of individual black people is a finding worthy of some celebration. As Feldman and Zaller (1992, p. 297) point out, "supporters of the welfare state still lack a clear *ideological* justification for their positions." Nor can it be claimed that sympathizing with African-Americans to the extent of seeing them as victims of circumstance (whether or not the circumstances were brought about by the agency of others) insures support for social welfare programs, or programs targeted toward repairing the injuries of the past (Sniderman, Carmines, Carter, and Layman 1996).

With respect to the general question of welfare, even among those who make entirely external attributions, 40 percent favor spending less. White external attributers express significantly more anger "when people are treated unfairly because of their race." At the same time, among those who made exclusively external attributions for the causes of racial inequality only 87 percent favored "laws protecting [black] people from discrimination in hiring and promotion."[19] Nonetheless, those who make external attributions have overcome the fundamental attribution error, the dominant ideology of individualism, the dearth of coherent philosophical justification for egalitarianism, and a noticeable lack of forthright political leadership from the American mainstream.

NOTES

1. Mass-survey research has always displayed a healthy respect for the potential existence of a "social desirability bias" brought about by respondents' need to portray themselves, and the opinions they hold, in a socially acceptable fashion (Edwards 1990).

2. In a related paper Gilens (1995a) demonstrates rather neatly that this fairly widespread misperception is packaged for the public in media stories and photographs which distort the demographic characteristics of welfare beneficiaries.

3. See the Appendix for a complete discussion of coding procedures and rationale.

4. Throughout this presentation the parenthesis will be used to indicate an interviewer probe or comment.

5. Interviewers were instructed to try to type the response verbatim without worrying about spelling or grammar and to use neutral probes until the respondent indicated that he or she had nothing further to add. If the first response to the question was a simple tautology (e.g., "They don't got as much money") or made reference to nothing more than differences in education or income, interviewers were instructed to ask: "And how do you think these differences came about in the first place?"

6. The idea of "scripts" in the way it is used here seems to have originated with Tomkins (1965).

7. This kind of global coding of an entire response is similar to that undertaken in coding levels of conceptualization (Campbell, Converse, Miller, and Stokes 1960) or cognitive complexity (Tetlock and Hannum 1984). It differs from the conventional content coding of open-ended responses. It is based on the premise that any interested researcher can examine the exact content of the response to replicate the coding or modify it. Those who wish to peruse the content of the response by attributes of respondents can now do so, for example, to see how conservative southern Democrats articulated the reasons for racial inequality. However, during the coding process used here, attributes of the respondents were not available. Again, see the Appendix for further description of coding and information on the text data set.

8. Again, race of the respondent could not be ascertained during the coding process.

9. Note that Allport (1954) says that internal, or disposition, attributions "predispose" us to prejudice, not that internal attributions equal prejudice.

10. Of course, arguments by the likes of Wilson or Murray and Herstein may have re-legitimized the biological inferiority explanation, but this was not evident in 1991.

11. Note here that viewing black inequality as the result of the conscious and deliberate acts of individual white people would technically constitute another form of the fundamental attribution error. Thus, for example, explaining racial inequality as a conscious conspiracy by a small group of white people would be an internal attribution. However, recall that to avoid confusion the basic coding question was whether or not *blacks* could exercise control. Thus, discrimination, prejudice, racism, etc. are considered external attributions.

12. Further, societal discrimination, when it is acknowledged, appears to be the product of individual prejudice on the part of others—something injurious to equal opportunity, but not something to which the respondent is a party.

13. No significant differences in attribution were found by gender, or by gender within region, among white respondents.

14. Because of the smaller number of respondents who make internal attributions, one cannot really say that the percentages across the group descriptors are significantly different. The Pearson's correlation between causal attribution and agreement with the

statement is .19 when the group is described as poor, .41 when the group is described as blacks, and .33 when the group is described as poor blacks.

15. Means for the two categories of unqualified attributions are significantly different at the .05 level using the Scheffe test. Means for the two mixed categories are not significantly different from each other. Differences between the means for the unqualified categories and the ones for which the same attribution predominates are also not significant.

16. Means for all three other attribution categories were significantly different from the mean for internal attributers using the conservative Scheffe test. The same is true for all other comparisons where the term *significantly* is employed.

17. The twelve respondents who made unqualified external attributions for the most part cited simple issues like "discrimination" and "lack educational opportunity." These responses were generally short, and the respondents tended to be less educated and older. One should have been coded into the E/i category. The others make attributions to forces clearly beyond the control of African-Americans, including " . . . the Lord made whites before blacks." The following responses provide a general flavor:

Lack of education. (How did this difference come about in the first place?) Done by people, I guess, the media.

(Could you tell me more about that?) TV & political reasons & television, old laws. (Anything else?) That's it. That's actually allowing them to make mandatory rules on black minority employment that pisses off white folks. That gets them mad. . . .

Because they're black I guess. I don't know. (Anything else?) I don't know. (Else?) Because (mumble, missed).

They hire in more whites than (missed). I don't know. I can't prove that to be a fact, there's supposed to equal rights.

18. Responses quoted in this chapter have been edited further for grammar and presentation.

19. This datum comes from another experiment in question wording that randomly varied the description of the targeted for antidiscrimination protection: blacks, Asians, women. Full analysis is a story in itself (see Chapter 6).

REFERENCES

Allport, Gordon W. 1954. *The Nature of Prejudice.* Reading, Mass.: Addison-Wesley.

Bobo, Lawrence, and James R. Kluegel. 1993. "Opposition to Race-targeting: Self-interest, Stratification, Ideology, or Racial Attitudes?" *American Sociological Review* 58:443–64.

Campbell, Angus, Philip Converse, Warren Miller and Donald Stokes. 1960. *The American Voter.* New York: Wiley.

Feagin, Joe, and Melvin Sikes. 1994. *Living with Racism.* Boston: Beacon.

Feldman, Stanley. 1982. "Economic Self-Interest and Political Behavior." *American Journal of Political Science* 26:446–66.

Feldman, Stanley. 1995. "Answering Survey Questions: The Measurement and Meaning of Public Opinion." In *Political Judgment: Structure and Process,* ed. Milton Lodge and Kathleen McGraw. Ann Arbor: University of Michigan Press.

Feldman, Stanley, and John Zaller. 1992. "The Political Culture of Ambivalence: Ideological Responses to the Welfare State." *American Journal of Political Science* 36:268–301.

Fiske, Susan T., and Shelley E. Taylor. 1984. *Social Cognition*. New York: Random House.

Gilens, Martin. 1995a. "Race and Poverty in America: Public Misperceptions and the American News Media," Paper presented at the annual convention of the American Political Science Association, Chicago.

———. 1995b. "Racial Attitudes and Opposition to Welfare," *Journal of Politics* 57:994–1014.

Heider, Fritz. 1944. "Social Perception and Phenomenal Causality." *Psychological Review* 51:358–74.

Heider, Fritz. 1958. *The Psychology of Interpersonal Relations*. New York: Wiley.

Hochschild, Jennifer. 1981. *What's Fair?* Cambridge, Mass.: Harvard University Press.

Hochschild, Jennifer. 1995. *Facing up to the American Dream: Race, Class and the Soul of the Nation*. Princeton, N.J.: Princeton University Press.

Kahneman, Daniel, Paul Slovic, and Amos Tversky, eds. 1982. *Judgment Under Uncertainty: Heuristics and Biases*. Cambridge: Cambridge University Press.

Kinder, Donald R., and Lynn Sanders. 1996. *Divided by Race*. Chicago: University of Chicago Press.

Kluegel, James R., and Eliot R. Smith. 1986. *Beliefs About Inequality*. Hawthorne, N.Y.: Aldine de Gruyter.

Lau, Richard R., and David O. Sears. 1986. *Political Cognition*. Hillsdale, N.J.: Lawrence Erlbaum Associates.

Lodge, Milton. 1995. "Toward a Procedural Model of Candidate Evaluation." In *Political Judgment: Structure and Process,* ed. Milton Lodge and Kathleen McGraw. Ann Arbor: University of Michigan Press.

Lodge, Milton, and Kathleen McGraw, eds. 1995. *Political Judgment: Structure and Process*. Ann Arbor: University of Michigan Press.

Nisbett, R. E., and L. Ross. 1980. *Human Inference: Strategies and Shortcomings of Social Judgment*. Englewood Cliffs, N.J.: Prentice Hall.

Paulhus, Delroy L. 1991. "Measurement and Control of Response Bias." In *Measurement of Personality and Social Psychological Attitudes,* ed. J. P. Robinson, P. R. Shaver, and L. S. Wrightsman. New York: Academic.

Pettigrew, Thomas F. 1979. "The Ultimate Attribution Error: Extending Allport's Cognitive Analysis of Prejudice." *Personality and Social Psychology Bulletin* 5:461–76.

Schattschneider, E. E. 1960. *The Semi-sovereign People*. New York: Dryden Press.

Schlozman, Kay, and Sidney Verba. 1979. *Injury to Insult: Unemployment, Class and Political Response*. Cambridge, Mass.: Harvard University Press.

Schneider, Anne, and Helen Ingram. 1993. "Social Construction of Target Populations: Implications for Politics and Policy." *American Political Science Review* 87:334–47.

Schuman, Howard, Charlotte Steeh, and Lawrence Bobo. 1985. *Racial Attitudes in America*. Cambridge, Mass.: Harvard University Press.

Sigelman, Lee P., and Susan Welch. 1991. *Black Americans' Views of Racial Inequality: The Dream Deferred*. Boston: Cambridge University Press.

Sniderman, Paul M., and Richard A. Brody. 1977. "Coping: The Ethic of Self-reliance." *American Journal of Political Science* 21:501–21.

Sniderman, Paul M., Richard A. Brody, and James H. Kuklinski. 1984. "Policy Reasoning and Political Values: The Problem of Racial Equality." *American Journal of Political Science* 28:75–94.

Sniderman, Paul M., Richard A. Brody, and Philip E. Tetlock. 1991. *Reasoning and Choice: Explorations in Political Psychology.* Cambridge: Cambridge University Press.

Sniderman, Paul M., Edward G. Carmines, Geoffrey C. Layman, and Michael Carter. 1996. "Beyond Race: Social Justice as Race-neutral Ideal." *American Journal of Political Science* 40:33–55.

Sniderman, Paul M., with Michael G. Hagen. 1985. *Race and Inequality.* Chatham, N.J.: Chatham House.

Sniderman, Paul M., and Thomas Piazza. 1993. *The Scar of Race.* Cambridge, Mass.: Harvard University Press.

Snyder, Richard, and Glenn D. Paige. 1958. "The U.S. Decision to Resist Aggression in Korea." *Administrative Science Quarterly* 3:341–78.

Tetlock, Philip E. 1984. "Cognitive Style and Political Belief Systems in the British House of Commons." *Journal of Personality and Social Psychology* 46:365–75.

Tetlock, Philip E., and K. Hannum. 1984. *Integrative Complexity Coding Manual.* University of California, Berkeley, Institute of Personality Assessment and Research.

Tomkins, Sylvan S. 1965. "Affect and the Psychology of Knowledge." In *Affect, Cognition and Personality,* ed. S. S. Tomkins and C. E. Izard. New York: Springer.

Tversky, Amos, and Daniel Kahneman. 1974. "Judgment Under Uncertainty: Heuristics and Biases." *Science* 185:1124–31.

Weiner, Bernard. 1980. "A Cognitive-emotion-action Model of Motivated Behavior." *Journal of Personality and Social Psychology* 39:186–200.

Wright, Gerald C. 1976. "Racism and Welfare Policy in America." *Social Science Quarterly* 57:718–30.

Zaller, John, and Stanley Feldman. 1992. "A Simple Theory of the Survey Response." *American Journal of Political Science* 36:579–616.

Contributors

Edward G. Carmines is the Rudy Professor of Political Science at Indiana University.

Michael D. Cobb is a Ph.D. candidate in political science at the University of Illinois, Urbana-Champaign.

Martin Gilens is assistant professor of political science and a fellow in the Institute for Social and Policy Studies, Yale University.

Hosea Harvey is a Ph.D. candidate in political science at Stanford University.

Jon Hurwitz is professor of political science at the University of Pittsburgh.

Kathleen Knight is associate professor of political science at the University of Houston.

James H. Kuklinski is professor of political science and a member of the Institute of Government and Public Affairs, University of Illinois, Urbana-Champaign.

Geoffrey C. Layman is assistant professor of political science at Vanderbilt University.

Mark Peffley is professor of political science at the University of Kentucky, Lexington.

Thomas Piazza is manager of statistical services at the Survey Research Center, University of California, Berkeley.

Paul M. Sniderman is professor of political science at Stanford University and a research political scientist at the Survey Research Center, University of California, Berkeley.

Laura Stoker is associate professor of political science at the University of California, Berkeley.

Appendix

CHAPTER 4

Survey Measures

I. *Racial stereotypes.* Scales were formed to measure two central dimensions of whites' stereotypes of African-Americans: black work ethic (Cronbach's α = .765 for the items lazy, determined to succeed, dependable, hard-working, and lack discipline) and black hostility (aggressive or violent), which were found to tap distinct dimensions of whites' beliefs about African-Americans (r between the two dimensions is .45) and in preliminary analyses were found to play a significant, nonredundant role in predicting various policy attitudes in the survey, especially attitudes toward crime and welfare. Both scales are coded so that higher values indicate more negative assessments of "most" blacks.

All of the stereotype items except one (lack discipline) are based on the following item: "Now I'll read a few words that people sometimes use to describe blacks. Of course, no word fits absolutely everybody, but, as I read each one, please tell me, using a number from 0 to 10, how well you think it describes blacks as a group. If you think it's a very good description of most blacks, give it a 10. If you feel a word is a very inaccurate description of most blacks, give it a 0." Lack discipline is based on the Likert statement "Most black parents don't teach their children the self-discipline and skills it takes to get ahead in America," where responses to the 4-point scale are also coded such that higher values indicate more negative assessments of most blacks (i.e., agreement with the statement).

Others have used different measurement strategies. Bobo and Kluegel (1993), for example, subtract ratings of "whites in general" from ratings of "blacks in general" on five 7-point semantic differential scales (e.g., hard-working to lazy, violence-prone to not violence-prone, unintelligent to intelligent, etc.) to measure "prejudice," a concept which they argue involves attributing less positive characteristics to blacks than to whites. However, other studies have found that the impact of stereotypes of blacks on political evaluations is unaffected by stereotypes of whites (Terkildsen 1993; Hurwitz and Peffley 1997). Moreover, we control for more general forms of ethnocentrism (and other possible confounds) in our analyses of the consequences of racial stereotypes by including measures of social intolerance, conformity, and anti-Semitism as control variables.

II. *Social and political variables.* In the regression analyses in tables 4.2–4.6, we include a variety of social, political, and attitudinal variables in the analysis to remove any obvious sources of spurious covariance between racial stereotypes and our dependent variables. *Party identification* and *ideological self-placement* are measured using the standard 7-point scales. Household *income* is categorized in increments of ten thousand dollars per year. "South" is a dummy variable where 1 represents the "Deep South" (the eleven Confederate states) and 0 represents the "non-South." The *education* variable categorizes respondents into groups of eighth grade or lower, some high school, high school graduates, some college, college graduates, and some graduate work or a graduate degree. *Political sophistication* is a summed index based on a respondent's ability to place correctly the political parties on three issues (reducing unemployment, reducing rich/poor income differences, and permitting school prayer); to identify oneself as a liberal, moderate, or conservative; and to respond accurately to two factual questions (knowing that there are nine Supreme Court justices and that presidents can serve a maximum of two terms).

III. *Core beliefs and values.* Additionally, we incorporate various measures of basic values that have been linked with stereotypes, policy attitudes, or both, in prior research.

A. Individualism (Cronbach's α = .444; r = .285) was formed by summing ratings to two value scales ("Self-reliance—having everybody stand on their own two feet" and "Emphasizing individual achievement and excellence on the job") from a larger battery of value items where respondents were asked to rate various value statements on a scale from 0 (one of the least important values) to 10 (one of the absolutely most important things to you). Consistent with prior research (Sniderman and Piazza 1993), correlations between racial stereotypes and Individualism and Ideology are minimal (e.g., r's between black work ethic and individualism and ideology are .12 and .13, respectively).

B. Ethnocentrism.

1. *Social intolerance* (Cronbach's α = .363) was measured with two 11-point scales from the value battery ("Tolerating different beliefs and lifestyles" and "Allowing people to speak out for ideas that most people disagree with") and two 4-point Likert items ("We should be more tolerant of different groups in society, even if their values and behavior are very different from ours" and "Groups with very different ideas and values should try their best to fit in with the rest of society").

2. *Conformity* (defined here as a desire for an orderly world in which people obey authority and adhere to convention—Cronbach's α = .711) was assessed with three 11-point scales from the value battery ("Preserving the traditional ideas of right and wrong," "Respect for authority," and "Improving standards of politeness in everyday behavior") and three 3-point childhood value priorities ("Independence or respect for elders," "Obedience or self-reliance" and "Curiosity or good manners").

3. *Anti-Semitism* (Cronbach's α = .775) is measured by summing responses to the following Likert statements: "Most Jews are more willing than other people to use shady practices to get ahead in life," "Most Jews believe that they are better than other people," "Most Jews in general are inclined to be more loyal to Israel than to America," and "Most Jews don't care what happens to people who aren't Jewish."

CHAPTER 5: QUESTION WORDING AND VARIABLE CODING

Negative Stereotypes: Five Items Relating to Blacks

1. Aggressive/Violent—"How about 'aggressive or violent'?" (On a scale of 0 to 10, how well do you think it describes most blacks?)

        1—Disagree (0–4)

        2—Neutral (5)

        3—Agree (6–10)

        2. Lazy

        3. Boastful

        4. Irresponsible

        5. Complaining

—The Index of Negative Stereotypes was created by summing respondents' scores on these five stereotypes.

—In tables 5.1, 5.2 and 5.6, and in figure 5.1, the index was reversed so that higher scores represented less antiblack prejudice.

—In tables 5.3, 5.4, 5.7, and 5.8 and in figures 5.2 and 5.3, the index was trichotomized.

Party Identification: Four Questions

1. Generally speaking, do you usually think of yourself as a Democrat, a Republican, an independent, or what?
2. [If Democrat] Would you call yourself a strong Democrat or a not very strong Democrat?
3. [If Republican] Would you call yourself a strong Republican or a not very strong Republican?
4. [If independent] Do you think of yourself as closer to the Democratic party or closer to the Republican party?

—In tables 5.1 and 5.3–8 and figures 5.2 and 5.3, only the first question was used and party identification was coded as follows:

1—Democrat

2—Independent

3—Republican

—In table 5.2 and figure 5.1, all four questions were used to construct the following seven-point scale:

1—Strong Republican

2—Weak Republican

3—Independent, Leans Republican

4—Independent

5—Independent, Leans Democratic

6—Weak Democrat

7—Strong Democrat

Racial Policies (Tables 5.1–3, 5.6, 5.7, Figure 5.1)

Government Spending for Programs to Help Blacks Get More Jobs—"Some people feel that the government in Washington should increase spending for programs to help blacks get more jobs. Others feel that blacks should take care of their own problems. How do you feel—do you think the government should increase spending or do you feel blacks should rely only on themselves?"

> 0—Blacks should take care of their own problems.

> 1—Government should increase spending.

Fighting Discrimination Against Blacks in Jobs—"Some people feel that the government in Washington should do more to make sure that blacks are not discriminated against in getting jobs. Others feel that blacks should take care of their own problems. How do you feel—do you think the government should do more or do you feel blacks should rely only on themselves?"

> 0—Blacks should take care of their own problems.

> 1—Government should do more.

Welfare Spending—"Suppose you had a say in making up the federal budget, would you prefer to see more spent, less spent, or the same amount of money spent on welfare as has been?"

> 0—Less spent

> .5—Kept about the same

> 1—More spent

Job Quotas for Blacks—"There are some large companies where blacks are underrepresented. Do you think these large companies should be required to give a certain number of jobs to blacks, or should the government stay out of this?"

> 0—Government should stay out of it.

> 1—Companies should be required to make sure jobs go to blacks.

Preferential Admissions to Universities for Blacks—"Some people say that because of past discrimination, an extra effort should be made to make sure that qualified blacks are considered for university admission. Others say that this extra effort is wrong because it discriminates against whites. How do you feel— are you in favor of or opposed to making an extra effort to make sure qualified blacks are considered for admission to colleges and universities?"

> 0—Opposed

> 1—In favor

Social Welfare Policies (Table 5.8; all have been placed on a 0–1 scale)

No Medical Insurance for Unemployed—"[How about] the lack of affordable medical care for people who don't have jobs? (On a scale from 0 to 10, how much does this anger you?)"

Tax Breaks for the Rich—"How about special benefits like tax breaks going to the richest people and biggest businesses? On a scale from 0 to 10, how much does this anger you?"

Spend More to Reduce Unemployment—"How about more money being spent to reduce unemployment? Are you . . .

1—strongly opposed?
3—somewhat opposed?
5—somewhat in favor?
7—strongly in favor?

Narrow Gap Between Rich and Poor—"How about narrowing the gap in income between the rich and the poor? Are you strongly in favor, somewhat in favor, somewhat opposed, or strongly opposed to these programs?"

1—Strongly opposed
3—Somewhat opposed
5—Somewhat in favor
7—Strongly in favor

Welfare Dependency (Figure 5.2—placed on a 0–1 scale)

"Most (poor people/blacks/poor blacks) these days would rather take assistance from the government than make it on their own through hard work." Do you . . .

1—disagree strongly?
3—disagree somewhat?
5—agree somewhat?
7—agree strongly?

Black Housing in White Suburbs (Table 5.4—placed on a 0–1 scale): Two Questions

Q1: "How do you feel about blacks buying houses in white suburbs?"
Q2: "And how do you feel about (programs set up by religious and business groups that . . . / government subsidized housing to . . . / the government putting its weight behind programs to . . .) encourage blacks to buy homes in white suburbs?"

1—"Somewhat opposed" to Q1 or Q2
3—"Strongly opposed" to Q1 or Q2
5—"Strongly in favor" of Q2
7—"Somewhat in favor" of Q2

CHAPTER 6: QUESTION WORDING AND INDEX CONSTRUCTION

Attributions of Blame in Explanations for Racial Inequality

The respondent was first asked an open-ended question: "Statistics show that the average black person in America is worse off than the average white person. What do you suppose caused this difference?"

After the respondent answered, he or she was then asked for a closed-end summary: "To sum up, whose fault would you say it is that blacks are worse off than whites—would you say that white people are mostly to blame, that blacks themselves are mostly to blame, or would you say that they both share the blame equally?"

[If whites:] "Even though you feel it's mostly the fault of whites, would you say blacks are partly to blame, or that blacks should bear none of the blame?"

[If blacks:] "Even though you feel it's mostly the fault of black people, would you say that whites are partly to blame, or that whites should bear none of the blame?"

The responses were coded to range from 0 to 1, as follows:

0.00	Whites entirely to blame
.25	Whites mostly to blame
.50	Whites and blacks equally to blame
.75	Blacks mostly to blame
1.00	Blacks entirely to blame

Old-Fashioned Racism

The measure of old-fashioned racism combined responses to three questions. Two of the questions were part of a longer stereotyping battery and tapped the respondents' perceptions of blacks as intelligent or unintelligent (see below). These were averaged to form a subindex where cases with valid data on only one of the components were accepted as valid. The third question assessed the respondents' support for racial integration or segregation. This question and the intelligence-stereotyping subindex were scaled to range from 0 to 1 and then averaged, yielding a scale that also ranged from 0 (least racist—blacks intelligent, advocate integration) to 1 (most racist—blacks not intelligent, advocate racial segregation). The average intercorrelation among the three component items was .29.

Component Items

Stereotyping items: "Now I'll read a few words that people sometimes use to describe blacks. Of course, no word fits absolutely everybody, but, as I read each one, please tell me using a number from 0 to 10 how well you think it describes blacks as a group. If you think it is a very good description of most blacks, give it a 10. If you feel a word is a very inaccurate description of most blacks, give it a 0."

"How about 'intelligent at school?' (On a scale from 0 to 10, how well do you think it describes most blacks?) How about 'smart with practical, everyday things?'"

Racial segregation/integration: "How do you feel about blacks buying houses in white suburbs? Are you strongly in favor, somewhat in favor, somewhat opposed, or strongly opposed to that?"

Work-Ethic Stereotyping

This index, also additive, was based upon the average response to five questions assessing perceptions of blacks vis-à-vis standards of behavior set out by the American work ethic. Four were stereotype items (see wording, above): (1) dependable, (2) lazy, (3) determined to succeed, and (4) hard-working. The fifth question followed a Likert format: "(How about) Most black parents don't teach their children the self-discipline and skills it takes to get ahead in America. (Do you agree strongly, agree somewhat, disagree somewhat, or disagree strongly?)" Each component was scaled to range from 0 to 1 before averaging, yielding a scale that also ranged from 0 (blacks meet work ethic standards) to 1 (blacks fail to meet work ethic standards). Cases with missing data on more than one component item were coded as missing on the index. The average intercorrelation among the five items was .40.

Racial Resentment

Respondents were asked to indicate, on a scale ranging from 0 to 10, how angry they felt toward "spokesmen for minorities who are always complaining that blacks are being discriminated against." The stem of the question read: "Now I'll read a list of problems facing the country. As I read each one, please use a number from 0 to 10 to tell me how angry it makes you. If something doesn't bother you at all, give it a 0. On the other hand, if the situation makes you extremely angry or upset, give it a 10. (Feel free to use any number between 0 and 10, but remember, the more something angers or upsets you, the higher the number you should give it.)" Responses were rescaled to range from 0 (not at all angry) to 1 (extremely angry).

Big Government

The big government index averaged three variables: a choice between government seatbelt requirements and individual choice about seatbelt use; a rating of how angry the respondent felt in thinking about "government officials interfering and trying to tell us what we can and can't do with our own lives"; and a measure of agreement with a statement about the government trying to do too many things "that should be left up to individuals and private businesses." Each variable was recoded to range from 0 to 1 before averaging. The overall index was scored to range from 0 (least objection) to 1 (most objection).

Individualism

The measure of individualism was based on responses to two questions. The stem read: "Now I'm going to read some statements about things some people consider important in life. Using a number from 0 to 10, please tell me how important each one is to you. If it's one of the absolutely most important things to you, give it a 10. If it's one of the least important things, give it a 0. (You're free to use any number between 0 and 10, but remember, the more important something is to you, the higher the number you should give it.)"

The two items were (1) "Self-reliance—having everybody stand on their own two feet," and (2) "Emphasizing individual achievement and excellence on the job." Responses to the two questions were averaged and then rescaled to range from 0 (least committed to individualism) to 1 (most committed to individualism).

Social Services Spending

The social services spending index averaged four variables: the rated importance of "taking care of the homeless" on a 0–10 scale, approval or disapproval of "more money being spent to reduce unemployment" (from strongly favor to strongly oppose), approval or disapproval of programs focused on "narrowing the gap in income between the rich and the poor" (from strongly favor to strongly oppose), and preferences about the level of money spent on "welfare" (favor more, same, or less spending). Each variable was recoded to range from 0 to 1 before averaging. The overall index was scored to range from 0 (most supportive) to 1 (least supportive).

Social Tolerance

The social tolerance index averaged four variables. Two of the variables asked the respondent to report the importance of "tolerating different beliefs and lifestyles" and "allowing people to speak out for ideas that most people disagree with" on a 0–10 scale. The other two variables in this index were Likert-scaled items about toleration of groups in society: "We should be more tolerant of different groups in society, even if their values and behavior are very different from ours," and "Groups with very different ideas and values should try their best to fit in with the rest of society." Each variable was recoded to range from 0 to 1 before averaging. The overall index was scored to range from 0 (most tolerant) to 1 (least tolerant).

Party Identification

The party identification variable was based on a standard branched series of self-designated party identification questions, and scored to range from 0 = strong Democrat to 1 = strong Republican.

Liberal/Conservative Ideology

The ideology variable was based on responses to a branched series of questions concerning whether the respondent thinks of himself or herself as a liberal, moderate, or conservative, and was scaled to range from 0 = strong liberal to 1 = strong conservative. Respondents refusing to identify themselves ideologically were scored at the scale midpoint (.5).

Political Information

Political information level was measured by an additive index built from six items: Whether or not the respondent (1) identified the Democrats as more likely than the Republicans to support federal spending to reduce unemployment; (2) identified the Democrats as more likely than the Republicans to favor reducing the income gap between rich and poor; (3) identified the Republicans as more likely than the Democrats to favor prayer in the public schools; (4) correctly identified the number of members of the Supreme Court; (5) correctly identified the number of terms that the U.S. President can serve; and (6) identified himself or herself ideologically (as either liberal, moderate, or conservative). The average intercorrelation among these six items was .19. The overall index was scored to range from 0 (lowest information level) to 1 (highest information level).

Demographics

Variables used to control for the socioeconomic characteristics of the respondents included:

age, scored 0 (youngest in sample) to 1 (oldest in sample);

female, a dummy variable scored 1 if female;

education, scored 0 (eighth grade or less) to 1 (postgraduate education);

family income, scored 0 (lowest) to 1 (highest);

unemployed, a dummy variable scored 1 if the respondent was unemployed;

region, a dummy variable scored 1 if the respondent lived in a southern or border state.

CHAPTER 8: USING NATURAL LANGUAGE RESPONSES

The impetus to make more use of the kinds of things people tell us *in their own words* developed as a result of my opportunity to read and code the open-ended responses to the so-called "likes/dislikes series" in the American National Election Studies (ANES). Because of state human subjects research regulations, obtaining access to the interviewers' verbatim record requires special permission, and a promise not to retain or reproduce the raw responses in other than statistical form. Yet reading the verbal responses fifteen hundred people provided to a set of general questions about the candidates and parties during the campaign season makes it clear that no coding scheme can truly capture the richness of the raw text. The "SRC Master Codes" try, but that effort has been likened to "instant coffee" by Robert Luskin (1987), and rightly so. Even with several hundred discrete coding categories it is impossible to reconstruct the sense of what a respondent says. Context, qualification, and nuance are irretrievably lost.

The ANES open-ended response data have traditionally existed as a paper record in the interviewers' handwriting. Some of the recent years' responses have been transcribed to electronic files. However, it is still the case that no quoting or extended characterization of what the respondent actually said is permitted.

The Race and Politics Study (RPS) was designed to include a brief opportunity for open-ended comment. After several options had been examined it was determined that a single broad causal question would fit best with the rest of the endeavor. Prior to the "why are black people worse off than white people?" question, respondents had been asked a large number of fixed-response-format questions and randomly assigned to some experimental versions of question wording. In this context the open-ended responses to the general question can be seen as an opportunity for the respondents to summarize their views and to qualify or otherwise elaborate on their perceptions of race relations.

The opportunity to speak in one's own words provides the respondent a brief respite from a long list of fixed-format items and some sense of control in the interview situation. No argument is being made here that interviewees are not influenced by the content of the interview to this point, or that they would respond in the same manner in the absence of the cognitive context of the previous questions. Since the idea is to allow respondents to elaborate on the general issue of race relations in their own words, the question was deliberately phrased in a way that allowed individuals some latitude in interpretation.

The best way to experience the richness of the verbal responses is to read them directly. At present they can be obtained as a single electronic file (text only) from ICPSR as part of RPS, from the Survey Research Center at the University of California at Berkeley, or directly from the author. Such a random walk may suggest any number of alternate themes suitable for systematic analysis that may not be captured by the coding scheme employed in this chapter. In such circumstances, establishing a new coding scheme for the verbal data is easy and relatively quick. It takes about twenty person-hours to read and code the responses by hand. The electronic text can also be processed by common content analysis software, but users should consider the implications of natural language responses, as opposed to documentary-style text data, for the software they wish to employ.

Although random walks may be enlightening, a means must be found to efficiently communicate the resulting observations. As detailed in the text, the attribution coding scheme employed here seemed (to this researcher) to arise naturally from the nature of the question. It can be viewed as an obvious starting point for examining peoples' perceptions of racial relations in the United States, and has also served as the source of much theorizing about the nature of prejudice.

One can view the degree of blame for racial inequality as a continuum running from purely internal, or dispositional, attributions to purely external, or situational, attributions. It would be presumptuous to claim to be able to accurately order all the verbal responses along such a continuum, although this might be the ultimate goal of a detailed content analysis. It might also be noted that in a question asking directly whether blacks or whites were to blame for racial inequality posed after the open-ended question, 67% of whites said both races were equally to blame.

Partly in order to compensate for the somewhat overpopulated neutral category in the fixed-format item, a four-value attribution coding scheme was employed. Two of these categories are referred to as *unqualified* internal and external attributions. This means that the response includes no direct indica-tion of ambivalence or ambiguity in the attribution. Where the respondent's explanation for racial inequality included both dispositional and structural features, the coder was instructed to decide which response predominated. In cases where the decision was at all in doubt, the essential distinction between internal and external attribution was posed in terms of *volition*. In other words, in cases where both attributions were made in the same response, coders asked themselves whether the internal attribution implied that black people would not want change if they *could* control the outcome. (Is the behavior causing the unequality under the control of the actor? If it is *not*, is there indication that the behavior is willful or preferred?)

The most common examples of a purely external attribution provided by the interviewees were discrimination, prejudice, and racism. These are circum-stances entirely beyond the control of black people, either individually or as a group, that they would wish to change, if they could. At the opposite extreme, the most common purely internal attribution was laziness. This is a behavior assumed to be entirely under the control of the individual. When it is viewed as a matter of choice, and particularly a choice more likely to be made by black Americans as a group, it engenders punitive moralism. In this view, blacks *deserve* to be worse off than whites because they violate norms of individual responsibility and industry.

REFERENCES

Bobo, Lawrence, and James R. Kluegel. 1993. "Opposition to Race-Targeting: Self-Interest, Stratification, Ideology, or Racial Attitudes?" *American Sociological Review* 58:443–64.

Hurwitz, Jon, and Mark Peffley. 1997. "Public Perceptions of Race and Crime: The Role of Racial Stereotypes." *American Journal of Political Science* 41:375–401.

Luskin, Robert C. 1987. "Measuring Political Sophistication." *American Journal of Political Science* 31:856–99.

Sniderman, Paul M., and Thomas Piazza. 1993. *The Scar of Race*. Cambridge: Harvard University Press.

Terkildsen, Nadya. 1993. "When White Voters Evaluate Black Candidates: The Processing Implications of Candidate Skin Color, Prejudice, and Self-Monitoring." *American Journal of Political Science* 37:1032–53.

Index

Abramowitz, Alan I., 38, 125
Abramson, Jill, 93
Abramson, Paul R., 55n.12
Ackerman, Norman, 25, 26
Adorno, T. W., 61, 64, 69, 90
Affirmative action opinion: of African-Americans, 165n.8, 166n.12; and color-blind ideal, 143, 161, 163; compensatory action versus preferential treatment in, 143–45, 155, 164–65n.6; conditional nature of, 11, 13; of conservatives, 3; contextual factors in, 28, 137–38, 140–42; economic inequality beliefs in, 146, 148, 149–51; in election campaigns, 135; fairness judgments in, 137, 142, 160, 167n.18; individual beliefs and attitudes in, 136, 145–59; old-fashioned racism in, 146–47, 151–53, 161, 162; and party identification, 3, 101–2, 104–10, 124, 126–27, 163; principle-policy gap in, 21, 22–23, 135–36;

question-wording strategy about, 159–61; remedial context to, 11, 138, 139, 142, 149, 153, 160, 161, 165n.7, 167n.20; resentment in, 147, 154, 158, 162; and reverse discrimination, 137; socio-demographic characteristics in, 122–23, 124, 126–27, 154, 158–59; of southerners, 124; and Supreme Court rulings, 11, 137, 138–40, 142, 163, 165n.7; work-ethic stereotype in, 147, 148, 153–54, 157, 161, 164n.3. *See also* Job quotas; University admissions, preferential

Age: and affirmative action opinion, 159; and causal attribution of inequality, 221, 226; and prejudice, 46–47, 48; and regional differences, 95n.4; and stereotyping, 66, 68, 75; and welfare spending preferences, 183

Aggressive/violent stereotype, 62, 63, 65, 68, 90, 104, 195, 237–38